REVIVE
THE
AMERICAN
DREAM

EDWARD CORCORAN

Copyright © 2024 by Edward Corcoran

All rights reserved. This book or any of its portion may not be reproduced or transmitted in any means, electronic or mechanical, including recording, photocopying, or by any information storage and retrieval system, without the prior written permission of the copyright holder except in the case of brief quotations embodied in critical reviews and other noncommercial uses permitted by copyright law.

Printed in the United States of America
Library of Congress Control Number: 2024921437
ISBN: Softcover   979-8-89518-395-3
          e-Book   979-8-89518-396-0
Published by: WP Lighthouse
Publication Date: 10/05/2024

To buy a copy of this book, please contact:
WP Lighthouse
Phone: +1-888-668-2459
support@wplighthouse.com
wplighthouse.com

For Carrolle Rushford

Many thanks for very helpful
reviews and encouragement

TABLE OF CONTENTS

PREFACE	xi
INTRODUCTION	xv
CHAPTER 1 - NATURAL THREATS	1
Asteroid Impacts	2
Volcanoes	5
Earthquakes	8
Other Violent Events	9
GLOBAL WARMING	10
Rising Sea Level	11
Storm Systems	14
Extreme Precipitation	16
Wildfires	19
Overview	20
PANDEMICS	25
SUMMARY	31

CHAPTER 2 - DOMESTIC CHALLENGES 33

ROUTINE THREATS TO LIFE 35
- Aircraft Accidents 35
- Traffic Accidents 36
- Murders 37
- Drugs 38

PERSONAL LIBERTY 39
- Religious Freedom 41
- Free Press 44
- Guns 46
- Search, Seizure, and Surveillance 52
- Speedy Trial 54
- Prison System 56
- Voting 58
- Regulations 59
- Erosion of Freedom 62

THE AMERICAN DREAM 63
- Wealth Inequality 65
- Health 69
- Financial System 73
- Capitalism Versus Socialism 75
- Employment 85

- Education 92
- Immigration 95
- Demographics & Economic Growth 98
- Discrimination 102
- DEMOCRATIC DYSFUNCTION 106

CHAPTER 3 - GLOBAL COMPETITION 111

GLOBALIZATION 112
RUSSIA 119
- Cyber Threat 123
- Public Opinion 126
- Summary 128

THE ISLAMIC WORLD: CLASH OF CIVILIZATIONS. 129
- Afghanistan 131
- Islam and Governance 135

TERRORISM 142
- Industrial and Terrorist Threats 143
- Summary 148

CHINA 148
- Economic Dominance 149
- Regional Influence 153
- Domestic Control 155
- Global Influence 157

Summary 159
OTHER NATIONS 160
    India 162
    Latin America 162
CONFRONTATIONS 164
    Nuclear Threats 164
        Strategic Nuclear Exchange 165
        Local Nuclear War 168
        Individual Weapon Detonations 169
        Radiation Dispersal Incidents 175
        Improvised Nuclear Devices 177
        Electro-Magnetic Pulse (EMP) 181
        Nuclear Overview 184
    Non-Nuclear Threats 187
        Conventional War 187
        Electronic Disorder 189
MILITARY-INDUSTRIAL COMPLEX 194
    National Security 195
    Money 200
SUMMARY 202

CHAPTER 4 - NATIONAL STRATEGY 207

    FIX AMERICA FIRST 209

        American Dream 210

        Resilience 211

        Equality 214

        Government 221

    REALIGN FOREIGN POLICY 225

        Prominence Not Dominance 227

        Democracy Promotion 228

        Latin America 230

        Russia 232

        China 235

        Muslim World 238

        Other Countries 240

        Global Warming 241

    STRATEGY DEVELOPMENT 242

PREFACE

When I was writing *Revive the American Dream*, I built on an earlier book that emphasized the problems facing America, all the threats and challenges in front of the nation. But now I have come to realize that the most important element is not the problems, but the impact the problems have on everyday Americans. And nothing demonstrates that better than the American Dream. When I was growing up in the 50's and 60's, the dream was vibrant. Everyone was aware that if you work hard you can have a prosperous life.

But through the years this dream has faded. The threats and challenges the nation faces have undermined many of the two elements that made America great in the first place. The first was the American Dream, providing a Beacon of Freedom promoting America's fundamental principles of democracy and equality. This is the same dream that Martin Luther King spoke about, a dream of freedom and equality. The second was America's postwar leadership critical to the formation of both a peaceful united Europe and a global framework of allies promoting peaceful development and prosperity.

I have always had a deep interest in our country's interaction with the rest of the world. When I was a young boy as an Eagle Scout, I was encouraged to get all the data and information I could gather before deciding what to do next. I have been involved in security assessments for some 60 years since enrolling in a Soviet studies program at Columbia University. After being commissioned in the Army, I entered a four-year training program of language and cultural training as a Soviet Area Specialist. This led to a tour with intelligence staffs in Germany and then two years as a Liaison Officer to the Commander-in-Chief, Group of Soviet Forces Germany. This was essentially spying on Soviet forces to minimize the possibility of an accidental outbreak of warfare. My three daughters were all born in Germany during this period: Lisa in Munich, Kimberly in Heidelberg, and Lara in Berlin. I was then stationed at Ft. Ord, California, where my son Brian was born as I was being sent on my second tour to Korea. During this period, I also received my doctorate in International Relations from Columbia University. On my return from Korea, I began my final Army assignment as a Strategic Analyst at the US Army War College. There I chaired studies for the Office of the Deputy Chief of Operations. Contributing to assessments at the national level opened my eyes to broader issues of national policy.

My original military specialty as a Nuclear Weapons Officer had involved several overseas assignments. Experience with these tours was significantly broadened after retirement by serving as a core member of the Secretary of Energy's Safeguards and Security Task Force evaluating security throughout its nuclear complex. I was also a National Advisory Board member for the ALSOS Digital Library for Nuclear Issues, a comprehensive reference library on nuclear issues. So, I am familiar in depth with issues of nuclear strategy.

After retirement from the Army, I was a Rapporteur of the Defence of Europe Working Group of the Common Security Programme, based in Oxford, England. This involved extensive discussions with European specialists on NATO defense issues. I also have a degree in Chemical Engineering and ran an energy efficiency company in Budapest, Hungary, for ten years, interacting extensively with other regional managers and specialists. Altogether my European experiences impressed on me the importance of the postwar integration of Europe into a peaceful compact of nations.

In recent years I have been actively involved with the foreign policy community in the Washington, DC, area. I have been promoting economic development in Afghanistan with the Afghan-American Chamber of Commerce. Then the war in Ukraine dramatically highlighted the importance of interaction with Russia, the need to promote its transition to a modern nation and ally.

Through all these years, I have continued to follow America's strategic planning and I am constantly struck with the short-sightedness in our strategies. Presidential administrations from Eisenhower through Biden have stressed the need for strong military capabilities but have not paid nearly enough attention to important topics where military approaches are not helpful.

INTRODUCTION

The core national objective is to ensure its survival and prosperity: "life, liberty and the pursuit of happiness," in the words of the Declaration of Independence. Achieving this has always been a challenge both domestically and internationally.

Domestically, the challenge of economic development was initially entangled with slavery. Even Thomas Jefferson, the author of the stirring words "all men are created equal" was himself a slaveholder. It took a Civil War to resolve this issue at a governmental level, but residual racism continues to hamper national development. Through the Nineteenth Century, the economy absorbed millions of immigrants, but was dominated by the top levels of society – industrial monopolists often referred to as Robber Barons who relentlessly exploited the workers they controlled.

Internationally, the United States initially faced a major challenge from its former colonial master, Great Britain. But through the Nineteenth Century, wide oceans and a Monroe Doctrine opposing European colonialism in the Western Hemisphere generally protected the country from foreign aggression. However, shrinking global connections meant that the rise of Nazi Germany threatened the entire global balance that was becoming increasingly important to US commerce. This was directly responsible for US involvement in World War I.

In the immediate aftermath of World War II, the United States led the effort to integrate Germany and Japan into the Industrialized World, establishing a new European Union and ending centuries of warfare among neighboring countries. The United States also led the formation of the United Nations, dedicated to fundamental values of human rights and democracy, as well as a number of international agencies promoting democracy and development. Domestically, broad social involvement in war fighting led to a much more equitable economy. Corporate profits were spread much more widely. Americans began to focus on a vison of an American Dream, providing the opportunity for individual prosperity and success, as well as upward social, achieved through hard work in a capitalist society with few barriers.

Unfortunately, the Soviet Union posed a major military threat to West Europe while reasserting its claim of global domination. This led directly in 1949 to the formation of the North Atlantic Treaty Organization (NATO), including America, Canada, and the major West European powers. The focus on military opposition to the Soviet Union took precedence over everything else, including economic development and democracy. This was vividly demonstrated by US involvement in numerous regime changes and the neglect of economic and democratic development in the Global South. For a number of years, Soviet missiles actually threatened our national survival.

The collapse of the Soviet Union in 1989 dramatically minimized this threat. It also collapsed the basic rationale for NATO but the Western focus on military superiority remained strong. NATO initiated a totally unnecessary expansion while there was a monumental and almost unrecognized strategic blunder: the failure to integrate Russia into the Industrialized World. The Russian people had vague but optimistic hopes that the end of the Cold War would lead to a new era of prosperity. But those hopes were immediately destroyed. As Bob Kuttner and Walter Shapiro detailed, the West stood by as former elites used Soviet practices to seize control of the country.

Russia's 2022 invasion of Ukraine transformed what been a great power squabble into a fundamental attack on universal values. Russia does not pose a direct military threat to the United States, but it is systematically undermining the structure of international order that is critical to US development and to global peace. Nevertheless, the overall strategic situation has been transformed. The threat of nuclear devastation has receded dramatically, though it remains a concern. The most significant threats of violence to the nation are no longer from hostile nation states, but from a loose collaboration of transnational criminals and terrorist elements, many motivated by radical Islamic beliefs, that threatens to disrupt the critical networks that underpin modern life. Military forces have limited utility against such threats of violence, while the nation faces a whole new range of threats of economic disruption. Nothing illustrates this blurring of the boundary between violence and economy better than the COVID-19 pandemic.

So instead of a clearly defined threat to survival that dwarfs all other threats, America now faces a world full of challenges, often vague, amorphous, and ill defined. Many of these are not from hostile actors, but from threatening situations. Globalization, in particular, means that the wider world has a much more direct impact on the nation than ever before. For two centuries, broad oceans protected the country from almost all external threats, but the oceans are now marginal to newly emerging threats. It is clearly impossible to totally address all the threats and challenges to the nation. It is difficult to even define them, much less describe what actions are necessary and how to balance such actions against one another.

The 2006 [National Security Strategy](#) of [George W. Bush's](#) presidency recognized that the world had changed significantly and that new approaches were needed. Its first specific task focused on championing aspirations for human dignity, and that strategy included a strong sense that promoting American ideals would promote a stable and prosperous world. Still, the challenges of the twenty-first century were cast largely in military terms. Global economic growth and international cooperation were set against this background. Enemies were hostile actors, not impersonal forces or harmful conditions. [President Obama's](#) National

Security Strategy in 2010 presented a view of sweeping change with a new global perspective. It recognized the core role of the economy and the importance of strength at home and of cooperation with allies, as well as the need for an all-of-government approach with a decidedly lower emphasis on military capabilities.

[President Trump's](#) National Security Strategy in 2017 focused on restoring America's advantages in the world by protecting the homeland, promoting prosperity, preserving peace, and advancing American influence. The main challenges were seen as hostile actors, including revisionist powers (particularly China and Russia), regional dictators, and jihadist terrorists, as well as transnational criminal groups. The strategy stressed the need for military overmatch along with more creative diplomacy. American leadership was presented as central to shaping multinational arrangements and international rules. Democracy promotion and protection of human rights were minimized. President Biden finally issued an updated [National Security Strategy](#) in 2022. It described out-competing our rivals to shape the international order while tackling shared challenges as the two biggest challenges facing the nation. It moved away from a total focus on military approaches, concluding:

> By leveraging our national strengths and rallying a broad coalition of allies and partners, we will advance our vision of a free, open, prosperous, and secure world, outmaneuvering our competitors, and making meaningful progress on issues like climate change, global health, and food security to improve the lives not just of Americans but of people around the world.

The National Security Strategy has traditionally focused on security concerns, particularly military ones. So it is encouraging that the most recent one takes a broader view of national requirements. A central problem is that there has been no system for developing a comprehensive National Strategy, addressing what the nation wants to achieve and how to do it. Broadening the National Security Strategy to address the fluid, evolving, and dispersed threats the nation faces is a major step forward. The first requirement is for a comprehensive assessment of the totality of threats and challenges facing the nation and how we can address them. That is what this book is about.

1

NATURAL THREATS

Nature is generally friendly and supportive. But there are times when unexpected events suddenly burst into view and astound the world with their impact. Protecting life is the first requirement of national security. The life of the nation is clearly the top priority but protecting the lives of individual citizens is close behind, especially in the face of threats to large numbers.

Natural disasters result from the environment we live in, from our galaxy down to our neighborhoods. The most serious are catastrophic events that could kill tens of millions of Americans and destroy the nation. Thankfully, these are all of low probability. Extreme events are those which could cause a million or more deaths as well as major damage to the nation. They are certainly more likely to occur and could take a high toll on the nation, but they would not threaten its very existence. Beyond this are routine events from risks we accept as a matter of course. They are part of our everyday existence, but they can still impact heavily on the nation.

EXTREME VIOLENCE

Our cosmic setting contains a potential for violence at a level that humans have never experienced. This potential is based on the structure of our own Milky Way galaxy and solar system down to the composition of the planets, including Earth. Events here are episodic; they follow no schedule, and we can only react to them as they happen to take place.

Asteroid Impacts

Four hundred people a year are killed by impacts of asteroids, large meteorites. Actually, that is only a gross average, and no asteroid deaths have happened yet. But the geological record suggests that every 20 million years or so we can expect an impact of a magnitude that would kill most humans, perhaps eight billion—an average of 400 a year. This is an unusual catastrophic threat since we know enough to actually estimate both consequences and likelihood.

Asteroids are a galactic threat that Earth has faced throughout its long history, a threat that can never be eliminated. Even a cursory glance at the moon's heavily cratered surface gives an immediate impression of the magnitude of impacts that Earth must have suffered through the eons. Nor is this just a theoretical threat. We now know that an impact some 60 million years ago of an asteroid perhaps ten miles in diameter was instrumental in killing off the dinosaurs and many other life forms. Another recent evaluation has identified a probable impact off the coast of Madagascar, a mere 4,800 years ago, which raised a 600-foot tsunami and was attributed to a large asteroid or comet, the kind that could kill a large portion of the world's population.

Looking ahead, a NASA calculation on near-Earth asteroid 2004 VD17 assessed it as about a third of a mile in diameter with a possible impact on May 4, 2102, while Russia assessed that asteroid Number 2907, a half-mile-wide chunk of space rock, "with a large degree of certainty" will strike the Earth on December 16, 2880. A similar recent calculation initially showed that a 1000-foot-wide asteroid named Apophis would pass as close as 15,000 miles to Earth (less than a tenth of the distance to the moon) on April 13, 2029, and an impact was possible, though later assessed as unlikely. On March 22, 2022, another asteroid that size, 2013 B076 actually came within 3 million miles of earth, a "close approach," a reminder that they are all around us.

In fact, the direct effects of a large asteroid impact (physical destruction, enormous tsunamis, global earthquakes) would only be the beginning. The great extinction that destroyed the dinosaurs resulted from massive amounts of dust thrown into the atmosphere, creating years of deep winter, which collapsed the food chain and starved hundreds of species into extinction. A similar winter from another major asteroid impact would inevitably starve the overwhelming majority of humankind. The apparent 20-million-year cycle of impacts also raises the possibility that part of the threat is from more distant sources, with our solar system regularly encountering some cloud of galactic debris.

Smaller asteroid impacts are much more frequent. The Meteor Crater in Arizona was caused some 50,000 years ago by a meteor that apparently broke apart before hitting Earth. The largest fragment, about 60 feet in diameter, struck with a force estimated at 2.5 megatons and created a crater over a half-mile wide. This provides a good illustration of what could be expected from medium-sized impacts.

Another illustration is a 1908 explosion over Tunguska, Siberia. This event has generally been attributed to a stone meteorite some 100 feet in diameter. The explosion has been estimated at 10-20 megatons. Because it was such a remote area, only one death was directly attributed to it, but it felled trees over more than 500 square miles. More recently, there were two relatively small asteroid events on February 15, 2013. The 150-foot-wide asteroid 2012 DA14 passed within 17,200 miles of Earth, inside the orbit of some satellites. That same day, a 50-foot diameter asteroid exploded over Chelyabinsk, Russia, injuring over a thousand people and causing considerable damage.

The good news is that such impacts would have mainly a local effect. They would not raise enough material into the atmosphere to produce a significant global influence. And even if, or when, such an impact occurs, it is unlikely to take place in a heavily populated area. However, a smaller asteroid impact could trigger earthquakes, volcanoes, tsunamis, or other regional effects.

Smaller asteroid impacts are probably separated by thousands of years or less, rather than millions. Nevertheless, it is unlikely that America would suffer significant damage. The land area of America occupies less than 4 percent of the Earth's surface. With population and resources concentrated in some 30 major metropolitan areas, the high-density portions of the nation make up far less than 1 percent of the Earth's surface. Medium-sized impacts outside these high-density areas would be unlikely to have an extreme effect on the nation. Impacts anywhere on the globe could significantly degrade solar radiation, stressing the global food chain.

NASA is addressing the asteroid hazard by carrying out a comprehensive telescopic search for near-Earth asteroids (NEAs). A 1990s program, the Spaceguard Survey, was tasked to find 90 percent of the NEAs larger than one kilometer, roughly a half mile, in diameter—a task completed in 2010. Today no known asteroid is clearly on a collision course with Earth. The current NASA budget funds a [Near-Earth Object Surveillance Mission](#) (NEOSM) that will fly a small space telescope into space along with an infrared camera. The aim is to identify any asteroid or near-Earth objects that are at least 500 feet in diameter (big enough to inflict damage on a regional or a global scale). Some [25,000](#) objects of this size pose a threat to Earth.

If an asteroid is discovered on a collision course, then NASA has anticipated that we would apply appropriate technology to deflect it before it hits. Unfortunately, such technology is only now being developed. Anti-missile technology could be adapted to this task, but no such systems are currently configured to escape Earth's gravity or to intercept an object travelling up to a thousand miles a second. Nor is it clear what such an intercept would really accomplish. Russia has also considered such development, so there is an opportunity for a cooperative effort. Concern on Apophis spurred more attention to developing anti-asteroid systems with serious international meetings. NASA and the European Space Agency are working together on an asteroid-deflection project. Most recently, a NASA probe named DART—the Double Asteroid Redirection Test—crashed into an asteroid Dimorphos and altered its orbit, demonstrating the possibility of asteroid deflection. Work on protection systems continues.

The asteroid threat vividly demonstrates the concept of risk. Although the consequences could be clearly catastrophic, the negligible probability means a minimal risk. Because of the potential consequences, $35 million has been allocated to NASA for detecting asteroids and managing a Planetary Defense System.

Volcanoes

The volcano threat is based on the structure of Earth. A Ring of Fire, hundreds of volcanoes where geologic plates meet, stretches around the Pacific Ocean. The Hawaiian Islands have been formed by a local volcanic hot spot deep in the ocean floor continually erupting lava as the geologic plate moves above. A new island named Loihi, now only 3,000 feet below sea level, is already in the process of formation southeast of Hawaii Island.

For a number of years, scientists puzzled over Yellowstone National Park. Its famous geysers and hot spots gave striking evidence of subsurface volcanic activity, but they were not able to identify any associated caldera (a subsurface chamber of magma characteristic of active volcanoes). Gradually, it became evident that their vision was too small; the entire Yellowstone area is one gigantic caldera. Scientists now understand that this is a massive supervolcano that most recently erupted about 630,000 years ago when ground-hugging flows of hot volcanic ash, pumice, and gases swept across an area of more than 3,000 square miles. When these enormous pyroclastic flows finally stopped, they solidified to form the Lava Creek Tuff, some 250 cubic miles of lava spread over adjacent states. Ash from this eruption was dropped as far away as the Gulf of Mexico.

Another catastrophic Yellowstone eruption is possible. The effects of such a disaster are hard to even comprehend. One geohazard specialist, Bill McGuire of the University College of London, has estimated that magma would be flung 30 miles into the atmosphere. Within 500 miles virtually all life would be killed by falling ash, lava flows, and the sheer explosive force of the eruption. Lava pouring out of the volcano would be enough to coat the whole USA with a layer five inches thick. As McGuire said, this could again bring "the bitter cold of Volcanic Winter to Planet Earth. Mankind may become extinct."

Fortunately, the probability of an eruption occurring at Yellowstone within the next few thousand years is exceedingly low. A National Volcano Hazards Program being developed by the US Geological Survey to monitor the most threatening volcanoes in America partly addresses this threat. It could provide some warning of such an event. However, as distinguished from the asteroid threat, there is no appropriate technology even waiting in the wings that could deflect a supervolcano eruption. Moreover, since the core threat is a global Volcanic Winter, supervolcanoes anywhere in the world pose a direct threat to the nation, with 5-10 estimated to exist. For now, this is a threat we simply have to live with. Perhaps with a gradually cooling Earth, there will be no more supervolcano eruptions.

As with asteroids, the most significant threat is from a volcanic event that drastically blocks sunlight for an extended period. Lesser events—the volcanic events that humanity has faced through history—pose mainly a localized threat.

One of the largest volcanic explosions in recorded history was Krakatoa, an undersea volcano in the Sunda Strait in Indonesia that exploded in 1883. The combined effects of pyroclastic flows (turbulent clouds of hot gas and rock fragments), volcanic ash, and tsunamis killed over 35,000 people. The eruption produced a worldwide volcanic dust veil which acted as a solar radiation filter, reducing the amount of sunlight reaching the surface of the earth. In the year following the eruption, global temperatures were lowered by as much as 1.2 degrees Celsius on average. Weather patterns continued to be chaotic for years, and temperatures did not return to normal until 1888.

There are few places in America where volcanic activity could reach this level of destructiveness. A relatively small explosion of the Yellowstone supervolcano would certainly affect the nearby area, which is relatively sparsely populated. Another possibility would be in the Hawaiian Islands, where undersea volcanic activity could conceivably mirror the Krakatoa event. The Krakatoa explosion was preceded by many smaller eruptions, so it did not come without warning. An explosive eruption in Hawaii combined with seawater penetration could result in widespread casualties. But even in this extreme case, casualties would be unlikely to exceed several hundred thousand. Honolulu is over 100 miles away and has a population of under 400,000; the entire state of Hawaii has less than a million and a half people.

The largest explosive eruption on Hawaii within historical time occurred in 1790. This eruption produced pyroclastic surges that originated at Kilauea's summit and flowed several miles to the southwest. The thick deposits of ash exposed at many sites on the island indicate that even larger explosive eruptions occurred in prehistoric times and probably originated from Mauna Kea as well as from Kilauea. Explosive eruptions of any size take place infrequently in Hawaii, but the possibility of one occurring in our lifetime cannot be totally discounted. Such eruptions are unlikely to begin without some warning. The most widespread hazard from an explosive eruption would be windborne ash, which could damage structures, machinery, and agricultural crops. Since 1912, the Hawaiian Volcano Observatory has monitored volcanic activity on the islands for any signs of impending eruptions.

Earthquakes

The earthquake threat is also based on the structure of Earth and is simply not subject to human management. Although the image of a large portion of the California coast sliding into the Pacific Ocean makes for dramatic stories, there is no historical record of any such widespread direct earthquake impact. The entire Pacific Coast, along with Hawaii, southern Alaska, and the areas around Charleston, SC, and New Madrid, MO, are at high risk for earthquakes.

Damage projections generally focus on infrastructure and buildings. One estimate for a major quake in the Los Angeles area places damages at over $500 billion. Yet, except for an estimated 3,000 killed in the 1906 San Francisco earthquake, only a few American earthquakes have had more than 100 victims. But earthquakes elsewhere have had far higher tolls. The 2010 earthquake in Haiti claimed over 300,000 lives. Widespread shoddy building construction was a major factor; the earthquake was only magnitude 7.0 and did not result in any major fires or tsunami damage. On the other hand, the 2011 earthquake off the coast of Japan spawned a tsunami that killed over 15,000 people even though it did not hit a major population area.

The good news about earthquakes is that they are localized events and cannot rise to the level of catastrophic damage. Overall, the potential for the death toll from an American earthquake and/or tsunami to reach even 100,000 seems unlikely. Yet coupled with expected physical damage, the impact could certainly be extreme. To address this challenge, the American government operates a National Earthquake Hazards Reduction Program.

Other Violent Events

The moon was apparently formed by a head-on collision between Earth and a newly forming planet Theia. Most of Theia is now incorporated into Earth, but a huge cloud of cosmic debris eventually consolidated into our moon. There is also a theory that Saturn's moon Titan was formed from two large moons that fused. Both Jupiter and Saturn have dozens of small moons that are apparently captured asteroids. These violent events all happened during the solar system formation and seem unlikely to recur. But obviously another collision of Earth with a new Theia would be totally catastrophic.

So far as we know, humans are the only highly intelligent beings in the universe, but extraterrestrials are a possibility. Some researchers claimed that an extraterrestrial spacecraft and its alien occupants were recovered near Roswell in July of 1947, but extensive Air Force research did not develop any information that the "Roswell Incident" was an extraterrestrial event nor was there any indication of a "cover-up." Since 1985, there has been an active Search for Extraterrestrial Intelligence (SETI) program that screens distant astronomical bodies for electromagnetic radiation patterns indicating intelligent direction and NASA is running an independent study team. So far we have not found any extraterrestrials, but perhaps we don't even know how to look. By a recent estimate there are up to 300 million habitable planets in the Milky Way, and perhaps a trillion other galaxies. Our own societies emit a prodigious amount of electromagnetic radiation at thousands of frequencies. Earth would stand out like a bright beacon for any extraterrestrial beings looking for a new home on some hospitable planet. If SETI itself makes any sense, then clearly so would a wariness about what such a contact might bode for humanity. The vast expanse of the universe does provide some protection; hostile extraterrestrials would certainly be hundreds if not thousands of light years away.

Astronomers believe that the sun will eventually explode in a gigantic nova fireball that will incinerate and maybe even vaporize Earth. Thankfully, they assure us that this is some billions of years in the future.

Other violent threats can be identified, but none of them seem to have a probability above the level of negligible. We cannot really identify all the threats we face. There is always a possibility that some unforeseen event will emerge to wreak havoc. For example, scientists know that dark matter is all around us, but they have no idea what it really is or how it directly affects us. And humanity relies on the current oxygen level in the atmosphere; some future phenomenon that significantly decreased this would be catastrophic.

GLOBAL WARMING

Atmospheric conditions on the Earth's surface produce the day-to-day weather that impacts everyone. The Earth's surface itself is in constant flux, changing incrementally as time moves forward. Global warming is the ongoing rise of the average temperature of the Earth's climate and drives much of this change. It is not a disaster in itself, but rather intensifies the impact of individual disasters and can drastically alter local economic conditions. While there have been prehistoric periods of global warming, observed changes since the mid-twentieth century have been unprecedented in rate and scale. In the decades ahead, global warming could make COVID-19 look like a stormy day at the beach, an unpleasant but temporary disruption of life versus a fundamental shift in conditions of life.

Several decades ago, it was just becoming apparent that global warming would be a major challenge. Scientists were alerting the media as the dangers of global warming came to the fore at the 1988 Congressional hearing of James Hansen, Director of the Earth Institute at Columbia University: "Global warming has reached a level such that we can ascribe with a high degree of confidence a cause and effect relationship between the greenhouse effect and observed warming.... It is already happening now." There was broad agreement on the low end of effects, but projections became increasingly controversial as their severity increased. Scientific research on climate change expanded. The Intergovernmental Panel on Climate Change (IPCC) was set up in 1988 to provide formal advice to the world's governments. Thousands of scientists from all over the world contribute to its work on a voluntary basis. Even an early comprehensive report in 2007 judged climate warming to be unequivocal and discussed a wide variety of expected impacts, including shifts in agriculture and forestry patterns and disease vectors.

Trying to evaluate long-term trends in the middle of short-term fluctuations is obviously difficult and models of climate responses to varying conditions are both complex and still rudimentary. The report was immediately controversial, raising questions on the projected extent of warming and even on the central factors causing it, espceially the rise in greenhouse gases, particularly carbon dioxide. On the other hand, the Environmental Protection Agency strongly supports the projection of serious global warming and the central impact of carbon dioxide. Overall global warming is expected to intensify natural disasters and to significantly change population and economic patterns.

Rising Sea Level

Sea level rises are perhaps the most readily measurable impact, one with primary effects that can be easily understood. Sea level has risen about a foot in the last century and is projected to rise perhaps two more feet this century, partly due to thermal expansion of warmer oceans. But even this relatively modest rise can have dramatic effects in small island countries. Paleoclimate records indicate that during the last interglacial period 120,000 years ago, sea levels eventually rose 20 feet (six meters) higher than today. No scientists expect such a dramatic increase in the immediate future, but this shows the possible magnitude of potential changes. The 2007 IPCC report projected sea level rises ranging from 0.18 to 0.59 meters (almost two feet) by the end of the century. Later reviews show that ice is melting at alarming rates globally. The 2019 special report on the oceans projects an increased sea level rise from 0.43 to 0.84 meters (close to three feet) by 2100, associated with scenarios of greenhouse gas emissions.

Arctic sea ice has shrunk dramatically, much faster than anticipated. Melting of this floating ice will not affect sea level but does affect salinity and temperature since floating ice reflects solar radiation, which open sea readily absorbs. Arctic summers could be nearly ice-free in the decades ahead. The crucial question on melting concerns not sea ice, but land ice, particularly the Greenland ice cap and the Antarctic glaciers and ice shelves. Melting of these huge water reservoirs could raise sea levels by six feet or more by the end of the century. Effects of such magnitude had generally been considered unlikely, but recent rapid melting of Arctic ice reduces confidence in these judgements.

The Greenland and Antarctic ice sheets are continuing to lose mass at an accelerating rate, and glaciers are continuing to lose mass worldwide. Sea rise from global warming could render the Marshall Islands and the Maldives uninhabitable and flood Norfolk, Virginia, half the year, while temperature increases will char places like Australia and California during longer and more intense wildfire seasons.

America, with its long coastline, is particularly vulnerable to impacts of rising sea levels. The direct threat to life is modest, but the economic threat is huge. Florida planners address a potential sea-level rise of up to 6.5 feet by the end of the century. Among the most vulnerable places is Miami. "I cannot envision southeastern Florida having many people at the end of this century," says Hal Wanless, chairman of the Department of Geological Sciences at the University of Miami.

On the West Coast, a comprehensive report by San Francisco State University used a sea level rise this century of only 1.4 meters (about four feet) as its median planning projection, but evaluated rises up to 2.0 meters (over six feet). This study calculated likely economic costs for five specific communities. It assessed the most significant economic impact to be flood damages exacerbated by the sea level rise. This study looked at only 15 miles of the 2,000-mile California coast and provided projections of roughly a billion dollars of likely damages, not to mention costs of interim protective structures and much larger indirect costs. For Ocean Beach city alone, flood damages from a 1.4-meter sea level rise would be roughly $20 million by the end of the century for residential structures, but another $540 million to address erosion and sinking land levels. Along the coast, extensive and expensive coastal reinforcement could stave off some effects, but "managed retreat"—relocation inland of threatened structures—is already happening with the relocation of several miles of coastal Route 1. Overall, it is clear that a relatively modest sea level rise could cause something on the order of a trillion dollars direct damage to America, along with considerable upheaval and turmoil in coastal areas.

Obviously, island countries including Japan, the Philippines, Indonesia, and numerous Caribbean and Pacific nations would be under real stress. Several Pacific islands have already experienced forced migrations. Bangladesh, with its densely populated, low lying coastal regions, also faces severe pressures. Venice, Italy, which has been slowly sinking for years, is the focus of a major protection program. From a geopolitical point of view, both China and Russia are primarily continental nations and would be relatively unaffected by sea rises. St. Petersburg and Hong Kong could be hit hard, but major population and production areas, as well as the national capitals, are well inland. In Europe, Holland is already under stress from its low-lying position and would be severely affected. Germany would be relatively less affected. Inland nations from Switzerland and Austria through the Czech Republic, Hungary and

Slovakia would not face any primary effects. Coastal nations worldwide would face major impacts. Overall, global economic and political patterns could be profoundly altered.

The national security implications are substantial. New research published in Nature Communications has estimated that rising sea levels will put up to 340 million people at risk of annual flooding or permanent inundation during the next 30 years, largely in Asian mega-cities. The World Bank, meanwhile, estimates that increased flooding, as well as food and water insecurity, in Latin America, sub-Saharan Africa, and South Asia alone could generate more than 50 million "climate migrants" by 2050. Alternatively, the Organisation for Economic Co-operation and Development estimates that by 2070, 150 million people and $35 trillion worth of property in the world's large port cities will be at risk from coastal flooding. It is clear that even low-end projections of sea level rise will cause significant relocations and could profoundly destabilize countries around the world.

Sea level rise of course is not the only concern. The more the sea rises, the more likely it is that changes in temperature and salinity will alter the course of major currents. The Gulf Stream, for example, could cease to bring warm water to the British Isles and northwest Europe. Agricultural patterns, rainfall, disease distributions, sea life patterns, and wildfire dangers will all be affected, but how much remains controversial. It is also unclear how much global warming will affect the frequency or intensity of major storms.

Storm Systems

Storm systems are a major economic threat to the nation. Katrina's strike on New Orleans in August 2005 caused well over 1,000 deaths and some $75 billion in damages and forced relocations of thousands of people. Beyond this, a significant portion of this major city will probably never be reconstructed, and tens of thousands of people have been displaced. In the immediate aftermath of Katrina, nearby cities like Houston and Baton Rouge willingly accepted thousands of storm refugees, providing temporary shelter, food, and other support. The Federal Emergency Management Agency (FEMA) supplemented this with emergency housing and relief payments to thousands. Thousands of other refugees scattered throughout the country, sometimes supported by relatives and friends, other times simply seeking a better place to live after homes were completely destroyed. Many refugees resettled in the nearby cities, putting a significant strain on social and other services. Various federal, state, and local agencies provided short-term assistance, but there was simply no system or planning for resettling disaster refugees.

When Hurricane Ike hit Galveston and Houston three years later, memories of Katrina promoted a large-scale evacuation, which helped to hold the death toll to about a hundred, though property damage reached almost $40 billion. The strike on Galveston could hardly have come as a surprise since a Category 4 hurricane in 1900 had put much of Galveston Island underwater and caused at least 6,000 deaths. Corpus Christi, Key West, Miami, Charleston, Newport News, and New York City can all expect to have their turn as a target for a Category 3-4-5 hurricane. Indeed, any random 50-mile stretch of coastline can expect to be essentially washed away sooner or later by a hurricane. These stretches of East Coast shoreline include some of the most expensive real estate in the country, so direct damage costs in the decades ahead will certainly be hundreds of billions of dollars. While Hurricane Katrina represented an extreme case, Hurricane Ike was only a Category 2 hurricane. Then in 2020, the hurricane season set the record for most named storms in a year. Along with extensive damage, over 400 people were killed, complicated by the ongoing COVID-19 crisis. Climate change intensifies the risk. Sea level rise obviously increases flood risk. Warmer seas can also fuel more intense storms; one recent analysis indicated that global warming will produce fewer but fiercer storms.

Tornado deaths average about 70 a year, though they are spread very erratically. There were only 15 fatalities in 1986, but 2011 was a difficult year with 1,691 tornadoes and a record 553 fatalities. The most significant impact of tornadoes is property damage, though fatalities can also be substantial. On May 22, 2011, for example, a devastating tornado struck Joplin, Missouri, killing over 100 people and causing almost $3 billion of damage in a few very long minutes. A year later, President Obama visited, and newspaper reports showed areas that had already been reconstructed. Judging from the photos, they were reconstructed wood frame buildings, the same type as those destroyed, although improvements such as stronger trusses or safe rooms would obviously not be visible. But the pictures certainly seem to show new buildings just waiting to be destroyed again by the next violent storm. In fact, tornado-resistant buildings can be built. Although protecting from an EF-5 category would be very difficult, buttressing against more routine EF-1 or EF-2 tornadoes is entirely possible but seems to be rarely done. As with hurricanes, there is a potential link between tornadoes and climate change. Changing atmospheric and oceanic conditions underlie the changing patterns of weather and can set the stage for more severe storms, including more punishing tornadoes. On the other hand, a top official at the National Oceanic and Atmospheric Administration in 2011 rejected claims that the outbreak of tornadoes, which ravaged the American South, was related to climate change brought on by global warming. Clearly the association between global warming and more intense storms remains unsettled.

Extreme Precipitation

Precipitation, like other climate and weather phenomena, is widely variable, and extreme events can cause considerable damage. Although a direct tie to climate change is still not clear, northern areas of the nation are projected to become wetter, especially in the winter and spring. Southern areas, especially in the West, are projected to become drier.

By mid-2020, much of America was in a sustained drought that could potentially last for an extended period. In Colorado, for example, there was a quick melting of a low snowpack. Crops and livestock were severely impacted. Such droughts especially impact field corn and push farmers to sell their cattle off early. Farmers often cannot pump their own ground water because water rights belong to downstream users, vividly illustrating the potential for looming struggles over water ownership. Historical rights favored agriculture, but the growth of cities combined with droughts is straining long-standing allocations. For agriculture, water supply is not the only problem. Water shortages coupled with unprecedented heat waves, as earlier projected at the University of Arizona, will force widespread adaptations to new conditions.

Drought conditions can also severely impact cities. Phoenix, in one assessment, now faces enormous uncertainties. It may be a worst case, but cities throughout the region are scrambling to increase water supplies. Las Vegas, for example, has been constructing a third supply tunnel—the "third straw"—to its Lake Mead water source because dropping water levels threatened to leave the upper supply tunnel dry, though water levels have since stabilized a bit. Looming clashes between cities and agriculture may well overturn a century-old agreement on Colorado River water and are now involving major financial players.

But not everyone is short on water. At the other end of the spectrum are areas at real risk for serious floods. In June 2008, major portions of Iowa were under water in a "500-year flood," causing over $60 billion of damages. Just a few months later, downtown Louisville was under water with much of the main library destroyed. Less than a year later, Fargo, ND, was seriously threatened by a flood. Only an intensive, sustained effort saved the city from severe damage but left it with millions of used sandbags and a deep concern about preparing for the next challenge. It seems that because Fargo survived, it will be less likely to receive the $800 million necessary to reinforce its levees, since aid typically goes to places that suffer disasters, not areas that work to avoid them.

In fact, there are over 450 protective levees in the country and changing precipitation patterns undoubtedly put many of them at risk. Sacramento is one city seriously threatened. Nearly $5 billion in state bond money was spent to protect 100 square miles, including the California state capitol complex, from going under water. The city continues to pursue billion-dollar projects of river control and levee construction. Perhaps if Fargo were a state capital it also could promote a program of that magnitude.

But even when they hold, levees can be a problem. In 2011, the American Army Corps of Engineers blew open levees on the Mississippi, flooding some 130,000 acres of farmland and 90 homes to protect Cairo, Illinois. About 600 homes in this city of about 3,000 people were faced with a 22-foot flood, but the decision by the Corps of Engineers was strongly opposed in court by the state of Missouri. This is just one more example of conflict on water rights between farmers and city dwellers. Floods are a continuing concern; in 2019, floods on the Mississippi alone directly affected some 14 million people.

Flood protection is expensive and only partly reliable. Fargo's levees held, thanks to massive reinforcement, but if the next storm is just a little bit stronger, they may not. The ones in New Orleans failed; the replacements are somewhat stronger, but so may be the storms (Katrina was only a Category 3 hurricane when it made landfall). However, even lesser measures can be helpful. For example, after high water in 2001 caused significant damage by flooding the downtown tunnel system, a company in Houston initiated a broad program introducing flood proofing technology into the residential and light-commercial building markets. Such relatively simple measures might have saved the Louisville library and are certainly applicable to thousands of structures at risk. By and large, protection is an individual, local, or state responsibility. During a period when these budgets are all very tight, it is inevitable that protective measures are inadequately funded.

When Hurricane Harvey hit the Houston area in 2017, over 200,000 homes were damaged, most outside of the recognized flood plains and without insurance; total damage was over $155 billion. A major reason for the high damage was earlier runaway development in a city with low taxes and little government. It is a patchwork of counties and municipalities with different rules and minimal coordination. One local engineer, commenting on federal flood insurance, characterized it as "subsidized floodplain development." There have been disjointed efforts at recovery with nobody clearly in charge.

Wildfires

Wildfires had been more of a national annoyance than a serious threat. Dramatic pictures of the town of Paradise, California, burning in November 2018 vividly brought the threat of wildfires to national attention. Almost 20,000 structures were destroyed, with total losses well over a hundred million dollars. And this was only one, though the worst one, of dozens of wildfires burning in the West, leaving some 70,000 victims, many with no insurance. Yet it did not result in widespread abatement plans.

The result was a totally disastrous fire season in 2020, driven by a combination of population growth, high temperatures, very low moisture, and dense forests with a lot of underbrush and dead trees killed by beetles. Another problem was that homeowners had taken only minimal individual mitigation efforts, though even limited measures prove useful. This produced some of the largest fires ever recorded in California, Colorado, and Oregon. Another small town (Phoenix, Oregon) was totally wiped out and shortly after, a wildfire raging north of Denver destroyed over a thousand buildings, including a shopping center. These exceptional fires are forcing state and federal officials to reassess how to best manage wildfires, including a wider use of prescribed fires. The continuing inadequate governmental fire protection efforts were dramatically highlighted in August 2023 when a power line snapped in high winds and ignited Hawaii's historical capital city, Lahaina, killing over 100 people and destroying over 2000 buildings. This was the fourth major destruction of a town in a few years.

Decreasing resources devoted to mitigation, including thinning of forests and clearing of underbrush, certainly did not help. For a century, the emphasis on fighting fires downgraded the importance of wildfire management. A reliance on seasonal firefighters lowers costs but increases mental health problems and creates a systemic brain drain as experienced fire fighters leave for other jobs.

The good news about wildfires is that they have been largely concentrated in areas of relatively low population, so there was less impact on the national economy. Some of the direct losses are also covered by insurance, but not the cost of firefighting nor the impact on local economies. The 2020 wildfires also had a broader impact due to widespread smoke and ash. As with other natural hazards, risk mitigation and response resources are important, but expensive and often neglected.

Overview

Insurance is a primary means of protection for individual homeowners and businesses. Basically, the individual joins with a large number of other individuals in a similar situation. Each pays a yearly premium into a pool that pays for the claims of members who suffer from the designated casualty. The key is that the premium level needs to cover the expected risk. So, if a $200,000 home has a one in a thousand chance of being destroyed this year, the premium should be on the order of $200, or somewhat more, to average out the fact that some homes in the group would be destroyed in earlier years, and the company needs to show some profit. But if the risk grows to one in ten, then the premium would have to rise to an impossible $20,000. As the risk increases, insurance becomes untenable. In fact, as risk goes up and uncertainly increases, insurance companies become less and less willing to write insurance in the first place, and governments are pressured more and more to cover the insurance deficit.

Most state insurance programs charged rates that did not fully reflect the risk of loss, potentially discouraging private market involvement and mitigation efforts by property owners. Proposals for federal support could give state programs access to capital at reduced or below-market costs, allowing state programs to continue to charge premium rates that do not fully reflect risks or even to lower their premium rates, but could also increase taxpayers' exposure to the potential costs in the event of state financial difficulties. The federal government's fiscal exposure from the National Flood Insurance Program remains high because its premium rates also fail to reflect the flood risk of its insured properties.

When a disaster strikes a concentrated area as it did with Katrina, individual insurance cannot cover all the losses. Relief falls on the government, and disaster aid covers much of the shortfall. In effect, everyone pitches in to help the victims, and the government becomes the ultimate insurer. Everyone pays for that insurance since some percent of their taxes is set aside for disaster recovery. Some people decline expensive private insurance, counting on disaster aid to compensate them. But even for government insurance, the premiums can rise too high for homeowners to afford. If all the oceanside homes and businesses on the Atlantic coast are engulfed by the sea, who will pay what? Florida's shortage of about two trillion dollars only addresses direct losses and would only be a small portion of overall Atlantic coast claims. It is easy to argue that people who choose to enjoy the joys of an oceanside or forested home should also enjoy the risks. Yet literally millions of homes that were built in what were prudent locations are now vulnerable, some modestly so and some more severely. One recent estimate is that four million homes along the Atlantic and Gulf coasts are at risk for storm surge. If the flood threats increase, the way the wildfire threat did in the 2020 season, so will the risks. Deciding who should pay what will be a major national challenge.

The federal government is clearly responsible for federal lands and for programs it is required by law to carry out, including extensive flood control work by the Corps of Engineers. Katrina found government at all levels unprepared. For days, various agencies and even commercial firms and nonprofit groups struggled to assist, but no one was in charge. Local emergency workers, state agencies, and numerous federal agencies were involved in the Katrina recovery, and they used a jumble of different communications equipment and frequencies, often incompatible with one another. National Guard units had trouble responding partly because some units had earlier been called to federal service and were unavailable. Additionally, National Guard units are primarily trained, configured, and equipped for combat operations against enemy ground forces. There were also some legal problems using National Guard troops to maintain law and order.

Even now, in the event of some sudden major disaster, it is unclear how a coordinated Command Center could be established and how its composition would be determined. A detailed review of the 2017 hurricane season showed there are still significant shortcomings responding in the first critical days after a disaster strikes.

But the biggest long-term economic threat is not from individual natural disasters, but rather from global warming, which magnifies all the individual threats as well as incorporates large-scale threats of its own. Climate changes since the mid-twentieth century have been unprecedented in rate and scale. Shifting agricultural patterns, water shortages, desert increases, and new disease patterns are challenging already stressed societies. Even modest sea level rises and more powerful storms might well produce widespread devastation in some areas. Major sea level rises could inundate coastal cities worldwide.

Reducing greenhouse gases is intertwined with energy policy. The development surge of the Industrialized World was based heavily on fossil fuels. Electricity generation began with coal-fired units and then oil-fired units. Most recently, there is a wide use of natural gas, less carbon intensive but still significant. Vehicles as well as heating and air conditioning units for buildings have also been dependent on fossil fuels. Some of the most powerful companies in the world have naturally been reluctant to reduce the use of fossil fuels as their entire financial position depends on them. Corporations have strong incentives to look out for their own interests so have naturally opposed many actions aimed at reducing the use of fossil fuels to lower emissions of carbon dioxide.

Renewable energy sources have become cost competitive, but large capacity facilities require large fields of solar panels or wind turbines. Their output is erratic and often at locations far from demand, requiring both transmission lines and significant electricity storage capacity. Battery technology remains expensive and heavy. Hydrogen technology could address some of these challenges but is largely undeveloped. Carbon capture technologies might also allow some continuing use of fossil fuels, but this is also undeveloped at the moment. Other new approaches, such as using tidal or ocean current energy, could also increase renewable resources.

In the middle of all this are the fossil fuel workers, millions of them. They expected to have nice paying jobs for life; instead, many are now out of work without benefits or even retirement. These jobs are often in isolated locations with few alternative employment possibilities. The expanding renewable technologies need new workers, but in new locations with new skills; transitions are difficult and comprehensive efforts to address them have not had much impact.

The natural result is that for years traditional energy companies and their workers have opposed efforts to reduce the use of fossil fuels along with their environmental impact and have undermined efforts to expand the use of renewables. Companies, local towns, unions, and individual workers have consistently fought for continuing fossil fuel activities and done little to help workers transition to jobs requiring new skills. These efforts have naturally supported skeptical scientific assessments of global warming and its causes, including the role played by CO_2. These assessments stress the high costs of restricting fossil fuels and attribute much of climate change to natural variations or simply dismiss some major changes, such as the global disappearance of ice and significant rises in sea level.

As scientists struggle to understand the complex interplay of the atmosphere, the oceans, and global flora and fauna, advances in computer technology allow them to develop increasingly detailed models of the range of expected effects and the key variables affecting them. All this is supported by satellite observations and worldwide data collection. Unfortunately, the models are still developmental. For all their efforts, scientists remain unable to give definitive judgments on causes or effects.

International efforts to address climate change have largely focused on controlling carbon emissions. The Kyoto Treaty obligated signatories to control carbon emissions and reduce them to 1990 levels. Unfortunately, the treaty did not include developing nations, including China, and some other major contributors to the global carbon dioxide release. Costs to meet treaty objectives were significant, while projected short-term improvements were modest. For these and other reasons, America declined to participate in the treaty. The Kyoto Protocol, even with 192 participants, was unable to make any real progress. So at a 2015 UN conference on climate change in Le Bourget, France, almost 200 countries adopted a Paris Agreement, pledging to limit warming "well below" two degrees. That basically required the world to move rapidly toward 100 percent clean energy, producing zero net greenhouse gas emissions between about 2050 and 2080. While there has been some progress, President Trump directed America's withdrawal from the treaty in November 2020; incoming President Biden promptly committed America to rejoining the agreement, but a coordinated global approach is still lacking. The December 2023 COP28 climate summit approved a global pact to transition away from fossil fuels, but the outcome is still uncertain.

PANDEMICS

Pandemics are a completely different type of natural threat, not a threat from the physical environment, but from its organic subsystem. This is the threat in which some newly evolved infective agent, one that is both highly virulent and highly transmissible, could kill tens of millions of Americans. Past pandemics show the potential for such an effect. The Black Death which swept through Europe in the mid-fourteenth century killed about half of Europe's population. Although modern antibiotics would probably reduce the impact of such a bacterial disease, this is not assured. More recently the influenza pandemic of 1918 killed an estimated 50 million people worldwide; it infected some 28 percent of the American population, killing nearly 700,000 with a lethality rate of 2.5 percent, much higher than the 0.1 percent of previous epidemics. Since then, there have been a number of worrisome diseases, culminating with COVID-19, which emerged in China in late 2019. It claimed over 7 million deaths globally and more than a million in the United States. Thanks to an exceptionally rapid vaccine development, the United States was able to keep the epidemic in check, but control measures (such as mask requirements) stirred wide political disagreements.

Acquired Immune Deficiency Syndrome (AIDS) first came to the attention of medical authorities in June 1981. Since then, the virus has infected some 65 million people and killed 25 million of them. Initially it was invariably fatal. Now drugs have made it treatable in many cases, but it continues to take a heavy toll, especially in Africa. Humankind is fortunate that AIDS requires intimate contact for transmission. But AIDS is a stark reminder that new and highly virulent diseases can emerge unexpectedly.

With its restricted transmission, AIDS was not a prominent candidate for a new pandemic. But in November 2002, the first severe infectious disease to appear in the twenty-first century surfaced in China. As it spread to several hundred people, the World Health Organization became alarmed at this previously unrecognized disease, which became referred to as [Severe Acute Respiratory Syndrome](#) (SARS). By July 2003, there had been 8,096 known cases in 29 countries and 774 deaths (a mortality rate of 9.6 percent). By late 2003, the disease seemed to have run its course, thanks to close and proactive international cooperation. There was no vaccine or treatment; it responded to traditional treatment tools: isolation, infection control, and contact tracing. An epidemic did not seem likely, but development of effective drugs and vaccines takes considerable time. The virus has been characterized as sufficiently transmissible to cause a large epidemic, but not so contagious as to be uncontrollable with good public health measures.

Against this background, 2006 outbreaks of [avian influenza](#) were very sobering. In its initial appearance, it infected only 256 people in 10 countries, mostly people in close contact with chickens in Asia. Yet the pathogen had a staggering 60 percent mortality. Conditions also existed for the disease to become highly contagious. One possibility was that the avian influenza virus might exchange genes with a common form of flu that routinely infects people. Should this happen, it could acquire the basic genetic blueprint for spreading quickly—and explosively—through human populations. Scientists believe a similar [exchange of genetic material](#) occurred with the 1918 influenza virus. More recent research has clearly shown that such a [possibility exists](#) and might even be achieved by some rogue biologist.

Also, a number of African filoviruses (including Marburg fever and Ebola) have a potential for causing global disaster, particularly if viral mutations make them more transmissible. Ebola had apparently spread from Central to West Africa in 2004 from an animal host and then went quiet until 2014 when a serious outbreak killed more than 11,000. The tragic death toll was mainly due to a late global response and totally inadequate health care systems. A single infected person did show up in America and the incident, despite some initial problems, was contained without any serious impacts. More recently, an Ebola outbreak in eastern Congo escalated in part because locals do not trust health workers and government officials.

These disease outbreaks were put in stark perspective by the emergence of COVID-19 in late 2019. Originating in Wuhan, China, it probably mutated from bats or another animal source. As medical personnel there began to recognize it as a new disease, local authorities immediately suppressed public information and even allowed large events to go forward, resulting in significant numbers of infected people allowed to travel. Authorities at local World Health Organization (WHO) offices, including integrated American specialists, became aware of it in early January 2020. Although the WHO officials initially downplayed its significance, the integrated American personnel began directly notifying Washington by January 3, 2020. The concerns were brought to President Trump's attention but were dismissed as being overblown.

The American government had long recognized the urgency of a pandemic threat. As early as 2005, President Bush proposed a $7.1 billion program for pandemic flu protection and issued a new National Strategy for Pandemic Flu. This effort stalled and in October 2015 a Blue Ribbon Study Panel commented on the "insufficiency of our myriad and fragmented biodefense activities" due to a lack of focused leadership. The Obama administration developed a detailed "Playbook for Early Response to High-Consequence Emerging Infectious Disease Threats and

Biological Incident" in 2016, passing it to the incoming administration. In 2018, the Trump administration issued a comprehensive National Biodefense Strategy, but failed to fund it even as it dissolved the White House's pandemic office and provided only minimal funding to the national emergency stockpile.

By the end of January 2020 as COVID-19 spread, some 300,000 people had travelled from China to America. As the first American casualty surfaced in Seattle on January 21, President Trump took initial steps to address the challenge with a ban on some travelers from China but delayed a more important ban on travelers from Europe who were a much larger source of infections in America. It quickly became evident that the American supply of emergency medical equipment was totally inadequate. Without broad testing, the virus silently spread throughout America in February, even as President Trump insisted that COVID-19 cases would soon drop to zero, and his aides mocked questions about whether the administration had successfully contained the outbreak. President Trump continued to hold large-scale rallies, including a February rally in New Hampshire attended by thousands where he declared that "by April, you know, in theory, when it gets a little warmer, it miraculously goes away."

By early March, President Trump was assuring the nation that anyone could get tested, though supplies for this were totally inadequate. In mid-March, even as he was finally initiating restrictions on travelers from Europe, some politicians were still denouncing the threat as a hoax, complicating congressional efforts to address the issue.

By the end of April, over a million people in America had been infected and more than 60,000 had died, the highest numbers anywhere in the world, although the statistics were very uncertain. A large number of excess deaths compared to previous periods indicated that many people who died had never been tested for COVID-19, so deaths were significantly undercounted. Outbreaks in nursing homes, prisons and on board major naval vessels were particularly problematic. On the other hand, available testing showed that there were large numbers of infected people who showed no symptoms, and so infections were also significantly undercounted. Through most of 2020, the outbreak appeared to be contained, but starting in November, cases surged to far higher levels than seen earlier in the year and spread much more broadly across the nation. By the end of 2020, over 20 million American cases of COVID-19 and almost 400,000 deaths were confirmed. This peak in cases came at the same time that vaccines were being initially distributed, though with widespread problems and little national direction.

Globally, there was a wide variation in early impacts. In China, once stringent controls were initiated, the rates dropped significantly; by late April there were days with no additional infections reported. Total infections for a population of 1.4 billion stood at 88,000, with 4,600 deaths. Vietnam (95 million population), which initiated strict controls early, reported less than 300 infections and zero deaths by mid-2020. South Korea (52 million population), which also initiated early restrictions and widespread testing, only reported 10,800 infections and 247 deaths. Italy (60 million population), on the other hand, was slow to put restrictions in place and reported 205,000 infections and 28,000 deaths. By the end of July, America, with just 4 percent of the world's population had more than 20 percent of the world's coronavirus deaths, a vivid commentary on how poorly the disease had been managed. Globally, cases had generally stabilized by mid-2020, but they surged again later in the year with over 90 million total cases and almost two million deaths by early January 2021.

The economic impact has been considerable. In America, even at the end of the first quarter of 2020, gross domestic product dropped almost 5 percent, with a much larger drop expected in the next quarter as over 30 million jobless claims had been filed. By early April as business restrictions were having a major impact on the economy, public demonstrations, encouraged by President Trump, already began to demand loosening of the restrictions. Inadequate testing supplies made balancing commercial pressures with medical concerns difficult. Without any comprehensive national direction, individual states, cities, and localities began various efforts to roll back restrictions. By mid-year, the economy had plunged 31.4 percent; an expected rebound vanished as a second surge of infections began in October. By the end of the year, job losses were the worst since 1939.

The lessons are clear even though the final tallies are yet to come. COVID-19 is considerably more transmissible than yearly influenza and has a higher fatality rate of several percent. But avian influenza and Ebola have had rates over 50 percent and AIDS originally 100 percent. Even with relatively modest rates, COVID-19 has severely impacted the economy, both domestically and globally, and provided a dramatic demonstration of how catastrophic a more virulent disease could be. The impact in America was certainly exacerbated by the slow response as it was over two months from the initial warnings before President Trump initiated significant travel restrictions, but never organized a cohesive national policy. Almost all the response came from state and local officials. Long-term underfunding of pandemic readiness and inadequate stockpiling of emergency supplies also complicated responses. This slow response meant that America had one of the highest death rates in the developed world. All this reinforced the same conclusion drawn after earlier epidemics and then ignored: extensive preparation is needed in advance of an epidemic

Overall, the outbreaks this century of influenza, AIDS, Ebola, SARS and COVID-19 make clear that virulent pandemics pose a catastrophic threat not just to America but globally. These recent pandemics have all been virus based, but the increasing ability of bacteria to develop resistance to antibiotics means they cannot be neglected. With widespread international travel now common, one lesson of the SARS epidemic was how quickly it spread to almost 30 countries, despite being under international medical scrutiny. COVID-19 also spread very rapidly. A highly transmissible disease with a longer incubation period could spread widely before anyone even recognized its presence. Once such a pandemic got started, the deaths of tens of millions of Americans is certainly within the spectrum of possibilities. The probability of such an occurrence is also not quantifiable due to the variability of both pathogen lethality and transmissibility. Considering the variety of possible infective agents and the record of past and current epidemics, the pandemic threat is probably the highest catastrophic threat the nation faces.

SUMMARY

Natural threats are part of the everyday challenge of life. Risks vary widely by location but almost everyone is affected, directly or indirectly. Disasters are a significant burden, not only locally but on the national economy. The initial responsibility for disaster planning falls on individual landowners and companies.

Physical protection starts with reasonably sturdy construction in reasonably safe locations. Partly as a result of disasters over the past decades, local construction codes have been significantly strengthened to require buildings that can better withstand stresses. Codes also discourage building in high-risk zones. Yet individuals are often ready to accept seemingly unrealistic risks and build (or re-build) in danger areas without any significant protection or mitigation.

Medical protection is more difficult, even at an individual level. The COVID epidemic included a wide variety of objections against locally required actions (such as masks, vaccine requirements and event closures). This obviously made it difficult for officials to address risks. Especially early in the epidemic, the medical community was overwhelmed and treatment was not available for all those who needed it. This improved substantially as time went on and vaccines became available. Businesses shut down many offices and group activities, widely using remote work for employees as economic activities generally continued to function. At the national level, the unexpectedly quick vaccine response demonstrated the importance of prior preparations and concerted government management.

Overall, even this cursory overview makes clear that there are hundreds of billions of dollars of requirements for disaster mitigation and preparedness and many of them are not being met because of budget problems for individuals, as well as for governments at all levels. Preparations invariably cost much less than losses and recovery, as well as the costs of re-aligning local economies and individual lives, so shortfalls now inevitably mean larger expenses later. This is a classic Penny Wise, Pound Foolish situation, but it is not just money that suffers. Individual deaths and major life disruptions have an even bigger and more personal impact. The nation needs to give much more attention to building resiliency; governments and organizations at all levels need to be better prepared to manage responses to the threats they face.

2

DOMESTIC CHALLENGES

The central domestic challenge is to create a society that works for everyone. In Thomas Jefferson's words in the Declaration of Independence, society needs to support the "pursuit of happiness." This is a subjective quality. Lincoln famously commented that, "Most folks are about as happy as they make up their minds to be." Happiness depends in large measure on each individual's assessment of his or her own unique situation.

A comprehensive British study of happiness agreed that individual personalities and demographics have a major impact on happiness as well as living in a well-managed, democratic society. Liberty is an important element of happiness. Other major factors included income levels, job satisfaction, health, and an active social life. Unemployment had a significant negative impact. Education *per se* did not seem to have a real impact. Income inequality is associated with low levels of life satisfaction in Europe, but less so in America. Partly this is attributed to higher levels of American social mobility, basically agreeing with an American commentator who noted that equality of opportunity was more important than equality of results. More recently, a broad survey of Americans showed that while money can't really buy happiness, it can help a lot. The correlation between income and happiness has steadily risen over the years.

Opportunity in America can be summed up in two words: American Dream. Work hard and you do well. You can create a comfortable life, own your own home, look forward to a retirement pension, and you can set up your kids for an even better life in the future. National prosperity is the glue that holds everything together. Critical to national cohesion, it is the economic dimension of happiness, and it also provides the resources to address threats and challenges to life and liberty.

The American economic system drove two centuries of impressive growth. Coming into the twentieth century, automobiles were something new—most people had never even seen one. Telephones were just beginning to catch on with strictly local applications. Commercial radios were brand new, but there was no such thing as broadcasting to a wide audience. Cities were just beginning to use electric power in public buildings, businesses, and public transport, such as trams and trains. Airplanes were unheard of. Coming into the twenty-first century, television was common, many people had computers and the internet as well as cell phones, and the country had even put men on the moon. Contemporary cellphones actually outperform computers from the 1990's. They can replace cameras, direct you to a specific destination, or let you know the distance to your favorite store. A century of innovation continues at an astounding pace.

The American economy is dauntingly complex and intertwined in many ways with the global economy. The key question is sustainability: Can the economy continue to function at a high level of satisfaction in the years ahead? This requires facing a number of major challenges. As the threat of national annihilation has receded and threats of major damage remain unlikely, economic well-being becomes more and more the focus of government actions.

Economic challenges are often diffuse in that their impact will not result from some specific major events, but rather from the cumulative effect of thousands or even millions of individual actions. Their consequences can be off in a hazy future. Assessing costs depends on very uncertain projections while necessary countermeasures are typically unclear and often controversial and expensive.

Internal challenges can undermine the economy's ability to function efficiently. The government can control some of these challenges and influence others. Maximum economic efficiency is important, but the key requirement is that the economy work for everyone.

ROUTINE THREATS TO LIFE

These are threats from risks that we accept as a matter of course. They are part of our everyday existence, but they still impact heavily on the nation.

Aircraft Accidents

Aircraft accidents are a major concern for some people who would rather drive from Boston to New York because they are afraid of flying, even though the associated risks are much higher driving. The last fatal American airline crash was a decade ago, although one passenger was killed in a 2018 emergency landing. Even the worst aircraft accident in history—two planes colliding in the Canary Islands in March 1977—killed "only" 578 people. Overall, it would be very unlikely for fatalities from aviation accidents to rise into the thousands. But because they tend to occur in large discreet groups, they have a disproportionate impact on the general psyche.

Traffic Accidents

Traffic accidents are one of the most visible of these routine threats to life. They killed 42,939 people in 2021, the highest number since 2005. That's over a hundred people a day, every day, year in and year out, relentlessly. Many people know a family badly impacted by a traffic accident. These yearly numbers have increased in the last decade. Several major accident causes are well known. Addressing them is a state responsibility, so there are 50 different responses, some better, some worse. As a result, deaths per 100 million miles driven also vary widely, from a low of from 0.71 in Massachusetts to 2.08 in South Carolina.

- Alcohol was involved in over a third of fatal accidents, sometimes by repeat offenders. Cultural tolerance for drunken driving, laws against it, enforcement of these laws, and local driving conditions vary widely.

- Inexperienced youthful drivers are responsible for a disproportionate share of fatal accidents. In the last decade, a number of states have enacted legislation specifically aimed at this aspect of the problem. Typical measures include limiting driving privileges to daytime hours, prohibiting youthful passengers, and requiring expanded driver training.

- Distractions significantly increase the accident rate. In 2020, crashes involving distracted drivers killed 3,142 people. Any non-driving activity increases the risk of crashing. Sending a text, for example, may only take a person's eyes off the road for 5 seconds, but at 55 mph, that's like driving the length of an entire football field with your eyes closed.

Murders

Murders accounted for about 22,941 deaths in 2021. Some categories, such as those that are gang- and drug-related, are concentrated in cities—murders in major cities per hundred thousand inhabitants varied from 0.3 in Irvine, California, to 88.1 in St. Louis, Missouri, in 2020. Other categories, such as domestic arguments, are spread more evenly over the entire country. Some significant categories are as follows:

- Gang- and drug-related murders mostly affect people who have some association with gangs or drugs. Unfortunately, the association can be both innocent and peripheral. Relatives, friends, neighbors, co-workers, local merchants, and random bystanders are all affected by these murders. Sometimes entire neighborhoods are involved. Often other criminal activities (such as prostitution, extortion, gambling, and human trafficking) complicate the situation. Counteractions depend on both state and local authorities and can be severely hampered by budget issues.

- Arguments are responsible for over a third of all murders. These include domestic violence, often following long periods of verbal and physical abuse. Typically, this involves abused wives, but girlfriends, husbands, children, and aged relatives also become targets. Addressing these situations requires very different approaches than other crime-related murders. State and local agencies as well as private organizations provide a wide range of badly needed services that vary widely by location.. Privacy concerns as well as a frequent reluctance of people to prosecute relatives greatly complicate these issues.

Drugs

The United States is suffering the deadliest drug epidemic in its history. Overdoses claimed the lives of more than 100,000 Americans between August 2021 and August 2022 alone. Over the span of just a few years, drug deaths have doubled. What had been a long-term problem has suddenly emerged as a national challenge, no longer just an opioid epidemic but an addiction crisis. COVID reduced the availability of medical support for anything outside the pandemic as drug companies pushed the availability of opioid anti-pain medicine. Growing economic distress has pushed thousands to use drugs to escape reality. Most importantly, a broad range of new drugs and an intensified supply of fentanyl have made addressing this challenge much more difficult. Governments at all levels struggle cracking down on suppliers while supporting treatment. Different localities have decriminalized possessing small drug quantities, supported needle exchange programs and safe injection sites. Results are often hard to measure.

Much of the drugs used, including almost all the fentanyl, is produced abroad and often entangled with other activities, such as wildlife trafficking and illegal fishing. International efforts at stemming the flow of drugs is greatly complicated by linkages between organized crime and foreign governments, as well as the resilience of international criminal networks. A whole-of-government approach is badly needed.

A central problem is money. At the individual level, economic difficulties push more and more people to drugs, while making low-level trafficking an attractive option in disadvantaged populations. Local, regional and state governments simply do not have the resources to support disadvantaged populations and provide appropriate mental health and rehabilitation organizations.

PERSONAL LIBERTY

Liberty is America.

The Statue of Liberty graces the entrance to our major immigration port, a gift from the people of France in deference to the principle of liberty (Liberté)—revolutions in both countries fought for it.

Americans take pride in their country as the Land of the Free. Despite many shortcomings, initially including slavery, America was recognized globally as a new type of nation, a nation founded on the principle that "all men are created equal." American economic success sprang from the dynamism of a free society; the statue became a beacon of freedom for millions, living up to its formal name, Liberty Enlightening the World, and its inscription: "Give me your tired, your poor, your huddled masses, yearning to breathe free, the wretched refuse of your teeming shore, send these, the homeless, tempest- tost to me."

With its participation and leadership in World Wars I and II, America established itself not just as a beacon of freedom, but as a fighter for it. It led the world in the struggle against tyrannical Nazi Germany and the Communist Soviet Union. Thanks to America's idealism and vision of freedom, the world was generally tolerant of its excesses and its arrogance: a deeply ingrained feeling that America knew what was best for the world. Even critics of this arrogance recognized that without American leadership, international crises were often unresolved. As one example, when America stood by during the genocide in Rwanda, so did everyone else. A resolution of the war in Bosnia took shape only when America stepped in after the European Union proved impotent.

America celebrates an innate urge to freedom as the driving force of history, a force that will displace tyrants and bring representative government to all. The opening line of President George W. Bush's National Security Strategy stressed that it is the "policy of the United States to seek and support democratic movements and institutions in every nation and culture." As noted above, President Trump's National Security Strategy prioritized the interests of American citizens and protecting our sovereign rights as a nation, but also recognized that promoting American values is key to spreading peace and prosperity around the globe. President Biden's subsequent version stressed working with allies to shape the international order. Freedom is not free, and America now faces serious challenges, both external and internal, challenges that directly attack the basic premise that liberty is indeed a common goal of mankind.

America has always been a country where individuals are not subject to arbitrary or capricious restrictions. The Constitutional Bill of Rights defines the core concepts of internal freedoms. The stark simplicity of its statements contrasts strikingly with the realities of a complex society. Now, even a casual glance at a typical law library drives home the vast scope of laws and regulations at national, state, and local level which restrain all our freedoms. Many of these are necessary so that a complex society can function smoothly. With a multitude of freedoms defined, it is inevitable that they will be in conflict in some situations and there will be a need for balancing one freedom against another. Courts at all levels are continuously addressing such questions of balance. Several subjects pose major challenges to individual freedoms within the country.

Religious Freedom

The very first words of the Bill of Rights address this core freedom. Although the Declaration of Independence references a "Creator," the founding fathers carefully worded the First Amendment to establish a secular state that prohibited any "establishment of religion." Its language clearly supports that people are free to believe what they choose, but not to force their beliefs on others. Yet laws, and the education system, inevitably have a moral grounding and this is tied to religious sources as well as legislators' individual beliefs.

From the earliest years of the nation, there has been a significant non-Christian element in the population, including Native Americans and Jews; then Asian laborers added to this mixture. Non-Christian beliefs have become more pronounced in recent years. Now only [64 percent](#) of the American population consider themselves Christian; over a quarter profess [no religious affiliation](#), but rather humanist, deist, or even atheist beliefs. Others associate with minority sects or cults. The association with the Islamic world reaches deep into our nation, which now includes well over [three million Muslims](#). Nevertheless, polls show that a large portion of the country still considers America to be a Christian nation; about a quarter of the population would favor legislation based on a [Biblical view rather than a popular vote](#). Christian beliefs and practices retain a strong hold on the population.

Against this varied background, further tensions are inevitable, all the more so in a society that has become prone to legal challenges. Many current controversies, including abortion, contraception, and civil unions, reflect the tension between religious principles and secular society. These controversies undermine social cohesiveness and make it increasingly difficult for governments at all levels to remain religiously neutral. People holding strong religious views typically see other views as simply wrong, undermining tolerance which is an essential value of a free society.

- Abortion. Conception starts a new life. Birth brings a new human being into the world. But there is no simple correlation between fertilized eggs and human beings. A fertilized egg may simply fail to implant in the uterus and simply be washed out of the body, or may implant in a Fallopian tube. Many fertilized eggs are naturally rejected in early miscarriages. A single fertilized egg can also develop into two (or more) separate embryos. Such embryos normally develop into identical siblings, but occasionally one embryo envelopes and encapsulates the other. This may come to light years later when a troublesome cyst is removed and found to be the remnant of a sibling twin. Clusters may also fail to totally separate and produce a variety of odd situations, including various types of conjoined twins. For example, Abigail and Brittany Hensel are clearly two persons with one body and not one person with two heads. In other recent cases, one girl born in India had one head but two faces; another had eight limbs. In individual cases, it may be difficult to decide whether there is one person or two. Equating conception with personhood is a religious judgement that is not shared by the majority of citizens or even specifically by major religions. From a theological point of view, a new person emerges when God infuses an immortal soul. Exactly when this occurs is something that religion has historically treated as ambiguous. Religions generally do not consider an early-stage fetus as a person and rarely hold a funeral for a miscarriage at this stage. Biology cannot answer this theological question. This is the central question that society has to address, deciding when a fetus becomes a person that society should protect.

- Marriage is a religious concept. It legitimizes sex between a man and a woman, essential for procreation which some churches see as the primary or even the only legitimate purpose of sex. Churches should be free to marry, or not marry, whomever they see fit, and indeed they are. Supporting the commitments of couples to one another and to their children, the government does have an interest in stable families. And so governments recognize marriage as an important civil commitment. Civil marriages performed by public officials also address this public interest. Similarly, many states recognize Common Law Marriages, granting couples who have demonstrated commitment and devotion to one another many of the rights and privileges afforded married couples. A number of states also recognize a status of civil union, allowing people to make a public commitment to each other without the necessity of meeting religious criteria, including gender. Civil unions are what governments have a legitimate interest in, recognizing stable commitments that support stable family units. Religious organizations may object to civil unions that do not meet their marriage criteria, particularly in regard to gender arrangements. But in 2020, even Pope Francis supported civil unions. That same year, Utah decriminalized polygamy which had been criminal throughout America.

Strongly held religious views have historically promoted civil legislation clearly at odds with civil rights in a free society. Numerous laws discriminated against women, who were only given the right to vote in 1920. Firm believers have also regularly turned to violence, particularly against abortion providers, gays and transgender individuals. The Supreme Court's recent decision that abortion is not a constitutional right has opened the road to a wide variety of state actions limiting abortions and restricting the availability of abortion pills. This is clearly an area where religious views are having a major impact on legislation.

Numerous instances have occurred where individuals or organizations offer public services but refuse to serve individuals who do not meet their religious criteria. Then these criteria take precedence over equal treatment under law. Similarly, in 2014 the Supreme Court decided that corporations are persons and has allowed Hobby Lobby to refuse legally required health insurance coverage to employees based on <u>religious criteria</u>. A multicultural society simply cannot function smoothly without broad respect for other views. Freedom of religion has to include freedom from having religious views imposed. Tolerance is a central social requirement.

Free Press

The First Amendment also prohibits Congress from making any law "abridging the freedom of speech, or of the press." A free press is an essential element of democracy, providing a check and assessments on government actions. The free press in America faces several major challenges:

- Newspapers are financially stressed as fewer people get their regular news from newspapers, so subscriber and advertising income drops even as expenses increase. This has steadily forced individual papers to close, especially those run by <u>for profit organizations</u>. In 2020, both <u>Salt Lake City daily newspapers</u> shifted to a weekly format while maintaining an online presence. <u>Nationwide</u>, the newspaper industry has lost more than a quarter of its newspapers and almost 60 percent of its newsroom employees since 2005.

- The Trump administration regularly denounced any critical postings as fake news. The President systematically put out questionable information, by one count 20,000 false or misleading claims. Newspapers naturally critiqued his commentaries, giving him a basis to claim that the mainstream media was prejudiced against him. This began right after his inauguration when his press secretary falsely claimed that his audience was the "largest audience to ever witness an inauguration" and his senior adviser defended this as "alternative facts." It culminated in January 2021 when a mob of extremists stormed the American capitol following weeks of President Trump wrongly insisting that the election had been stolen from him and directing his followers to exert pressure on their elected representatives.

- The rise of the internet has given millions of people alternative sources of news, often inaccurate versions that spread very quickly. This was well illustrated by an article tracking how three false election commentaries rapidly gained traction on Facebook and Twitter, generating tens of thousands of shares and comments. Newspapers are generally responsible for what they publish, but social media is largely not responsible for content created by their users. The rise of extremist rhetoric leading to the mobbing of the capitol resulted in some major social media companies shutting down selected accounts. It has also intensified discussion on the degree that social media should censor content.

The profusion of often contradictory news sources can leave the broad public uncertain of just what to believe. Individuals naturally tend to accept reports that support their own beliefs. In this state of affairs, not only do falsehoods flourish, but even outlandish narratives, such as a QAnon conspiracy that presents Trump as battling a cabal of deep-state saboteurs who worship Satan and traffic children for sex.

Social media sites have an incentive to allow controversial or even false information because it can help generate traffic and increase ad revenue. Ad revenue is also facilitated by the collection of large amounts of personal information on users. Journalism is no longer restricted to newspapers but is practiced by many public policy and social media sites. Free speech allows organizations and individuals to distribute a wide range of questionable information. Some of this is moderated by governments and some by the media outlets themselves. The most important moderator has to be the user, assessing the validity of the flood of information threatening to overwhelm everyone.

Guns

The Second Amendment is short and succinct: "A well regulated Militia, being necessary to the security of a free State, the right of the people to keep and bear Arms, shall not be infringed." But it is also ambiguous; it took a 2008 Supreme Court decision to determine that the right to bear arms is an individual right. The central problem is that bearing arms is not a fundamental human right (like, say, free speech or a right to a trial) or even a fundamental collective right (like the right to assemble). Rather the Second Amendment was a reflection by politicians some two hundred years ago of what would be appropriate for America in the society of that time. And that society is now fundamentally different in two major aspects:

First, the need to bear arms:

- Then: Several factors supported the need for individuals to bear arms. In 1776 a viable citizen militia was an important element of national defense. There were significant collective dangers, and foreign invasions were not unlikely. In the War of 1812, the British invaded and burned parts of Washington. Indian wars at that time meant that individuals needed to protect themselves in case of local attacks. Guns were used by slave holders to maintain control over their slaves and to quell potential rebellions. Many people depended on hunting as a food source and attacks by wild animals on the frontier were often a daily threat.

- Now: America has a well-established armed force of over 1.3 million. It is almost unconscionable to think everyday citizens would need to jump individually to the defense of our nation. In fact, each state has its own National Guard at the ready to be called to active duty, and they also can serve as a local militia. For the most part, Indian wars ended with the Wounded Knee Massacre in 1890. The need to control slaves ended in 1865. People can still hunt for food, but that doesn't require an automatic weapon. And wild animal attacks are certainly less prevalent these days.

Second, the arms themselves:

- Then: Guns were single-shot, muzzle-loading weapons firing low-velocity lead balls. At the time, modern weapons were not even dreamed of—the first fully automatic machinegun was not invented until around 1884. The manufacturing of rifles and handguns was slow and laborious, so most citizens owned only one weapon.

- Now: Rapid fire, even automatic fire, weapons with high-velocity, high-lethality bullets are available to most citizens. The purchase of semi-automatic weapons is legal in most states, as are automatic weapons made before 1986. The Founding

Fathers had no idea that one person could stash a horde of automatic weapons and, in a period of ten minutes, injure over 800 people and kill almost 60 more (October 17, 2017—Las Vegas, Nevada). Let's not even go into the Columbine or Sandy Hook school shootings

Although the Constitution was well-drafted, it is neither infallible nor sacrosanct. This is, after all, a Constitution that legalized slavery and ignored women's rights. The Second Amendment was a political response to the security situation two centuries ago. Even if it were well worded, even if we knew exactly what the drafters had in mind, it could not provide meaningful guidance for our modern society. It is probably the single most outdated part of the entire Constitution. Instead of quibbling over the exact meaning, scope, or intent of the Second Amendment, what is needed is a new consensus on what constitutes a reasonable role for guns in modern society.

Society is much more complex with dense concentrations of people in sprawling mega-cities. In America, gun ownership is more deeply embedded in society than anywhere else in the world. It is tied to the spirit of individual freedom that was so critical to the nation in its early years.

Why even allow any private ownership of guns? It is certainly not an inalienable human right. The original main justification of a well-regulated militia has long ago disappeared, particularly with the nation's extensive armed forces well able to protect it. Hunting is clearly still important, though now more for outdoor experience or trophies than for actual food need.

A major reason for gun ownership is recreation—target practice, skeet shooting, and competitive shooting. Guns can also provide a sense of power and control. Of course, anyone able to blow targets away can also blow people away, and some will. In 2023 alone there were 656 mass shootings, an average of 118 deaths per day due to gun violence. Many gun owners form into groups, even groups organized on militia lines. Often it is not easy to even judge if a group has formed to enjoy guns or to use guns to promote some radical agenda. Or both. In recent years individual militia groups speak of civil strife, and right-wing extremists are now the major domestic terrorist threat. This has raised deep concerns about potential armed riots after elections. A 2020 militia attempt to kidnap and possibly execute Michigan Governor Gretchen Whitmer was another striking example of the threat posed by these groups. Then on January 6, 2021, a mob of several hundred, including a number of armed militia groups, stormed the national capitol at President Trump's encouragement, overwhelming the police and vandalizing the building. Some people died. Numerous arrests were made, including some on weapon charges. Less than two weeks later, at an annual rally in Richmond, Virginia, hundreds of gun rights proponents from many of the same militia groups openly displayed guns in defiance of state law, intimidating both police and bystanders. Overall, recreation is a terrible justification for gun ownership, especially assault guns, and gun groups are posing a challenge to national order.

Self-protection is now the central justification. Criminals can always get guns, though the harder it is, the fewer will succeed. From an individual point of view, it clearly is attractive to own guns for self-protection. A central problem is the fact that many people injured by guns are not injured by criminals but by other legal gun owners. In some cases, it is simply due to accidents or carelessness: a small child shooting somebody, a stray bullet, or an accidental discharge.

Herein lies the central paradox: the more people who own guns for self-protection, the more they will need them, the more shootings there will be. In addition to accidents, normal, everyday people occasionally lose control of themselves; some are more hot-headed than others, or more depressed, or have more suppressed rage. So domestic problems, friction at work or school, a dispute with a neighbor, racial slurs, or road rage can lead to gun violence. Certainly the situation is worsened if fueled by alcohol or drugs, or by someone's gradual decline into despondency or dementia. These concerns are magnified in an economic situation that puts people under significant stress.

Background checks try to weed out the most obvious cases of concern, but the central problem remains: any person buying a gun can be perfectly normal today, or at least seem normal, but what about tomorrow? Some percent of those who legitimately buy guns for protection will eventually use them for destruction. In two studies, one found that a gun is 12 times more likely to result in the death of a household member or guest than in the death of an intruder. The other found that gun ownership creates nearly a threefold risk of a homicide in the owner's household. Armed individuals may interrupt a mass shooting, but this rarely happens; more likely the person interrupting will also be shot. What's more, all gun owners are subject to the risk that someone else will take control of their gun; many guns are simply stolen.

All of these factors create the Protection Paradox: the widespread ownership of protective weapons increases the risks for everyone. Owning a gun can indeed provide personal protection and can make sense for individuals but does not make sense for society as a whole. Even for many individuals, the benefits of protection may be overshadowed by the risks their own gun ownership creates. There is no answer to this paradox, no solution to the challenge it poses. More stringent checks can help, but inevitably will provoke much vocal dissent. In the longer run, a more widespread awareness of the low level of actual protection that guns provide, coupled with the risks involved, could lead to lower ownership levels, especially if people are basically comfortable with their economic situations. It seems for the foreseeable future the Protection Paradox will continue to confound society. The more people who have guns, the more people will need to have guns.

Specific actions have to be taken as there are far more guns than are rationally needed. One study showed that incorporation of background checks at a federal level could cut gun mortality in half. Further, expanding them to include ammunition purchases could reduce mortality in half again. Background checks keep guns and ammunition away from those who should not have them, reducing both homicides and suicides. There also needs to be restrictions on particularly dangerous weapons, especially assault rifles, specifically designed to kill people in military operations. A buy-back program could be helpful but could take decades to have a real impact. When Australia passed a very strict gun control law that included such a program, the country recovered 600,000 assault rifles and other arms—20 percent of all the known firearms in Australia. Homicides by firearm plunged 59 percent between 1995 and 2006, with no corresponding increase in non-firearm-related homicides. The drop in suicides by gun was even steeper: 65 percent. Studies found a close correlation between these sharp declines and the gun buybacks. The most stunning statistic was on mass shooting. In the decade before the new gun controls, there had been 11 mass shootings in the country. There hasn't been a single one in Australia since.

There is clearly no simple solution to the gun control problem. It has been over two centuries in the making and results of controls are often not visible for years. Many gun control arguments do not hold water, but they hold money, lots of it. Despite the fact that most Americans are in favor of gun controls, opposition is intense, another example of the impact of money in the political arena.

Search, Seizure, and Surveillance

The Fourth Amendment prohibits "unreasonable" search and seizure and sets requirements for judicial warrants which have long been used to authorize wire taps, communications intercepts, and physical searches. Criminals have always taken advantage of these rights to protect their own nefarious actions. The public has accepted this complication of crime fighting as a necessary cost of maintaining individual freedoms.

The situation has gotten much more complicated with the proliferation of electronic means of communication and the rise of international terrorism, largely based in radical Islamic groups. The increasing vulnerability of society has made intelligence gathering and analysis much more critical to the nation. The 9/11 attacks, followed by bombings in London and Madrid, starkly demonstrated the perils of inadequate intelligence. Protecting against these very substantial threats has inevitably intruded on personal freedoms. Nowhere is this more evident than in New York City, the epicenter of terrorist attacks. Between 2005 and 2013, the New York Police Department aggressively conducted hundreds of thousands of "stop and frisk" encounters with young men and monitored potentially disruptive groups, particularly Muslim organizations. Lately such "stop and frisk" encounters have been curtailed due to nationwide protests against police excessive use of force, chiefly against minorities. It has also become clear that terrorist activities can be carried out by white nationalists as well, further complicating the intelligence challenge.

The situation is greatly impacted by the ways that modern technology has increased the potential for surveillance. Cameras are now commonplace not only at traffic intersections and in airports, but in stores, homes, and even doorbells. These cameras store data but are also often linked with recognition software that can identify license plates and individuals. Telephones are no longer just for calls; they are powerful miniature computers that store extensive data from calls and messages. They can also show where a person is located; law enforcement agencies are apparently collecting this data globally. Since the calls are wireless, they can also be intercepted and monitored. Social media companies collect expanded amounts of personal data and sell it to marketing companies, but this data is also susceptible to surveillance monitoring. Police now use drones for surveillance. Body cameras, though they reduce the potential for misconduct, also record large amounts of private information. An economy that depends increasingly on credit cards rather than cash also puts large amounts of private information in the electronic cloud where it is susceptible to surveillance.

Congress has tried to address police surveillance by creating special secret courts and specific exemptions from warrant requirements to meet the diffuse threat from terrorists and other international adversaries. America has assembled a vast domestic intelligence apparatus to collect information about Americans, using the FBI, local police, state homeland security offices, and military criminal investigators. This inevitably touched innocent and unaware citizens and was the central reason that Edward Snowden released thousands of classified documents in 2013. The intelligence community naturally denounced him as a traitor, even though a federal court ruled that the mass surveillance program he exposed was illegal and possibly unconstitutional. The central questions have become: To what extent should we give up our freedoms to protect our freedom, and how much surveillance is appropriate? There are no obvious answers, but several key observations are pertinent:

- The terrorist threat is relatively low level so does not clearly justify a high surveillance level.
- It is unclear to what extent various surveillance programs actually contribute to critical intelligence assessments. The

programs are helpful in addressing everyday criminal activities, but this does not show an intelligence need.

- Judicial and congressional overview was minimal until 2020 protests energized by the Black Lives Matter movement erupted

The increasingly complex issue of search and surveillance calls for a broad public consensus on what is reasonable and what is not. Regular judicial oversight and periodic national reviews to assess the continuing need in light of real risks are a minimum requirement. Nationwide protests have cast light on ingrained problems in police forces across the nation. This has forced conversations on various reforms to help police better maintain law and order.

Speedy Trial

The Bill of Rights provides "any person" the right to due process, to a speedy trial, and to confront witnesses. At times these rights have been suspended for national security needs with the most nefarious example being the WWII incarceration of thousands of Japanese-Americans. In addition, these rights have not generally been accorded to prisoners of war who, after all, are not usually accused of any individual criminal actions but are held until the cessation of hostilities.

Providing a speedy trail is immediately problematical for several reasons. The first is staffing. It takes a lot of resources to provide the personnel needed to run an efficient court system. The system has to assemble and pay for jurors, provide lawyers for many defendants, and be prepared for delays from unexpected circumstances. A busy court simply means a slow trial schedule. Bail can also be a major problem. Everyday people are often unable to post bond. Courts are reluctant to release people facing trial, even for minor offenses, that could result in jail time – a problem exacerbated by excessive prison sentencing as discussed below.

Radical Islamic terrorists have made determinations in this area highly problematic. Even when caught on the battlefield they rarely qualify as "prisoners of war," but more correctly as international criminals. As with many criminals, they will often loudly proclaim their innocence and challenge their status. A number who have been released have subsequently been found once again engaging in active hostilities against American forces. Evidence against individuals is often circumstantial or ambiguous and rarely would meet courtroom requirements. This evidence often includes data that if disclosed would directly undermine further intelligence efforts. Additionally, some information was obtained by torture, particularly waterboarding. After World War II, the Allies executed Japanese officials for waterboarding Allied prisoners, but the Bush administration defended the practice. This provoked much controversy and certainly helped undermine American prestige abroad, as well as greatly complicating any use of evidence at trials..

This challenge has been particularly difficult in regards to terrorists seized in international situations and then held outside the United States at the Guantanamo Bay Naval Base in Cuba. Although regarded as some of the worst of the worst, much of evidence against them would be difficult to present in court and is often tainted by charges of torture. Efforts to close the prison have been moving slowly for years.

Criminals, terrorists, and deranged individuals and groups continuously seek ways to use civil freedoms against society. Society continuously seeks ways to avert their efforts in order to maintain freedoms while blocking abuse of them. The courts are where these competing efforts get resolved so an efficient system expeditiously moving case through, is a critical function for society.

Prison System

The largest group of people in the nation who are clearly not at liberty are those who are incarcerated. Wrongdoers of various sorts are put in prison to punish them for serious crimes and to protect the general population. Ideally, the punishment will get convicts to see the drawbacks of a life of crime and to resolve to be contributors to society. In individual cases there are such alternatives to prison as community service, fines, or probation periods, but no modern government has been able to eliminate the need for prisons. Nevertheless, it is incongruous that the Land of Freedom is also the nation that has the highest incarceration rate in the world with some 1.9 million imprisoned, a rate of 664 per 100,000. The rate is now seven times higher than the median rate (102) for other rich democracies and more than ten times higher than the rates in Scandinavia.

The prison system itself has serious problems:

- Minorities have typically received harsher sentences and been more heavily impacted by specific guidelines, such as a three-strike rule mandating life sentences for repeat offenders, or simply a requirement for monetary bail. They have also been convicted more often than white defendants for similar crimes and are given longer prison terms.
- Rehabilitation is an objective, but prison often has the opposite effect, serving as a school for criminals, an opportunity for negative networking and building relationships that facilitate a criminal life. It is not unusual for people needing mental help to end up in prison.

- There is widespread abuse within the prison system. Sexual abuse by other prisoners is prevalent, also occasionally by prison staff. Solitary confinement certainly has justifications, but there are presently some tens of thousands of prisoners held under these conditions. When used for extended periods of time, it can literally drive prisoners insane.

- Released convicts have difficulty reintegrating into society. Not only are their voting rights often taken away, but the stigma of being an ex-convict is a major impediment to finding a job, even in good economic conditions. Reintegration is even more difficult, certainly helping to encourage ex-convicts to turn back to a life of crime. Some programs, like Homeboy Industries, work to solve this problem, but it is an uphill battle to even keep the program funded.

- Prison administrators and staff have a vested interest in maintaining high prison populations. This interest is even starker with commercially operated prisons which have an obviously strong interest in high inmate levels. Nearly half a million people are in pre-trial confinement, by far the highest rate in the world.

- Sexual predators are a particularly difficult challenge to the system. Rehabilitation is not easy, but mandatory life sentences are clearly out of the question. A wide range of crimes can result in someone being classified as a sex offender and it is unclear, to say the least, how to best structure sentencing and living restrictions.

The prison system is a drain not only on the idealism of America, but obviously on its resources. The direct economic cost is significant. Yet the direct cost is only half of the problem; the lost opportunity cost is even higher, what the convicts could be contributing if they were productive members of society. Beyond these purely economic costs are the social costs of disrupted families and broken communities. Overall, it is distressing that the American prison system is one of the worst in the world.

Voting

Voting is a central element of democracy. In theory, it is quite simple—on election day voters go to the polls and cast their votes and the votes get counted. But each state and some subordinate elements have their own systems, often heavily dependent on volunteers, as well as weather and traffic. Simply getting to the polls can be difficult for some in rural areas. Individuals may be without transportation, disabled, or unable to get time off work. Mail-in ballots can ease some problems but create others. Despite a lack of any evidence, in the 2020 election President Trump continually denounced mail-in ballots as a source of [massive fraud](). This was the underlying reason he gave for promoting the mob attack on the capitol building.

Concerns about fraud bring increased controls on ballot collections, stricter individual identification, and restrictions on specific classes of people such as felons, current or past. What seems like perfectly reasonable requirements can prove quite difficult for some. Simply getting an identification card can be problematic for someone born at home or who lives on a reservation.

Voting oversight is complicated by the fact that people in political control of an area may want to suppress some classes of voters by strict enforcement of controls as well as manipulation of times and places for polls. On a broader scale, officials in many areas have traditionally manipulated election district boundaries to favor the party in power. Such gerrymandering has gone on since the earliest days of the republic, addressed in some states by setting up independent electoral commissions, but not addressed at all in others. It remains an area of constant court battles. The Voting Rights Act of 1965 restrained many questionable practices, but it was essentially gutted in 2013, resulting in a surge of restrictive efforts.

Overall, voting suppression remains a problem in many areas of the country. Some of this is a natural result of election controls, but often voting practices are intentionally manipulated for political advantage. So, for example, a requirement for street addresses significantly impacts Native Americans on reservations where there are no street addresses. Of course, election campaigns themselves can encourage or discourage individual citizens from voting. Texas, for example, restricted collection points for mail-in ballots to one location per county in the 2020 election.

Voting problems go back to the earliest days of the republic with writing of a constitution that supported slavery and held back the vote from women. Its writers were wary of open democracy and restricted it in a number of ways, including with the composition of the US Senate and the Electoral College. Thanks to that there have already been a couple elections where the Presidential candidate getting the most votes failed to win the Presidency. America cannot celebrate real liberty without some basic changes in its Constitutional structure. Its electoral system is among the weakest of any advanced democracy. The Electoral Integrity Project rated it at rock bottom, 57th among Western democracies.

Regulations

Regulations are intended to protect broad public interests from narrower commercial interests. Few of them prohibit or require specific actions by individual citizens. Most of them are industry requirements. The Code of Federal Regulations and additional state and local regulations attempt to prohibit specific actions which would be detrimental to the nation. Noncompliance generally results in fines or access restrictions. There are thousands of topics upon which regulations are applicable to corporate operations. A few current ones with high visibility include:

- Agricultural Use of Antibiotics. Antibiotics have had a huge positive effect on public health, greatly reducing the impact of harmful bacteria. They are in wide use at low dosages to keep farm animals healthy, significantly reducing costs to farmers. Unfortunately, low level usage tends to eliminate bacteria most susceptible to the antibiotics and so systematically promotes the development of a more resistant bacterial community, which can then spread to the general human population. Because of this, agricultural use of antibiotics has been regulated. But with the continuing growth of resistant bacterial communities, there is a growing push for stronger regulations. This is a good example of how a situation can evolve over time with measures that were once appropriate becoming outdated.

- Banking Excesses. A major cause of the housing bubble in 2008 was the movement by major banks into increasingly complex derivatives and other financial instruments that aggregated debt and made risk difficult to assess. This was facilitated by the repeal of earlier regulations and by systematic manipulation of remaining ones. The financial system itself has become a problem.

- Food Safety. There is a wide array of regulations pertaining to food safety, inspections, and best practices, ranging from local restaurant inspections to federal food standards. These programs cost money, and it is easy to cut funding when budgets are tight, as exemplified by a proposal to eliminate the national Microbiological Data Program, which tests fruits and vegetables for disease.

- Mercury Emissions. These have posed a huge challenge in recent decades as their deleterious effects on children have become clear. One result has been strong regulations on the disposal of fluorescent lamps, thermometers, and other mercury-containing items. The most difficult area concerns power plant emissions, as coal typically has some mercury content, which ends up in the stack emissions. Regulations in 2011 tightened emission standards on power plants, providing as estimated [by one analyst](#) up to $90 billion a year in benefits compared with around $10 billion a year of costs. But the figures are controversial, and there are determined efforts to [modify the standards](#) which can be quite costly for individual companies.

- Hydraulic Fracturing. A current major controversy concerns "fracking"— forcing high pressure water and proprietary chemicals into geological formations to free up natural gas deposits. This allows a significant increase in production, expanding both the national energy supply and jobs. Some evidence indicates, however, that fracking can also produce local earthquakes. More troublingly, the water and chemicals can contaminate ground water supplies and inadequate controls can result in large gas releases, particularly methane. Local geology and population density can make a real difference in assessing risks, so community regulations are often the most pertinent. By greatly increasing the supply of natural gas, fracking has helped to significantly reduce the use of coal. But fracking's environmental impacts push efforts for [tighter regulation](#), and it is now a central issue in addressing global warming.

It would be easy to fill a book with thumbnail sketches of individual regulations, their rationale, the effects they have, and how situations change over time. Regulations are invariably grounded in economics; often someone is restricted from doing something they see as profitable, so they have a vested interest in opposing regulation. This concern is obviously reinforced during times of economic distress when profits and jobs are hard to find anyhow. The costs of regulations are often clear because they fall on specific individuals or companies. But the benefits are typically unclear or too broad, for example, cleaner air or a less fragile banking system.

So specific groups have strong incentives to fight regulations and can make very persuasive arguments. It can be a <u>local issue</u>, such as intensifying air quality regulations on a power plant that is a central economic facility for a Navajo reservation, or a national issue, like proposed banking regulations where the six largest banks spent $29.4 million on lobbying. Wall Street and other financial institutions engaged <u>about 3,000 lobbyists</u>—more than five lobbyists for every member of Congress—and hired almost the same number to delay, weaken, or otherwise prevent implementation of banking regulations. Against well-funded lobbyists, proponents of a regulation typically have an uphill battle. It can take a crisis to produce change. How to balance competing interests is a constant challenge, complicated by the fact that one side is typically much better connected politically and financially than the other.

As with other topics, much of this is related to moneyed interests. A recent example was how lobbying by the <u>National Restaurant Association</u> resulted in large relief payments to major corporations while independent restaurants suffered. Interests of smaller organizations or the general public have a difficult time facing lobbyist groups.

Erosion of Freedom

Even this cursory overview shows that freedom at home is steadily eroding under the thrust of modernization coupled with a background of terrorism. As the global internet brings international criminal elements directly into our homes, and terrorists exploit our open society, new governmental restrictions will continue to affect our daily lives. An increasingly complex society requires an increasingly complex system of regulations to ensure a reasonable balance between freedom and safety.

Additionally, a burgeoning prison population plus millions of disenfranchised former prisoners and undocumented immigrants means that voting rights fall to an increasingly smaller percentage of the population, while economic distress sharpens internal conflicts and further constrains the benefits of liberty. Americans hold self-reliance and individual liberty in high regard, often slighting social responsibility. There is no obvious path toward an improved domestic situation, but these challenges undermine domestic cohesion, while the economic dimension increases tensions. Balancing competing interests becomes more difficult every day. America sets an example for the world, so shortcomings undermine American efforts at promoting a more equitable and prosperous world.

THE AMERICAN DREAM

For two centuries the American Dream of being able to work hard and prosper energized the country and gave the world a vision of a new kind of nation, a Beacon of Freedom. A Ladder of Success gave even those at the very bottom of the economy an opportunity to work up to more affluent levels. Some ten years ago there was an extensive assessment of the American Dream and how important it is to society, but there was little effort to invigorate it.

In recent years, this American Dream has faded as it has become increasingly difficult for workers to earn a living wage. Close to 40 million people are now at or even below the poverty level. Economic pressures promote social frictions; people lash out in anger, and desperate individuals turn to drugs and petty crime. They cling to their own social groups and seek others to blame for the situation. Overdose deaths now outnumber traffic deaths. There are roughly a half million homeless in this country, which also has one of the highest incarceration rates in the world. Militias and hate groups grow as the Ladder of Success disappears. Under these conditions, state and local governments find it difficult to raise the taxes they need to support operations, police and fire departments, education and parks, not to mention mental health services. The 2020 impact of COVID-19 drastically worsened the situation. Millions of adult workers were furloughed or simply released. America's problems are visible globally, all but destroying the vision of America as a shining example of democratic success.

The increasing concentration of wealth in the hands of a small minority undermines the social contract, a general agreement that the American Dream should be accessible to everyone. Joblessness leads to frustrations and then easily to violence, as attested by regular news of murders and mayhem tied to economic conditions. Frustrated individuals naturally band together to insist on improvements. This is essentially what the Occupy Wall Street Movement had been doing, branding itself as the 99 percent that will no longer tolerate the greed and corruption of the 1 percent. They were basically nonviolent and ineffective. Some kind of social explosion, as happened in Watts in 1965, seemed inevitable. The Watts rioters overturned and burned automobiles and looted and damaged grocery stores, liquor stores, department stores, and pawnshops. Over 14,000 California National Guard troops were mobilized. All told, the rioting claimed the lives of 34 people and resulted in more than one thousand reported injuries. Although initially blamed on the work of outside agitators, the McCone Commission, appointed by Governor Pat Brown, found it was economic and sociological conditions that escalated a routine arrest of a drunken driver into six days of violence. Racial inequalities fed the Watts riots and economic conditions only worsened them. A sequel to the Watts riots stormed into view in 2020 as the Black Lives Matter movement promoted nationwide protests against a police culture of excessive use of force resulting in numerous deaths of blacks. In both cases, black communities saw themselves as suppressed.

The fading of the American Dream is a central challenge for the nation, how to realign the country so that all its people are part of its active community, so that all of them appreciate living in a Beacon of Freedom where they can work hard and prosper.

Wealth Inequality

The core problem is that America has failed to demonstrate that democratic capitalism can lead to a peaceful and prosperous society. Distribution of wealth is the single best indicator of the scope of prosperity, and it has steadily become more and more lopsided, dividing society into haves and have-nots. After the 2005 recession, the top 1 percent captured 95 percent of income growth from 2009 to 2012 and that trend continues. People are generally aware of the concentration of wealth at the top of society, but they fail to appreciate its impact at the bottom. It is poverty there that drives minorities into crime and prison, a self-perpetuating cycle of frustration and destitution. If America can fix wealth inequality, minorities would be greatly advantaged because the poverty rate for Blacks in 2020 was 18.8 percent, for Hispanics was 15.7 percent and for whites was 7.3 percent. There are thousands of examples where minorities are disadvantaged, ranging from poor water quality in Flint, Michigan, to pervasive pollution in the Grays Ferry neighborhood of South Philadelphia.

In 2022, the bottom 90% of jobs averaged $40,845/year, while the top 5% averaged $344,667/year. Were income distributed as evenly as it had been in 1975, the median income in 2020 would have been $92,000/year. The share of the nation's wealth held by the less affluent 50 percent of American households is only 1.1 percent. By contrast, the wealthiest 5 percent of American households owned two-thirds of America's wealth in 2016. By 2017, the wealthiest 1% owned an estimated 40 percent of the total America wealth of over $100 trillion. Since then wealth accumulation has significantly increased with the richest 1% capturing almost two-thirds of all new wealth since 2020. Had half of this concentrated wealth been more broadly distributed, it could have provided 50 million American families each $1,000,000! Alternatively, it could have been applied to government programs—education, infrastructure, health care, and disaster preparedness.

As noted above, the impact of COVID-19 drastically worsened the situation. By May 2020, unemployment had soared to almost 15 percent, the highest level since 1948. The restaurant and fast food industry, the second-largest private employer in America, was hit particularly hard. At least 5.5 million of these jobs evaporated by the end of April; estimates indicated that at least 20 percent of independently owned restaurants would never reopen. And those restaurants uphold an ecosystem that extends to farms, meat and fish suppliers, florists, ceramists, wineries, and more. The most deeply affected were restaurant workers who often do not have access to health insurance, earn less than a living wage, and disproportionately include undocumented workers. The wealth gap was vividly demonstrated in 2020 as COVID-19 ravaged the working class but the stock market reached record highs, giving even more money to those who already had it. Employment rebounded dramatically after COVID; by late 2023 the unemployment rate was under 4 percent while hourly wages were rising steadily. But wealth inequality has barely budged. In the second quarter of 2023, the top ten percent of earners in the United States held two thirds of total wealth.

Public investments are of particular importance: they increase job demand in the short run and productivity in the long run. A realigned workforce development system could facilitate the economy's structural transformation, helping it move from sectors with declining employment (like manufacturing) to more dynamic sectors. Strengthening education could help restore the American Dream and help make the country once again a land of opportunity where the talents of our young people are fully utilized. But local and state governments, badly strapped for income, are cutting back on all these expenditures. The nation has enough wealth to support the needed expenditures, but too much of it is tied up in private accounts.

The potential for significant wealth does provide a high incentive for real improvements to society. America has long considered itself as the Land of Opportunity with individual prosperity depending on a person's own diligence and abilities. Few people begrudge Bill Gates his wealth—he is an American success story; his efforts have added significantly to the wealth of the nation and of the globe. But his wealth is excessive. Many other wealthy individuals have gotten their wealth not by contributing to society, but by an ability to exploit its imbalances and take advantage of their own positions. When company leaders have led their companies to new heights despite daunting competitive and regulatory requirements, they are generally accepted to have earned their pay. But when company leaders have manipulated subordinates and pliable oversight groups to obtain large rewards despite poor performance, the legitimacy of their wealth is called into question. Some have actually been prosecuted for stripping companies of assets; others have just quietly faded from the scene. Society needs to determine what level of wealth is appropriate for those who make major contributions to society.

Politically, there is every effort to deflect attention from excessive wealth accumulation by portraying it as perfectly normal and protecting those who support it. Immigration and refugees are widely blamed for economic and social shortcomings. Government support programs are pictured as a cause of economic problems rather than a result. Government regulations protecting the public and environment are pictured as undermining prosperity, while tax and subsidy programs heavily favoring wealthy interests are systematically downplayed. Widespread frustration with such unequal wealth distribution led to the election of President Trump, who stressed his independence from the establishment but did little to reduce the influence of moneyed interests.

As President, he compounded the underlying problems, promoting more wealth accumulation. The tax reform bill he promoted favored the rich, as [President Trump himself](#) bragged to club members at Mar-a-Lago, "You all just got a lot richer." That was certainly good news to help them pay their $14,000 yearly club membership.

Political discussions are widely covered in the press, but the central issue of wealth distribution is barely visible, covered over by the smoke of wealth acceptance and of distractions that focus attention on peripheral issues. In a market economy, wealth is certainly acceptable, even desirable. It is the incentive that motivates many to perform at their best, to work hard, to innovate and develop new opportunities. So it makes sense that [one observer](#) would be grateful for billionaire innovators and [another](#) would comment that America needs more billionaires. However, the situation calls for addressing more fundamental questions of the social contract. Wealth as a reward for contributions to society is widely accepted, but there are questions on its scope. How can someone actually **earn** a billion dollars? What does someone have to do to create a million dollars of value? Inheriting a family farm or a family business may seem perfectly normal, but how about inheriting $1 billion? Should this be accepted by society? The fundamental question is simply, what level of incentive is appropriate? If a major economic contributor were to receive, say, a modest hundred million dollars instead of a billion, there would be nine hundred million dollars available for wider distribution, including to the laborers creating the development. To what extent does the wealth **in society** actually belong **to society**? When does individual wealth get to be excessive and therefore undermine society as a whole?

Historically, there has been a wide range of top tax rates. Late in World War II, the [top rate](#) was 94%. Post war, it decreased slightly, but was not significantly dropped until the 1960's when Kennedy's tax reduction proposal set the top rate at 70%. These rates were seen as confiscatory, and indeed they were. What they did was cap the amount of wealth going to the top. This is the decision society has to make: what restrictions or caps should be placed on wealth accumulation?

One measure is the Gini Index which shows the degree of inequality in the distribution of family income in a country. By this measure, American inequality ranks far worse than the rest of the Industrialized World, even worse than many African nations, while the Nordic countries lead the world in equality. Promoting global prosperity remains a critical challenge for the twenty-first century and many of the problems, including those that drive illegal immigration into America, are grounded in wealth inequalities at home and abroad. It is obviously difficult for America to press Mexico, for example, to provide a better distribution of wealth when the American distribution is just as bad. Internationally, America ranks near the worst end of the inequality scale. Countries with comparable income inequality include Madagascar, the Congo, and Iran. Within the Organisation for Economic Cooperation and Development, American income inequality is on a level with Turkey, Mexico, and Chile.

Wealth inequality is now a major challenge for the period ahead for both domestic and foreign policy. In 2017, the holdings of the eight richest people in the world (five of them Americans) were greater than what half the rest of the planet owns. America used to set the global standard as the Land of Opportunity. It needs to reclaim that status by addressing the underlying problem: those with wealth work hard to protect their own situation, stressing that wealth is normal and avoiding any recognition that is can be excessive.

Health

Health, both physical and mental, is an obvious critical component of happiness. It is difficult to enjoy life when sick or depressed.

In 2022, America spent $4.5 trillion dollars on health care, almost 17 percent of Gross Domestic Product - far higher than all the other advanced countries. According to World Bank data for 2020, America's health expenditure is almost double the European Union's average. Similarly, the United States has a lower life expectancy than peer nations and has seen worsening health outcomes since the onset of the COVID-19 pandemic. Dozens of comparisons of the American healthcare system with those in comparable nations are notable. The French system, for example, is rated as the best in the world. With its universal coverage, responsive healthcare providers, and patient and provider freedoms, the French system costs about half as much as the American system. Comparative rankings indicate that the overall American national system is grossly inefficient; other countries with significantly lower per capita expenditures manage to provide significantly better health care. America is one of the only advanced countries that does not have universal (or almost universal) health coverage. Over a third of all health care costs go to administration.

Drug costs are a significant problem for the American system. Prescription drug spending in America is more than double the OECD average; 1 out of every 3 adults taking prescription drugs say that they've been unable to take their medication as prescribed due to cost. Not only is manufacturing concentrated in a few companies, but ingredient supply is also concentrated and the supply is distributed through by a small number of wholesalers. Complicating the situation, manufacturers can set prices at exorbitant rates thanks to protections (often extended) that they enjoy under the patent code. Overall, the system is manipulated to minimize transparency and maximize profits.

Medical shortcomings account for tens of thousands of excess deaths a year, certainly a major threat to life and a significant challenge for the nation. Some of these are due to simple inattention. One study, for example, attributed over 100,000 deaths a year to hospital acquired infections. More critically, much more could be done to reduce death rates, but there is little awareness of the problem.. Heart disease, for example, accounted for almost 695,000 deaths in 2021, about one third of total deaths. Progress has been made—between 1990 and 2006, cardiovascular deaths declined by 20 percent and life expectancy has recently improved slightly. But chronic conditions and premature deaths have reached the highest levels recorded in over 30 years, underlining the need for policies and actions that tackle disparities and help communities improve their health and well-being.

The steady drop in life expectancy is a clear indicator of inadequate health care. Rising obesity levels certainly have not helped. And in recent decades, deinstitutionalization has severely impacted mentally ill people. Since rankings are overall averages, it is important to look at comparisons between social and ethnic groups. A wealth of information is available on those comparisons and it is clear that health benefits are distributed very unequally. Some specific indicators include:

- The Indian Health Care system applies to over two million Native Americans and Alaskan natives. Among these groups, the death rate of people under 25 is three times the national average. Although the Trump administration pledged to make tribal health care systems more effective, health disparities between Native Americans and the rest of the American population are stark. Native Americans are 60 percent more likely to commit suicide, twice as likely to die during childbirth, and five times more likely to die from tuberculosis. Their life expectancy is five years less than other Americans.

- A mountain of research catalogues the complex and widespread effects that racism has on the health—and the medical care—of minorities. Those effects stretch back centuries and take different forms, from discriminatory diagnostics to institutional barriers to care. The spread of COVID-19 had a hugely disproportionate impact on blacks and Latinos. Much of this was due to poverty impacting health by its connection with inadequate nutrition, substandard housing, exposure to environmental hazards, and decreased access to health care facilities. Today, minorities in America are more likely than white people to live in food deserts, areas with limited access to fresh fruit or vegetables. They are less likely to be able to access green spaces, and more likely to live in areas without clean water or air. Black children are more likely to grow up in high-poverty areas. Minorities are more frequently exposed to greater occupational hazards, often working in frontline jobs that were significantly worsened by COVID-19.

A major reason for the poor standing of American health care versus other advanced countries and for the discrepancies between different population groups is the lack of broad insurance coverage. America is one of the only advanced countries that does not have universal (or almost universal) health coverage. In case of illness or injury, the uninsured are forced to turn to emergency rooms, which are generally required to treat them for free, but only for critical needs. This care is both expensive and inadequate, and it strains the resources available for real emergencies. In 2021 there were almost 30 million Americans without health insurance not even counting most of the ten million undocumented immigrants in the country. The Patient Protection and Affordable Care Act (Obamacare) signed into law on March 23, 2010, helped increase private health insurance to 218 million by late 2018. However, even with the increase, COVID-19 led more than six million workers to lose employer-provided health insurance. Since most workers have families, the total number of people who lost coverage is likely more than 12 million.

Affordable Care Act's 2010 enactment was expressly designed to significantly broaden the number of Americans covered by health insurance, but it was immediately mired in controversy, mainly because of projected costs. Although key provisions were upheld by the Supreme Court, eliminating it became a central objective of the Trump administration, but without offering any clear alternatives. President Biden reversed this trend, insisting that health care should be a right — not a privilege — for all Americans and noting record numbers of Americans enrolling in supported programs.

Financial System

Originally set up to provide resources to businesses, the financial system has gradually become simply a means of extracting wealth from the economy. An ultimate example is High Frequency Trading in which buying and selling at millisecond intervals allows specially equipped traders to skim money off the stock market without any contribution at all to society. As in any economic sphere, mergers allow economies of scale, but also provide a potential for domination, which only adds to the problem. Before the recession of 2007-2009, financial institutions used a wide variety of instruments, such as bundled mortgages, to gamble with customer assets. Their huge customer base meant that seemingly small individual charges got consolidated into major income streams, supporting out-sized salaries and benefits for many financial executives. This was a central contributor to the 2008 real estate bubble, but their status as "too big to fail" brought broad federal support to the financial sector and minimal support to the people actually affected.

Hundreds of innovative firms now provide payments, lending, and other consumer financial market services that banks used to dominate. These new entrants have lowered the cost and expanded the reach of financial products to Americans who were previously excluded. But their growth has also raised questions about the fitness of existing regulation. Hedge funds for example, have profited greatly off the financial distress of malls and have also devastated a number of newspapers.

A steady rise in the stock market does not reflect a rise in actual value of companies so much as a rise in valuation, benefiting those who already have capital. Thanks largely to a rise in the stock market, the world's wealthiest became $1 trillion richer in 2017, expanding their share of wealth at the expense of everyone else. This continued through 2023 as the stock market reached record highs.

Strong lobbying leads to the best Congress that money can buy, a Congress sympathetic to the concerns of the wealthy and often oblivious to everyone else. Much of the growth of income and wealth at the top in recent decades has come from activities directed more at increasing the share of the pie for the wealthy rather than increasing the size of the pie itself. Corporate executives take advantage of deficiencies in our corporate governance laws to seize an increasing share of corporate revenue, enriching themselves at the expense of other stakeholders; pharmaceutical companies successfully lobby to prohibit the federal government (the largest buyer of drugs) from bargaining over drug prices, resulting in taxpayers overpaying by an estimated half a trillion dollars in about a decade. Thanks to special benefits hidden in the tax code, mineral companies get resources at below competitive prices while oil companies and other corporations get "gifts" in the hundreds of billions of dollars a year in corporate welfare. These excessive gains are protected by a variety of financial measures, including:

- Limitations on the estate tax, tarring it as a "death tax" that resonates strongly with average citizens who naturally want to pass their own assets to their children and heirs. Yet estate taxes apply only to assets well over $12 million, so they are specifically limited to the very wealthy.

- Similarly, high income tax levels for top brackets are denigrated as confiscatory. Indeed, they are, and they should be. But "confiscation" has a nasty ring to it, implying that the government is taking away hard-earned monies to redistribute, presumably to slackers. In reality, the government is trying to get back monies drained from an increasingly manipulated system.

- Capital gains are taxed at very favorable rates, favorable especially to the rich. It is true that many average Americans also depend on capital gains for retirement income and everyday expenses. Nevertheless, it would be relatively easy to provide favorable treatment only up to some threshold so that higher rates would apply only to large capital gains.

- Even worse are tax loopholes, often almost invisible, and justified by nice-sounding words. President Reagan, for example, promoted "trickle-down" economics, claiming that a reduced tax burden for the wealthy would increase the money available for investment and create more jobs. He was half right—it increased money in the hands of the rich, but not jobs.

Overall, the financial system has morphed from a focus on supporting the growth of business to supporting the accumulation of wealth. Again, transparency is critical so that the public can evaluate the impact of government controls and policies. An active press is probably the most essential actor in building public awareness of efforts to manipulate the system.

Capitalism Versus Socialism

The American economy has traditionally been seen as capitalist, a system with private ownership of production operated for profit. This label has strong positive resonance with the population. Conversely, socialism is a system of public or government ownership of production, a label that elicits strong negative connotations from Americans.

Capitalism is based on the idea that each person works to maximize their own individual gains. [Greed](#) is its ultimate driving force. Private ownership supports the production of profits by the investment of capital. Two centuries ago, there was a belief that an Invisible Hand of the Market would somehow assure that a market left to its own devices would work to the benefit of all. This proved to be illusory. As early as 1890, the necessity for government to protect market competition was embodied in the Sherman Anti-Trust Act.

Capitalism has driven the innovation that supported America's rise to prosperity. Post-war America supported the American Dream and was a beacon to the world. It was a dynamic economy with strong unions and a prosperous society. It was a time of broadening equality, the rise of a more diverse society. But relative affluence proved inadequate for people in the top levels of society and they strongly pushed for further wealth accumulation. In a widely read 1970 article, a leading American economist [Milton Friedman](#) claimed "there is one and only one social responsibility of business—to use its resources and engage in activities designed to increase its profits." This legitimized a widespread belief that shareholders have every right to take care of just themselves.

Capitalism supports a relentless focus on profits. There is no better example than one of the major American corporations: Amazon, and its founder and CEO Jeff Bezos. The focus is vividly illustrated by articles, practically side by side in the Washington Post on November 24, 2017: [German, Italian Amazon Workers Strike on Black Friday](#) and [Jeff Bezos is Now Worth More Than $100 Billion](#). Amazon clearly favors management and shareholders over workers, many of whom earn barely over minimum wages. A whole army of transients, a [Camper Force](#), travels from location to location to provide Amazon a pool of poorly paid workers. Amazon also puts local governments under pressure. Its 2017 efforts to draw maximum tax and infrastructure concessions from cities interested in hosting a new processing center demonstrated how it heavily pressures local governments for financial concessions.

In 2020, 55 of the nation's largest companies had paid no federal income tax thanks to laws set by a Congress heavily influenced by monied interests. This changed in 2023 as President Biden signed a new law requiring large companies to pay a minimum of 15 percent tax. This will certainly initiate a huge corporate effort to maintain loopholes and exemptions. There are hundreds of examples of corporations focusing on profits at the expense of society. Regulations act as protectors for both people and the environment but are consistently denounced because of their impact on corporate profits. Continuous review is appropriate but must be done in full public view—an important role for the press. Capitalism focuses on corporations as the source of jobs for workers, rather than on workers as being the source of income for the corporations.

Capitalism has relied not on the Invisible Hand of the Market, but rather the Invisible Hand of the Government supporting the top of society at the expense of everyone else. Capitalism's manipulations undermine society as a whole. It has empowered hundreds of millions of people to climb out of poverty, but its underlying motivation of greed means that excessive inequality is not an accidental by-product. It is at the core of the system. These contradictions have become increasingly apparent in recent decades as monied interests have increasingly manipulated the system to their own benefit. Unregulated capitalism is deeply flawed. It needs to be drastically updated, as Nobel Prize-winning economist Joseph Stiglitz convincingly argues in his 2019 Progressive Capitalism. The economy has to exploit the benefits of market without exploiting workers. America needs to set conditions so that everyone can get a job; that is an essential element of dignity.

At the end of 2013, the stock market hit an all-time high. So did corporate profits as a share of Gross Domestic Product. However, wages slid badly. This lopsided distribution of wealth has been justified as simply the working of the market economy. It is not the market that promotes increasing stock prices, high profits, and low wages—it is the financial rules of the game as set by the government. Underlying much of this is the notion that the sole responsibility of corporations is to provide profits to the shareholders. This belief is fundamentally wrong. It is a basic distortion of corporate responsibilities and is an underlying reason for the growing wealth inequality in this country. Society facilitates the operation of corporations for the benefit of society as a whole. Corporations provide the goods and services society needs, jobs with wages that support the standard of living, and taxes that support government programs. Society supports corporations for all these reasons, recognizing that these activities will create considerable wealth. However, this wealth should be for the benefit of society as a whole. Indeed, Friedman qualified his comment on profit and social responsibility: a corporation must stay "…within the rules of the game, which is to say, engages in open and free competition, without deception or fraud." But he did not back off from profits as the central responsibility. The rules of the game should be much broader, ensuring that corporate efforts support all stakeholders.

In an extraordinarily complex socio-economic system, the rules of the game must also be extraordinarily complex. The Code of Federal Regulations with 170,000 pages is only one set of rules at the national level, not to mention state and local ones. Theoretically, these thousands of pages of laws and regulations protect the public's interests, including environmental standards, health and safety requirements, and mandatory quality requirements on production. They also set criteria for tax and royalty payments and provide tax benefits, a major tool to guide economic development. Many corporations engage in wider social support programs because of a strong sense of general obligation to society; such efforts are commendable, but supplemental. The core corporate responsibility to society is to pay the taxes and royalties that support overall government operations.

Thousands of regulations, of course, mean thousands of opportunities for corporations to advance their own narrow interests. Regulations are not set by some kind of unbiased, neutral evaluation, but by politics. Shareholders, often financial institutions that hold large blocks of stock, have a natural interest in maximizing profit, and so an interest in minimizing social support. One result of this is strongly focused lobbying efforts aimed at favorable treatment in the specific provisions of some law or regulation. Even the exact wording of some obscure regulation can provide major but practically invisible benefits to some corporation(s). Such lobbying efforts are typically backed not only by considerable corporate resources but also by a broad network of largely invisible ties among legislators, lobbyists, regulators, and officials. The public interest, on the other hand, is often diffuse, with no one to counter specific corporate arguments that, at any rate, are often invisible to the general public. The result is that thousands of corporations enjoy some level of dispensation from their obligations to provide social benefits.

As with corporate responsibilities to society as a whole, benefits to employees impose fiscal provisions which reduce profit to shareholders. So again, shareholders have a vested interest to fight such requirements. Stressing profit as the sole legitimate objective of corporate operations gives a sheen of legitimacy to reducing wages while raising profits. More importantly, politics is again a major player, and the same concerted lobbying efforts and networks of corporate influence which undermine rules supporting social responsibility also undermine rules supporting responsibilities to employees. One clear example is that the federal minimum wage has not risen since 2009 and stands at a low $7.25 an hour (roughly $15,000/year), far below the poverty level.

The situation is further complicated by outsized levels of executive compensation. Executives are part of the total employee collective and their compensation is ultimately set by the shareholders with minimal government direction. However, it is obvious that more remuneration to executives means less income available to distribute as wages and benefits to other employees. The extent to which senior managers deserve their outsized compensation has been regularly challenged. But just as legislation is complicated by interlocking networks of key players, setting executive pay is complicated by interlocking networks of corporate directors, senior managers, and wealthy shareholders. Major financial or social funds often comprise a significant proportion of shareholders, focusing on short-term profit and paying little attention to social or employee responsibilities. Individual shareholders who try to support such broader interests can find it difficult to oppose settled corporate policies and simply turn to invest elsewhere. The overall result is that the share of total corporate remuneration going to rank-and-file employees is steadily declining. Top corporate executives have seen their pay grow by more than 1,000 percent over the past 40 years, nearly 100 times the rate of average workers.

The most significant current trend is the intense effort to minimize any corporate responsibility to outside stakeholders, including customers and governments. In addition, several other trends facilitate minimal corporate attention to broader responsibilities:

- Corporate Consolidation was the focus of the Sherman Anti-Trust Act over a century ago. The obvious worst recent example was when banking institutions labeled as "too big to fail" received large government funding despite the fact they were the major cause of the market problems. But consolidation is rife; a recent example is the merger of United and Continental Airlines in 2010 creating the world's largest airline, just one of several mergers between large airlines. The mergers have been difficult for employees, but travelers have also suffered significantly by reduced price competition.

- Large companies can certainly increase efficiency by eliminating duplicative administrative and support systems. WalMart is a prime example: its supply and distribution system is a marvel of modern efficiency, reducing unit processing costs to levels that strongly support its low price policies. Unfortunately, WalMart and other large corporations not only diminish competition, they are also able to squeeze workers and suppliers, making smaller companies less profitable and putting some out of business. This can provide lower prices and better selections to the local market, but at the cost of weakening local community life.

- Technological advances continue to increase productivity and decrease the need for workers. But savings in labor requirements have not translated into increases in wages. Rather, reductions in aggregate wage levels have facilitated increases in profits and executive pay.

- The mammoth size of the Code of Federal Regulations and other rules is not simply due to an increase in requirements placed on corporations. It is also partly due to increased special treatments, resulting in a greatly expanded ability of corporations to avoid taxes based on special tax provisions that corporations can use to minimize their social responsibilities. Naturally, corporations will not pay more taxes than they are supposed to, but they often lobby very efficiently to minimize that amount.

The widespread notion that the sole responsibility of corporations is to make money for the owners is a major factor supporting the trend of increasing wealth at the top levels of society, at the expense of everyone else. It promotes policies and activities that squeeze income to both government and workers. The central economic task of government is to ensure a distribution of social assets that benefits society as a whole. As the main economic engine of society, corporations should rightfully distribute the wealth they create among all stakeholders—society, employees, and owners—and not simply retain it as profits for shareholders.

Capitalism is badly flawed. Its financial system has consistently been manipulated to support wealth accumulation. Stock Market growth is presented as a key indicator of national economic strength, but stock increases only enrich people who own stock. As the American population levels off, the nation is faced with zero or minimal domestic economic growth. This is not something from which we need to be rescued; it is something we need to learn how to live with. Reaching the limits of growth does not equate to reaching the limits of prosperity. The key question is not how to maintain growth as the population stabilizes, but how to maintain prosperity with a stable (or decreasing) population.

Socialism is also badly flawed, though it is more difficult to say exactly why because it is really a philosophy and not a single system. Its focus is commendable: doing what is best for society. Traditionally, socialism was characterized by social ownership of the means of production and workers' self-management of enterprises. But socialist economies where the government owned the nation's industrial organizations concentrated wealth for the benefit of influential individuals; without the benefit of market feedback mechanisms, resources were poorly allocated and innovation was stifled.

Communism is a socialist system that includes common ownership of the means of production and stresses an absence of social classes. Its triumph in Russia led not to a comfortable and prosperous society, but to famines, prison camps, and widespread, brutal repression. Worker self-management was totally absent as the elite enjoyed a privileged life in their hidden country houses. The collapse of the Soviet Union vividly demonstrated how inadequate such systems are. Socialist governments set up with Soviet support began with Cuba, Nicaragua and then Venezuela, which was once a prosperous state but by 2020 had an economy so degraded that several million people had fled the country.

Socialism in China did no better, with Mao's Great Leap Forward (1958-1961) resulting in at least 15 million deaths, mostly from starvation. Following Mao, the leadership of Deng Xiaoping relaxed control over citizens' personal lives and transitioned the nation from a planned economy to a mixed economy with an increasingly open-market environment and repressive government.

Socialist governments have certainly been failures, even dramatic failures, as both Stalin and Mao were responsible for millions of deaths. None of them were really socialist, focusing on the needs of society. So it is not surprise that modern socialists want to disassociate the word from its historical disasters. Democratic socialists flatly reject the belief that the whole economy should be centrally planned. They stress that both the economy and society should be run democratically—to meet public needs, not to make profits for a few. Social ownership could take many forms, such as worker-owned cooperatives or publicly owned enterprises managed by workers and consumer representatives. Democratic socialists favor as much decentralization as possible. Some form of state ownership might be appropriate for large capital industries such as energy or steel. While democratic planning would shape major social investments, market mechanisms are needed to determine the demand for many consumer goods. Corporations would need to be subject to greater democratic control with regulations and tax incentives pushing them to act in the public interest. Public pressure and unions could also make them more accountable. But there has never been a nation run as a democratic socialist state to demonstrate what this would actually mean in practice.

Socialist elements are prominent in the Scandinavian countries, which stress broad social programs and democratic accountability. However, they are identified not as democratic socialist states, but social democratic states. The shift in wording does more than just emphasize democracy rather than socialism. Their governments emphasize private property and do not have public ownership of major economic organizations; their economies are basically market systems that protect private property. Their programs are social rather than socialist, monitored by a strong press and active democratic institutions. These programs, such as universal health care, lengthy paid maternity leave, and strong unions and unemployment benefits, focus on significant social benefit to the population as a whole.

The American economy clearly needs major adjustments if it is to work for everyone. The central problem is the excessive concentration of wealth at the top. *E pluribus unum*, a single society uniting all, is only possible when everyone is doing well, when we can all embrace our neighbors without undermining our own families. A Colorado executive order puts it concisely: "We will only reach our potential as a state when all Coloradans can live, work, learn, play and thrive in healthy, inclusive, and equitable environments."

Both capitalism and socialism are badly flawed because they can be manipulated for the benefit of those at the top. The American economy has to use the best elements of both. Projects and proposals need to be assessed in terms of how well they can work for the country, not what label someone can put on them. Many programs clearly have to be social programs, supporting a broad spread of society's wealth. Such programs, like Social Security and Medicare, are neither capitalist nor socialist, they are simply humanist.

Employment

The most striking aspect of the employment situation is how the need for production workers has steadily declined.

The productive sector of the economy makes the products that the nation needs. It was long considered the essential foundation for the rest of the economy which includes a service sector supporting both production and society. In our modern economy it is difficult to decide what is essential and what is not. The productive sector is facing significant changes.

- Agriculture employment peaked at 32.5 million people in 1916, is now barely over 2 million. Larger (and more efficient) farms have replaced family farms and food imports have also climbed. Restrictions on water supply and competing demands from growing populations are forcing significant reductions in irrigated land, while changing climate patterns will force major shifts in agricultural regions. Energy will also have a large impact, raising production costs and making long-haul transport of agricultural products decidedly less attractive. One result may be the development of vertical farms in city skyscrapers. Another result may be a major increase in crops for biofuel production. Overall, there will be significant shifts in the agricultural sector, which will require large investments and further realignments of agricultural jobs.
- The manufacturing industry lost some 5 million jobs between 2000 and 2017. Much of this loss is the result of technological improvements as manufacturing has become substantially more capital intensive, requiring more equipment investment per worker. There have also been significant shifts of manufacturing abroad. Manufacturing provided around 17 million jobs in

2000, around 14 million before the 2008 recession and by 2022 around 13 million. There is no one simple reason, but overall, it is clear that manufacturing requires fewer jobs.

- The construction industry had already faced a severe challenge. It had grown from around 2 million employees post-war to almost 8 million before the 2008 recession. The recession resulted in a 30 percent drop from which it rebounded slowly but steadily, reaching pre-recession levels by 2018. The COVID-19 virus shut down or delayed many construction sites, but its impact was less here than for manufacturing. Much of the work is outside and the industry seems to have learned lessons from the prior recession. There will certainly be changes in union impact and in project types. In the years ahead, global warming may also have a major impact on the construction industry. Rising sea levels and more severe coastal storms could force relocation or abandonment of thousands, even millions, of buildings currently at risk. Coastal flooding could also result in large demands for protective structures, and a new attention on infrastructure could require construction activities. Whatever the eventual outcome, the construction industry is also facing significant realignments and major investments.

- The energy sector, a central player in the economy, is totally in flux. Almost all individuals depend on energy connections to their homes, while energy drives industrial production and provides a key support for the transportation and service sectors. The energy sector itself employs over 8 million people. Traditionally, this sector has relied on fossil fuels (coal, oil, natural gas) which, as discussed above, have some serious problems. Much of the work (coal mines, oil and gas wells) is physically demanding and dangerous. Extraction, processing, and use all have major environmental impacts including air and ground pollution, as well as contamination from accidents with off-shore wells and transport (pipelines, rail cars, oil tankers). Fossil fuels, emitting carbon dioxide and methane, are also major contributions to global warming. Green energy is attractive but is not yet sufficient to meet needs; much of it provides intermittent power at inconvenient locations. A transition to green energy is probably inevitable, but difficult. It requires shifting major investments from established facilities and activities to new ones. Even more difficult is shifting millions of workers away from traditional jobs, often at remote locations. How to arrange jobs for these workers and provide them new skills are long-term challenges that will require significant government involvement.

These four sectors are basically the productive core that supports the rest of the economy. However, it is not easy to specify exactly what is essential with production ranging from basic food goods to luxury items, from wheat to yachts. In all sectors there are major job shifts in process, partly driven by technological improvements decreasing the need for workers.

This productive sector supports the service sector, which itself encompasses a spectrum from essential to nonessential and is undergoing major changes.

- Computer and information services used to be peripheral but have become the essential backbone of the modern economy. They control manufacturing lines, manage projects, and greatly increase the efficiency of private and government offices while reducing employee requirements throughout the economy. These services also trail off into nonessential and even trivial, from teen-age text messaging to massive computer gaming. It has been a continuously expanding sector.

- Health services, physical and mental, are an expanding portion of the economy, extending from essential basic services that keep people alive to a range of elective procedures. Many of these services, such as dietary programs and gym memberships, improve health but require extra disposable income. The high costs of health care, discussed above, underline a need to realign jobs to more essential tasks. With an aging population, job requirements will rise, but many of these jobs are inadequately paid and have poor, if any, benefits.

- Military services protect the nation and its interests overseas. Much of this is open-ended and the importance of specific elements is widely questioned. What is clear is that military elements, including the military-industrial complex behind them, are nonproductive and use assets that could be applied elsewhere. As discussed in some detail below, this sector could face major realignment in the years ahead.

- Business services include management and office operations. The downsizing by many large corporations vividly demonstrated how flexible the concept of essential management is. COVID-19 has also forced a reassessment of needs for office spaces and associated jobs, intensified by technologies reducing the need for workers.

- Financial services range from essential mortgage and business loans through stock markets and pension funds to hedge funds and financial derivatives. Some of these services are essential for the functioning of the economy. Others undermine it by extracting wealth with minimal input.

- Government services not only provide essential coordination and justice activities, but also oversight and regulation of increasingly complex economic and social relations. At the municipal level these include basic education and utilities, as well as local parks and infrastructure. Upkeep and maintenance are also necessary but can easily be deferred for significant current savings but increased future expenses. American infrastructure has been degrading for years as elected politicians work to keep taxes low.

- Legal services range from support of basic court and justice functions to routine services provided to individuals. Specialized corporate services also included the complex financial transactions which eventually collapsed much of the economy.

- Hospitality services support business travelers, essential to a complex and widespread economy, as well as personal travel, vacations, and such simple pleasures as dining out. COVID-19 hammered this economic sector. It also starkly demonstrated how nonessential some of these services are.

- Childcare is essential for many parents to get into the work force. America notoriously lags other industrialized countries in investing in childcare and early education. The child-care system has been in bad shape, with many working parents unable to find or afford care. The problem, at its core, is that child care simply costs more to provide than parents can afford to pay.

- Religious and cultural services enrich many lives. They also include items that may be nonessential but are central elements of modern life: sports, entertainment, and art.

This is obviously only a partial list of the services that make a modern society possible. They all will have significant changes in employment, as will the productive sector. The underlying reality is that both production and essential services need only a fraction of available workers. Non-essential goods and services—luxury items, cultural services, entertainment, vacations, military—can only exist based on assets provided by the productive sector of the economy. Services offered have to be sufficiently attractive to induce the productive sector to pay for them. A small productive sector struggles to support an outsized service sector. So there have been voices, for example [Alan Tonelson](), arguing for a resurgence of manufacturing as the only credible route to full employment. The challenge is exacerbated by demographic projections which show an expanding retired population depending on a shrinking workforce.

Unskilled and low priority workers— meat processors, maids, elder care workers—were significantly impacted by COVID-19. Since its earliest days, the American economy depended on cheap labor. Many middle-class workers can maintain a reasonable standard of living only thanks to an underclass which is much worse off due to hard labor, woefully inadequate wages, no health or retirement benefits, and miserable living conditions. Since the growth of good American jobs has stagnated, so have the prospects for this underclass which includes large numbers of migrant laborers and undocumented immigrants, initially in agriculture but now also widespread in construction and service industries. The economy cannot function without them, but with its increasingly lopsided distribution of wealth, it cannot pay them adequately either. They have been particularly impacted by rising rents in many cities and by looming [foreclosures and evictions]() that may significantly increase the already large homeless population. Exploitation is embedded in the American economy.

Even allowing for all the ambiguities, there are now clearly millions of extra workers, qualified people who cannot find jobs; some [seven million]() were not even looking before the COVID-19 crisis. As noted above, COVID-19 drastically worsened the situation as unemployment soared, particularly in the restaurant industry. But employment has rebounded dramatically; by late 2023, over 160 million Americans were employed. Corporations and households are reevaluating just what is essential as remote work expanded significantly. The current employment level is satisfactory, but there is ample reason for skepticism:

- Many jobs have been lost to globalization, even in some service industries such as call centers. Foreign workers can now compete directly with American workers in many fields, enabling companies to get significant savings from wage differentials between America and the developing world. The more skilled the job, the higher the differential and so the higher the incentive to send the job abroad. Many of these jobs will never come back to America.

- The move of manufacturing jobs overseas is more complicated. Some of this production supported exports to nations where the production plants are now located. It is unlikely that much of this production will ever come back. Global investment (and job creation) is now much less likely to occur in America than a decade earlier. Other production shifts overseas, based on lower labor and raw material costs, may be challenged by gradually rising wages and material costs overseas, as well as increasingly higher transportation costs. So, some manufacturing jobs are gradually shifting back to America. President Biden's economic programs emphasize a thriving middle class and can be an important driver of economic growth.

- [A study by Oxford University](#) identified a number of jobs at high risk for automation, including cashiers, legal assistants, and taxi drivers. Expectations are that the number of [new jobs created](#) will be greater than the number lost. But skill requirements will be significantly higher, and workers will need to continually update their capabilities. Global competition will be based not on cheap labor and shoddy goods, but on sharp minds and long-term orientations.

Where new jobs will come from remains troublesome. Government supported jobs can ease the situation, particularly in areas such as infrastructure where more efforts are badly needed. Joblessness is a major challenge; a return to a steadily expanding economy seems well beyond reach. Unemployment benefits ease the situation for many families. Low-paying jobs requiring hard physical labor in agriculture, landscaping, and construction are unattractive to many. The problem is not so much a lack of visas, but a lack of good wages and benefits.

In the long run, only developing a globally competitive workforce will provide high employment and support American prosperity, and this depends critically on the American education system with its numerous shortcomings. Young companies and entrepreneurs have been particularly important in job creation. So, while the nation faces a wide range of external challenges, the most critical challenge is to fix America first. Without some very basic realignments, America faces the prospect of becoming a second rate economic power unable to compete in the new global market. Integrating emerging technology with jobs is a central necessity. This requires improved education and shifting out of legacy industries, especially in energy.

The overall economy needs to provide jobs so that everyone has one that provides a living wage. There should be no underclass of people locked into underpaid jobs. Whatever is done has to be a much more fundamental shift than simply expanding the economy, and this poses another major challenge for the nation.

Education

As more and more unskilled jobs vanish, more and more skilled jobs are being created. The days are long gone when someone could graduate from high school and take a well-paying job for life, gradually working himself—almost always men—up into management. The continuing evolution of work requires a continuing evolution of education, including lifelong requirements to regularly upgrade knowledge levels. Two major problems complicate this: the inequality of education availability and the utility of higher education.

Education inequality has been most directly tied with racism, but high cost levels are also a challenge. Rural areas, for example, are hard pressed to provide the education levels typically found in cities. There have also been focused efforts to re-segregate schools, especially in the South. For example, a four-year effort in Gardendale, Alabama, eventually allowed it to separate higher-income districts (mostly white) from lower-income ones (mostly black). Racial, socioeconomic, and gender disparities in academic performance and educational attainment are stubborn features of the educational system but are neither inevitable nor immutable. This is clearly illustrated by the impressive performance of a number of low-income school districts in Chicago. Education remains a real challenge. The 2001 No Child Left Behind program was a good starting point; what is needed now is a new program: Every Child Pushed Ahead that tailors education to each child, ensuring that all children are all pushed to maximize their potential.

Some elements of American society are certainly not doing well educationally, but the bigger problem is that the overall educational system is not doing well. It continues to be financially strapped everywhere and scores poorly in global comparisons. A 2022 report ranked it 28th in math, in the bottom half of the Organization for Economic Cooperation, with a continuing achievement gap between high- and low-performing students. COVID-19 had worsened the problem; a digital divide between those with internet connections and those without severely impacted low-income households. Simultaneously, there is an on-going effort to shift education support funds from public schools to private ones, including with education vouchers.

Higher education has largely maintained its traditional topics and course structures, even as society is continually evolving. The result is that a college education is becoming less relevant for some sectors of the economy. Jobs requiring a college degree often have duties or performance criteria that have no relation to higher education. Degree requirements disqualify non-credentialed workers, even if they have relevant skills and experience. This forces students and families to spend substantial time and money on degrees that can be irrelevant to the job. In fact, 41 percent of recent college graduates were working in jobs that do not require a college degree. Another analysis shows that as many as 30 million American workers without four-year college degrees have the skills to realistically move into new jobs that pay on average 70 percent more than their current ones. Reassessments of the need for a college degree as well as ways education can best be matched to national needs are clearly needed.

Colleges have worked to reduce racial disparities. Affirmative action's original intent was to incorporate more minority students, but blacks and Hispanics have actually lost ground and lawsuits are increasingly common, particularly at Ivy League schools. Admissions officers work to put together a diverse freshman class. Standardized tests are one tool, but colleges also seek a diversity of interests and backgrounds that will create a vibrant community. Colleges need to be more candid about their complex and idiosyncratic needs, rewarding applicants who have overcome disadvantaged beginnings, but not giving one race an advantage over another. They also need to reduce criteria, such as legacy connections, that help to perpetuate traditional disparities.

College has also become increasingly more expensive. Tuition has almost doubled since 2004, now standing at $42,162 yearly, including room and board, for a four-year nonprofit private institution and $23,630 for out-of-state students at public college but only $10,662 for in-state students. One result is that student loan debt is close to $2 trillion, the second highest consumer debt category, only behind mortgage debt. Federal programs to reduce education debts, particularly from for-profit colleges, have bogged down in extended court cases. With the impact of COVID-19, the Class of 2020 graduated into the worst job market in a generation, with high unemployment rates and over 20 million people filing for unemployment. Although the virus significantly affected college education, its long-term impact is still uncertain. Technology will certainly be more integrated with on-line education, and universities will certainly re-consider the whole structure of continuing and higher education.

Immigration

Immigration has shifted from being a strength to being a weakness. For years, immigration was central to America's reputation as the Land of Opportunity, reflecting the inscription on the Statue of Liberty, "Give me your tired, your poor, your huddled masses..." This situation was made possible by American expansion, both geographically into a largely Open West and economically with a major increase in industrial strength. Earlier immigrants provided a large pool of cheap labor. Largely of European stock, they could take advantage of the Ladder of Opportunity, working themselves into the middle class. The unskilled jobs they left behind were filled by a continuing flow of new immigrants. Immigration made a significant contribution to America population growth, in contrast to Europe where population growth had leveled off. But the Open West is long gone and economic expansion that needed unskilled labor has slowed dramatically. The ladder of upward mobility has all but vanished; the Land of Opportunity has become a Land of Stagnation.

Under the Trump administration, immigration policies were significantly tightened. Promptly after taking office in January 2017, Trump suspended entry to America from seven Muslim countries, called for the immediate construction of a wall across the US–Mexico border, and hired 5,000 new border patrol agents and 10,000 new immigration officers. A subsequent "zero tolerance" allowed children to be separated from adults unlawfully entering America. Immigration was further reduced by coordination with Mexican authorities and a policy of requiring many asylum applicants to remain in Mexico pending determination.

One commentator suggested that the inscription on the Statue of Liberty has been replaced by two stark signs at the border: HELP WANTED and KEEP OUT. This reflects the dichotomy of American attitudes, the continuing need for an underclass but the concern that immigrants will drain increasingly scarce resources from society at large. It is regularly stated that illegal immigrants take jobs from Americans. What is usually glossed over is that Americans do not want these jobs because they are very hard and grossly underpaid. As long as the economy depends on a large number of jobs that do not provide a living wage, there will be a demand for immigrants. Now, as good jobs become harder to find, more Americans are willing to accept lower paid jobs they formerly avoided, but these jobs still far outnumber the Americans willing to work at them. Those in the current underclass are stuck in it, in particular some 10 million undocumented workers. Their status with a constant threat of deportation severely hampers their participation in society. Because of their understandable reluctance to be involved with the police, they are often crime victims. On the other hand, lacking employment, young immigrants can easily turn to gangs, drugs, and crime. Freedom eludes them.

With globalization, immigrants are more and more consigned to a permanent underclass; merging with the chronic unemployed, they form a growing marginalized population, increasingly frustrated and miserable. Even as America works to improve security by better border controls, it continues to attract illegal immigrants by offering them undesirable jobs—low paying by American standards, but high paying by the standards of most of the world. Better controls on borders and workplaces could ease the problem, but the underlying cause is the gulf in standards of living between America and much of the rest of the world. The reluctance of undocumented immigrants to return to their home countries and the significantly increased inflow of new undocumented immigrants is stark testimony to the failings of home governments, particularly in Mexico and Central America. As bad as their situation may be in America, it still seems better than back in their home countries, as vividly illustrated by continuing immigration from Central America. Whenever a disaster hits in that region, there is a resulting wave of immigrants to America as happened after the December 2020 storms in Guatemala left thousands destitute. The same problem is visible in Mexico where a favored elite sits atop large numbers of impoverished peasants. In the past, America was the safety valve for unequal wealth distribution in neighboring countries. Now, immigration is part of a much larger global challenge that cannot be solved at home.

By 2016, there were thousands of immigrants from all over the world seeking to live in America; in 2022 about half were from outside Latin America—a stark testimony to how small the world has become and what a global problem immigration is. President Trump came into office in 2017 promising to build a strong border wall. A policy of separating families drew much condemnation but probably helped make immigration less attractive to people south of the border. However, a surge in immigration in 2019 led to a reinforced deterrence policy, including an agreement with Mexico to hold immigrants while refugee applications were being processed. The end of the COVID-19 crisis and a more flexible policy by President Biden has resulted in record numbers of migrant encounters at the southern borders. Texas began a high-profile campaign to bus migrants to other cities, overwhelming many of their systems. What is driving the current immigration crisis is that downtrodden populations globally are seeking better living conditions, sometimes even survival. America has a moral obligation to help them, particularly since as one of the dominant countries in the world it has a major responsibility for the repressive governments driving their populations. The American economy can no longer integrate large numbers of immigrants. This problem has to be addressed on a global scale, not a domestic one.

At the same time, American employers cannot find the skilled workers they need, so they have been importing them for years. Although the number of [H-1 B specialty visas](#) is limited to 65,000/year, there were 780,884 registration applications for 2024, vividly demonstrating the high demand for temporary foreign workers. These visas have raised considerable controversy over whether they provide necessary support to American employers or simply allow companies to hire cheaper foreign workers, but the available data clearly indicates that they do not drag down the wages of other workers, but they are a brain drain on the Global South. In 2021, the median wage of an H-1B worker was $108,000, compared to $45,760 for U.S. workers in general.

Demographics & Economic Growth

The concentration of good paying jobs in the Industrialized World in general and particularly in America is gone. Globally it is obvious that higher birth rates provide more mouths to feed without providing the employment opportunities to support them; [lower birth rates](#) are a prerequisite for increasing national wealth. In recent years population dynamics have shifted dramatically. Almost half the world is now below the replacement fertility rate—this applies to some 83 countries, including most of the industrialized world. By 2050, the global fertility rate is expected to be [below the replacement fertility level](#) of about 2.0 births per woman and the world population should slowly level off.

The overall demographic projections for America had two major components. The first was relatively high fertility. Back in 2008 it was slightly above 2.0, implying near-complete replacement from one birth cohort to the next and considerably higher than in Japan or Europe. But by 2021, the rate had fallen to 1.66, steadily declining for several years. It seems that births will never again be at a replacement level.

The second major factor is immigration (both legal and illegal). The high flows of net immigration explained much of the country's previous history of steady population growth. Population projections show an American population by 2060 of 404 million. The population is expected to grow with excess births over deaths until 2030; then growth would continue thanks to immigration. By around 2050, the white population in America will probably be a minority.

Another major aspect of the demographic projections is that the American population will grow significantly older. The Census Bureau projects that in 2030, one in five Americans will be over 65 and by 2034 older adults are expected to outnumber children for the first time in history. The pattern should continue in the coming decades so that by 2060 there will be 95 million older adults but only 80 million children. If immigration slows, the percentage of old people will be even larger. At the upper end, the number of Americans at least 90 years old has tripled in recent decades, a major shift in population that has implications for social policy, especially regarding housing and health care. Individuals within this aging population likely will have at least one disability, and many will live alone or in a nursing home.

This societal aging raises a whole range of challenges, with two areas being particularly difficult:

- The larger percent of the aged population means a lower percent of working age adults. This naturally raises questions of how well a smaller working population can support the total population. Automation of many production areas and improvements in agriculture mean that fewer workers are needed for essential services. Also, as the population levels off, there will be less need for construction workers. The biggest open questions are the effects of climate change and its impact on agriculture and coastal settlements. How will this affect job availability? The obvious question is how can retirement income be maintained for such a large older population when there are fewer contributing workers. When 65 was initially set as the normal retirement age, it was also near the life expectancy; retired people were not expected to live long. They do now.

- Health costs are the most challenging area and raise questions of health rationing, or the extent which government should support the large payments for minimal life extension in end-of-life situations. The core question is, to what extent should people be responsible for paying for their own care and to what extent should others be responsible for paying for them? So, it is not a question of who will decide to pull the plug on grandma, but of who will pay for the plug. If grandma and her family pay, then of course they decide. But if they cannot pay, should grandma's treatment be reduced or stopped? Should someone else—we the taxpayers—pay for continuing medical support? That is a major social question that needs to be addressed.

Demographics also underlie the question of economic growth. This has been the central driver of the American economy ever since early settlers built up the East Coast and moved into the Appalachians. By the middle of the nineteenth century, the California Gold Rush and the Transcontinental Railroad were at the end of coast-to-coast growth. This had been much more than geographic growth. America had become the world's leading economy, a position it consolidated in the twentieth century as two World Wars devastated Europe. This growth continued into the twenty-first century, though the effects of economic globalization became increasingly evident: American companies systematically moved manufacturing operations overseas, while an emerging global market for intellectual work gradually drained many good-paying jobs. Then the bursting of the housing bubble in 2008 brought first American and then global economic expansion to a screeching halt.

About 200 years ago, Thomas Malthus envisioned population growth outpacing the increase in food production; famine would limit population size. Thanks to continually improving agricultural technology, that has not happened—yet. Nonetheless, growth cannot go on indefinitely. World population has increased from one billion in Malthus's time to around seven billion today and will probably level off around the end of the century at about ten billion. As noted, it has already leveled off for much of the Industrialized World, as well as for non-Hispanic white Americans. Only immigration has kept the American population growing, though at a slower rate. As immigration slows, the American population will undoubtedly also level off.

But even now, without a steady population, American economic growth has been flattening under the impact of globalization. The American economy was a consumption economy, and this was an underpinning of the entire global economy. High unemployment and a new sense of economic wariness have significantly limited domestic consumption, complicating the resurgence of not only the American economy but also the global economy.

For years, the cornerstone of many investment portfolios for those who could afford them had been blue chip utility stocks, prized for their ability to provide steady income, year in and year out. Turmoil in the utility markets and volatility in the overall markets replaced a reliance on steady income with a search for capital gains. Just as the housing bubble caused an artificial rise in house prices, there was a parallel bubble in stock prices as capital gains drove the entire financial sector. New companies were established and their values inflated as quickly as possible so that an Initial Public Offering would provide the founders a financial windfall with minimal real economic benefit. Growth in financial valuations was driven by the pressure of capital markets looking for profits. It was not only an overpriced housing market that collapsed but also an overpriced stock market. The Dow Jones fell almost 50 percent from May 2008 to March 2009, decimating many retirement funds.

The nation has worked hard to regain the economic growth seen as essential to prosperity. But this is not going to happen. The key question is not how to maintain growth when the population stagnates, but rather how to maintain prosperity with a stable population. Not how to reignite growth, but how to maintain a high standard of living without it. A steady economy can still be a dynamic one; indeed, it must be. While supporting all stakeholders, companies need to put more emphasis on efficient and profitable operations rather than on steady growth. Some companies will inevitably grow and others decline. Economies of scale will drive some size increase, though rising transportation costs will counter this to some extent. New sectors will continually replace outmoded ones. The economy as a whole needs to stabilize, to accept that growth will no longer be the core driver of prosperity. This is a major challenge for the twenty-first century.

Discrimination

Racism is a central factor in the skewed distribution of wealth. For blacks, this traces back to slavery, which was central to the economy of the South in the early nineteenth century. The Civil War brought an end to slavery, but certainly did not make blacks equal. The post-war Reconstruction basically returned control to Southern whites. They used economic pressures, education deficiencies, voting restrictions and the simple threat of violence with hundreds of lynchings to keep blacks in a position of inferiority. Our racial dilemma is grounded in a political, economic, and identity-based devaluing of black lives that has persisted ever since the first enslaved African arrived in Jamestown in 1619. The ensuing history of America is built on both racial and economic injustice, two related but distinct problems.

Conditions improved in the twentieth century. Supposedly "separate but equal" education facilities were rejected by the Supreme Court in the Brown v. Board of Education decision in 1954. Laws against interracial marriages were only voided in 1967. The subsequent overturning of segregation laws and practices was a long process, spurred by the emergence of a strong civil rights movement led by Martin Luther King, Jr., and other activists. Although there were obvious improvements, there were also many shortcomings. Black–white residential segregation remains a major source of unequal opportunity, perpetuating an enormous wealth gap and excluding black students from many high-performing schools. This is mostly a result of deliberate public policies which were designed to subjugate black people and promote white supremacy.

Unequal education opportunities help to maintain a significant shortfall in income for blacks compared to whites. In early 2020, white households were 60 percent of the population but owned nearly 85 percent of total national wealth; black households owned just 4.4 percent, Hispanics 3.2 percent.

Racial disparities, of course, are not restricted to blacks. A recent influx of Hispanic immigrants from Central America has brought objections that they are taking jobs from Americans. This is almost completely unfounded as many of the jobs they take are jobs that white Americans simply do not want. This was vividly illustrated by the COVID-19 crisis that drove major virus outbreaks among workers in meatpacking plants, prompting 21 plants to close, sickening more than 4,300 workers, and killing at least 200. Workers at these plants are typically immigrants, including illegals, mostly from Central America. White Americans are not interested in these jobs, for two basic reasons: working conditions are horrible and the pay is very low, rarely with any benefits. This not only disadvantages minorities, but the concentration of meat purchasing also traps farmers in take-it-or-leave-it contracts that hold down the prices they receive and that dictate many aspects of their operations. All these elements are driven by the same factor—the need for corporate profits. Meat prices should be higher so that both farmers and processors can get a fair return on their labor. Overall, another striking example of the social impact of wealth inequality and racism.

Minorities still remain relatively sparse in high corporate, government and military positions; they hold roughly 20 percent of high official positions although they comprise some 40 percent of the population. In Congress, more than a quarter of voting members are minorities—the most diverse Congress in history. At the state level, relatively low levels of minority members give many legislators incentive to minimize minority voting to protect their own positions. Efforts to restrict voting continued in the 2020 Presidential elections with President Trump loudly denouncing mail-in voting and then contesting the election and spurring an ongoing election denial movement undermining voting rights

Minorities are far above their population percent in jails and prisons. Economic disparities push a disproportionate number of young minorities into gang associations and petty crime, worsened by a system that criminalized relatively minor actions such as possession of small amounts of drugs or marijuana. A common inability to pay bail keeps additional offenders in jail. Of course, higher infraction rates also mean higher police attention, often overbearing and oppressive. A police culture of excessive use of force has resulted in numerous deaths of blacks and has been the driving force behind nationwide protests led by a Black Lives Matter movement.

Although the movement stressed its peaceful approach, in 2020 protests in several cities, particularly Portland, OR, resulted in extensive vandalism and destruction of numerous small businesses. Similarly, in Kenosa, WI, activists justified the destruction of small businesses by rationalizing that insurance would cover their losses, even though it often did not. The Black Lives Matter movement failed to organize efforts to address the vandalism or help devastated businesses recover. This widespread destruction stood in stark contrast to earlier protests by Martin Luther King and associates, who not only denounced violence but actively avoided it. Some of this recent violence was due to overzealous protestors, as well as to various extremist elements and thugs taking advantage of the cover provided by the protests. One result was excessive reactions by police departments. Another was that President Trump highlighted the destruction to bolster his standing among whites. At the same time, he issued an executive order restricting the scope of diversity training in the federal government and its contractors, basically denying that any systematic racism even exists. This was immediately rescinded when President Biden took office.

A major element in this controversy is the rise of white nationalists, which the Department of Homeland Security characterizes as the country's biggest threat. These radicals have been partly driven by the demographic realization that whites will soon be a minority in the country. Recently a white nationalist commented that they would not even accept white Muslims because their loyalty would be to their religion first and foremost. Of course, putting loyalty to religion first certainly could be said of many Protestants, Catholics and Pentecostals; white nationalists practice a diverse range of Western faiths. Their Son of God, Jesus Christ, was not white, nor were his apostles. He was of Middle Eastern ethnic origin and Jewish. Exactly what he was, we don't know, but we do know what he wasn't: white. And he was supportive of other ethnic groups as vividly demonstrated by the story of the Good Samaritan. So, it would seem strange for a devout Christian to be a white nationalist.

It also seems that the white nationalist groups, as well as many other racist groups, are partly driven by economic distress and the need to find "others" to blame. If everyone were doing well, there would be much less incentive for racism—another societal problem where wealth inequality is at the base.

Discrimination is not only racial, but often based on gender. There are strong objections to some people choosing their gender, while treatment of women in America varies widely from state to state. In a ranking by inclusion and treatment in justice and security systems, New England states rank best and a number of southern states worse. In addition to educational and job discrimination, women often face intimate partner violence and poor health care affordability.

DEMOCRATIC DYSFUNCTION

As the size of a community increases, democracy inevitably transforms into representative democracy, which brings in a number of immediate problems. Many people, for example, become represented by persons they voted against. Government also becomes more remote, with individual citizens unaware of many of its intricacies. When a community is comprised of irreconcilable factions, democracy is hard pressed to produce good governance. But mature democracies in which leaders balance competing views and then compromise on issues can provide competent and respected governance. Unfortunately, several intrinsic elements undermine collaboration, particularly:

- Representatives have their own personal interests, as well as those of the local constituent majority that elected them. This affects elected officials and legislators and ultimately the staff and bureaucracy that support them. These interests may encourage neglect of local minority elements and can pit strong constituent concerns against measures that promote the overall community good. Tensions between local concerns (often short-term and pressing) and the overall social good (often long-term and vague) are unavoidable. Local concerns can easily be given precedence—after all, an elected official's position depends on maintaining support of the constituent majority.

- The situation is often complicated by capitalism which has everyone pursuing their own individual interests. An open market manages some of the undesirable results of such free-for-all competition, but regulation has proved essential: anti-trust, minimum wage, and anti-discrimination laws are only a small and highly visible part of this system of controls. The more complex a system becomes, the more complex the regulations working to control or moderate it and the easier it is for tensions to develop.

- Every decision has winners and losers. More vocal constituents naturally get more attention, so do favored groups, ranging from family to friends to associates to general supporters to brokers—persons whose support is contingent on obtaining specific favors. Ultimately, thousands of individual decisions provide thousands of benefits to thousands of favored individuals and groups.

In the end, all politics are not only local, but personal, with decision-makers understandably reluctant to take actions that hurt them individually and inclined to "trade favors" with others. Democratic institutions become more and more encrusted with legacy procedures, and democracy becomes more and more unresponsive to the general welfare.

After the 2008 stock market crash, America experienced an economic recovery that was disturbingly superficial. Many basic indicators were doing well, but unemployment remained stubbornly high, so for millions the recovery was no recovery at all. Against this background, the American legislative system has become increasingly dysfunctional and polarized. We have reached a point where accumulated entitlements and favored treatments are weighing heavily on the system. There is no simple description of the problem; rather it is a culmination of long-standing trends:

- The society with its embedded economic system has become so complex that it is difficult to manage coherently. This was obvious in the response to the COVID-19 unemployment crisis; no one really knew just what to do. Widely varying programs were proposed. Some were implemented. Employment gradually recovered, but no one knew exactly why or how this happened.

- The massive set of laws and regulations, including the Tax Code and the Code of Federal Regulations (all 50 titles), include thousands of individual favorable treatments. Many were initially put in place with good justification, but all of them are resistant to reduction.

- Economic problems mean short-term considerations have a higher salience. Policy changes often have a direct impact on individuals, who will loudly defend their own specific privileges. When they have only a diffuse impact on the general public, there is often no one to speak for the common good. Interests with strong financial support get represented in the public debate; those without financial backing have difficulty even getting public visibility, much less support.

Every day the news includes dozens of examples of groups, big and small, strongly protecting their own favored positions without balancing voices speaking for the general welfare—a few random examples:

- A new push to strengthen mine safety faced determined resistance from coal mine owners;
- Although most farm subsidies go to farms with average annual revenue exceeding $200,000, reducing them is extraordinarily difficult;
- Even though an alternate engine for the F-35 Joint Strike Fighter had been opposed by both the Bush and Obama administrations, it still enjoyed broad bipartisan support in the House because it provides jobs for constituents;
- Junk mail supposedly pays its own way, though it is hard to understand why it costs $1.16 cents to deliver a three-ounce letter but only 21 cents to deliver a three-ounce advertising letter;
- Lobbyists from the pesticide industry pushed the American delegation at a major 2020 international conference on antimicrobial resistance, to omit any references to fungicides, a stance that infuriated other participants and forced the final public health recommendations to omit any mention of antifungal drugs;
- Unions are intimidating companies to eliminate secret ballot requirements in union-organizing elections.

Vested interests naturally resist change. This does not simply apply to a handful of rich or powerful citizens, but to millions of everyday people who also protect their own individual interests, particularly personal, short-term interests—their organization sends junk mail, or their job depends on a government program, or their own small subsidy is more important to them than the outsized subsidy to someone else, or their company profits are squeezed by some regulation.

Politicians naturally see this as an opportunity. It is much easier to get votes with attractive slogans and simplistic answers than with thoughtful programs that cannot be explained in a short paragraph. Long-term programs need short-term money, and this can be difficult to articulate. A vivid example was the 2007 collapse of a major bridge in Minneapolis, killing about a dozen people as well as creating a momentous traffic problem. State inspections had rated the bridge as marginal, but the Minnesota governor twice failed to act, vetoing increases in the state gas tax to fund transportation infrastructure needs. The voters clearly got what they wanted: lower taxes and weaker infrastructure. Similar stories abound in all our states where infrastructure has been neglected for a half century. This was widely illustrated in February 2021 when a strong winter storm hammered the Midwest, shutting down power throughout the region. In Texas, people even froze to death and water supplies were severely impacted. The state power company had been disconnected from the regional network and had simply failed to build resilience into its system. The storm highlighted more than electric grid problems—the entire infrastructure of roads and railways, drinking-water systems, power plants, electrical grids, and industrial waste sites is at risk. Infrastructure is a particularly difficult challenge since problems are typically off in the future and the short-term costs significant. This is complicated by the fact that the American government is organized along functional lines with many responsibilities split between federal, state, and local officials. It is very difficult to address issues that require an integrated response.

It is the people who have to protect their own interests, supporting leaders who watch out for the common good and groups and organizations that support America's traditional values.

3

GLOBAL COMPETITION

America operates in the international environment. Its history shapes our relations with the other major international powers and our competition with them and indicates potential areas of cooperation.

Most Americans are generally aware of earlier civilizations that overextended themselves and then vanished, sometimes precipitously. Rome ruled for centuries and then the empire disintegrated. The Soviet Union dominated a large portion of Eurasia for 80 years and then collapsed in a few short months. Yet it is hard to appreciate the central historical lesson: the need to continuously adjust to ceaselessly changing external circumstances, to continuously re-invent the nation to fit each newly evolving environment. Coming into the twenty-first century, America was seen by Francis Fukuyama as representing the End of History—the culmination of governmental development in a free society with a free market economy. There were expectations that this model would gradually spread to the whole world and bring peace, stability, and prosperity. Unfortunately, this self-assured confidence in global peace and development proved to be premature. In actuality, the nation faces a range of daunting global challenges.

Threats to life and liberty have, of course, a direct impact on prosperity, primarily because of their call on resources. Besides overtly hostile challenges, the nation faces a range of socio-political and economic challenges that constrain American economic development. Additionally, the growing economic dependence on computerization raises a very different set of challenges that were unthinkable a century or so ago when electricity was first being integrated into the American economic system.

External challenges set the framework within which the nation operates. The global setting both supports and constrains what is possible for the nation. The government can influence these external challenges, but it cannot control them. Adapting the nation to its external environment is one of the key requirements of government.

GLOBALIZATION

Globalization is the interaction among people, companies, and governments worldwide, reflected in a growth in international trade and an exchange of ideas and culture. Although America had not really been a colonial power, it did take control of Puerto Rico, and for many years the Philippines. American business interests dominated several nations, particularly the "banana republics" of Central America and independent Hawaii. The pro-business governments they set up disenfranchised indigenous populations with drastic, long-lasting, negative impact on those countries, including the current flow of desperate immigrants heading to America. These business interests even overwhelmed the civil government of independent Hawaii, engineering its incorporation into the United States.

For over a century, economic conditions ensured that the Industrialized World, led by America, received agricultural commodities and raw materials at bargain prices. One result was a disproportionate American share of global production, profit, and high paying jobs. Many of the smartest people in the world naturally gravitated to America, so it also enjoyed a disproportionate share of the best brains. This "brain drain" was a cause of concern in the 1980s, but the concern gradually faded away.

After World War II, America and 22 other nations met in Geneva and set up a General Agreement on Tariffs and Trade (GATT). This created an open world trading system minimizing trade barriers. Lower tariffs promoted the rapid economic recovery of Europe and Japan. Economic growth allowed democracy to become firmly established in a way that had failed after World War I. Average tariff levels for the major GATT participants fell from about 22 percent in 1947 to 5 percent at the end of the century. The prosperity of the world economy over that period owes a great deal to the growth of world trade. In 1995, GATT was replaced by the World Trade Organization (WTO). Signed by 123 nations, it is the largest international economic organization in the world and provides a framework for negotiating trade agreements and a dispute resolution process.

The rise of the Organization of Petroleum Exporting Countries (OPEC) in 1960 put the first serious crimp in the control by the Industrialized World of critical imports. Oil was the lifeblood of the American economy, which was then heavily dependent on imports. The rising costs greatly increased the amount of American debt held abroad, undermining the entire American economy and restricting foreign policy options. At the same time, environmental concerns on fossil fuel usage and deep ocean drilling made oil usage less attractive, while turmoil in the Middle East and Nigeria and strained relations with Iran and Venezuela underlined the fragility of the supply.

Coal resources came with major environmental problems; and after the Fukushima nuclear power plant disaster, nuclear power appeared even less appealing. Biofuels held some promise, but corn-based ethanol only survived by being heavily subsidized. Renewable power sources could meet only a fraction of energy requirements. Then fracking upended the American energy system. Hydraulic fracturing of oil and gas deposits increased dramatically, bringing substantial benefits to the nation in terms of lower energy prices, greater energy security, reduced air pollution, and fewer carbon emissions. America became the number one oil producer in the world. Then the COVID-19 crisis severely undermined global demand; daily prices actually went negative. President Trump joined in a global effort to restrict production, and prices rose modestly. Oil is much less critical today, as natural gas is becoming much more prominent, and renewables will steadily increase. Solar energy must play a central role in any long-term effort to reduce energy dependence. A global realignment of energy use patterns is unavoidable. Whatever is done will inevitably produce short-term damage to some politically influential groups, and American leadership will be critical. As mentioned above under global warming, the international community has started to address this better; a December 2023 climate conference called for a transition from fossil fuels, but did not envision how this would actually happen.

Oil is not the only commodity that has seen rising prices. Since 2000, for example, coffee prices have more than doubled; copper has gone from under a dollar a pound to over three. Because of these steadily increasing prices of a wide range of materials with inadequate local supply, America imports a smaller share of global resources. While America has more than adequate supplies of some critical minerals (such as phosphate rock for fertilizers), it depends heavily on external supplies for other important minerals, such as lithium (negligible American production) and platinum group metals. Shortages of some critical materials, particularly rare earths, make the nation further dependent on international trade.

Although wages in developing nations have increased, they remain significantly lower than American rates. One result in the early 2000s was had been a strong tendency of American and multinational corporations to move management and manufacturing operations abroad, not only to supply those markets but also to export back to America. This sent investment, profits, taxes, and revenues abroad, increasing the vulnerability of supply chains and reducing the ability of American industry to respond to military and medical requirements.

It also resulted in the closing of American factories with devastating economic impacts on some individual towns. Technology development has also automated more and more industrial jobs, while rapidly growing artificial intelligence is even undermining a variety of white-collar jobs. America can no longer hold a disproportionate share of high-paying jobs; more and more work requirements in America can be satisfied by jobs abroad.

Globalization, with a newly networked world and burgeoning physical interconnections, means that America can no longer dominate the global economy and continue to enjoy a grossly disproportionate share of global resources. Around the world, citizens are demanding an increased share of global wealth. Economic inequality fuels the frustrations within which radical ideologies flourish and is a major underlying basis of unrest, challenging the entire world. Now, with information freely flowing on the internet and the rise of new economic powers, particularly China and India, the era of American economic dominance is drawing to a close. The economic turmoil caused by COVID-19 is having a major impact on the American economy, vividly demonstrating how interconnected the world is. America has benefited greatly from international trade, though increasingly negative aspects are making trade agreements more important than ever. There is even a potential for a trade war between America and the European Union.

In February 2016, America and 11 other nations joined in a Trans-Pacific Partnership, a comprehensive effort to harmonize the trade of nations operating in the region. It did not include China and was expected to shift more trade of regional nations from China to America. There was some opposition to the Partnership, particularly in its treatment of medical drugs as well as concerns on being too deferential toward corporations at the expense of workers. Donald Trump specifically denounced it as undermining the American economy and independence, and promptly withdrew America when he became President in January

2017. The remaining 11 countries signed a revised version which went into effect in December 2018. This was just the first of disruptive trade actions by the Trump administration.

The trilateral 1992 <u>North American Free Trade Agreement</u> had significantly increased American trade with Mexico, but also facilitated the transfer of industrial jobs from America. President Trump promptly initiated negotiations, resulting in a new <u>United States–Mexico–Canada Agreement</u> (USMCA), which entered into force in July 2020, increasing environmental and working regulations. It also incentivized more domestic production of cars and trucks and gave America more access to Canada's dairy market. Most importantly, a reduction of trade barriers among the USMCA's parties helped strengthen <u>investment,</u> but job growth is still problematical. President Biden's efforts under the Inflation Reduction Act represent a broad commitment to <u>revitalize neglected factory communities</u>, but results are still uncertain.

The challenges of globalization merge with the challenge of global demographics. Populations in the developing world have a high percentage of young, unemployed men, an imbalance unlikely to change significantly in the immediate future. The global internet ensures that they are aware of being exploited and gives them incentive to object. The current turmoil in the Middle East is driven partly by this imbalance, the lack of local jobs. There is no resolution in sight. Similar imbalances in Africa and the rest of Asia only portend more troubles. This naturally leads to domestic dissatisfaction that can be exploited by demagogues and lead to autocratic regimes.

Against this background, we are approaching a <u>flat world</u>, a level economic playing field on which everyone can compete. Well, actually, not everyone. The poorest of the poor are still left out and the underclass continues to grow. America has been undertaking piecemeal efforts to address these challenges but lacks a coherent vision. It is easy to envision by mid-century a world in which strife with disaffected domestic and international underclasses, global economic competition, and the pressures of energy shortages and overseas debt combine to bring a sharp drop in the American economy.

More broadly, this could be a world of turmoil with widespread conflict as militarized societies vie for increasingly scarce resources. Russia and China could both revert to stern, heavily militarized autocracies, challenging America. Rogue nuclear states would make the world increasingly perilous. Prosperity would be out of the question; survival would be the main objective. Such a projection lies along the main line of current trends. Avoiding such a global meltdown is a core challenge of the twenty-first century, a major political challenge of the future. This is also problematic for both India and China, where government legitimacy rests on economic performance. The situation with China is especially bothersome because it could easily drive a beleaguered leadership to adopt a strongly nationalist, confrontational stance, greatly complicating efforts to promote global harmony.

Within the global community, the decline in American prosperity and cohesiveness is readily apparent, thanks to the internet, with the most disturbing event being the storming of the Congressional offices in January 2021. This has all but destroyed America's reputation as a Beacon of Freedom and has undermined democracy worldwide. Current domestic economic problems—joblessness, decline of manufacturing, stagnation of household income—are exacerbated by evolving global market forces. The internet suddenly put Indian managers, Chinese engineers, and Russian programmers in direct competition with skilled American workers, often providing comparable services at a fraction of local wage and benefit costs. No longer able to exploit an outsized proportion of global resources, America must now seek other ways to maintain a highly competitive position in the world. Global modernization is the major political challenge of the future and requires

America to work more closely with its wide range of supportive allies, including the other major countries of the Industrialized World. America also has strong relations with most of the major governments globally, including Brazil, India, Indonesia, Israel, Egypt and Saudi Arabia.

The continuing concentration of wealth at the top of global societies is being facilitated by multinational corporations' focus on profit. Global economic inequality is a major underlying basis of the terrorist threat challenging the developed world in general and America in particular. It fuels the frustrations within which radical ideologies flourish. It is the result of hundreds of years of economic development and cannot be solved quickly or with simple fixes. In addition, American frustrations with the global trade system have led to trade disputes with a number of nations, particularly China. This has had a strong impact on the American economy, partly because concentrated supply chains made American companies dependent on Chinese supplies. Global standards on trade are increasingly disputed.

America's militarized approach to democracy promotion has further undermined its reputation. The failure of democracy to demonstrate broad prosperity has facilitated autocrats globally to promote alternative systems, often giving lip service to democracy and using nationalist appeals to distract attention from autocratic repression and surveillance. For the first time in American history, military forces are not central to addressing the major challenges facing the nation. In the newly globalized world, prosperity depends on global stability. The tide is now running against this with turmoil in the Islamic World, worldwide economic shortages, Chinese and Russian protection of failed states, and the uncertain impact of climate change.

Although the global challenge is driven by economics, it is more fundamentally a challenge of good governance, as autocrats drive their populations into poverty while building their own personal fortunes. A main reason these nations can continue to operate is the support they get from China and Russia, which resolutely refuse to judge the actions of other sovereign rulers. Both countries have numerous internal problems, and their leaders are working hard to suppress any dissent. Both are becoming increasingly authoritarian, justifying this internally by the need to have a strong government in the face of external challenges. America, working with its allies, can support the alternative development approaches that are so badly needed.

RUSSIA

As the lone superpower, American leadership was first tested by its relationship with Russia, and it failed the test miserably. The collapse of the Soviet Union had been followed almost immediately by one of the major strategic blunders of the twentieth century, a blunder still barely recognized. This test was the need to integrate Russia into a coalition of democratic nations. The Russian people had vague but optimistic hopes that the end of the Cold War would lead to a new era of peace and prosperity. But any sense of a new world was immediately destroyed when the West stood by as the fragile democratic effort was overwhelmed by the former elites, who took control of the nation's assets while millions descended into poverty. Underemployment was replaced with widespread unemployment; inflation destroyed pensions; criminal gangs expropriated economic assets. The West provided advice on capitalist development, but zero actual financial support. The West had no concept at all of integrating Russia and offered minimal support to struggling democratic elements. The Russian population came to see democracy and market capitalism as Western ploys designed to suppress and humiliate Russia.

Besides the failure to promote economic integration, the Western strategic blunder also had a military dimension. After World War II, Soviet consolidation of control over Eastern Europe and then a Soviet-supported war in Korea led to the formation of the NATO military force, including America, Canada, and the major West European powers. When this expanded to include West Germany in 1955, the Soviet Union responded by forming an opposing Warsaw Pact alliance. Europe settled down into an uneasy stalemate. The unfavorable balance of conventional forces pushed NATO to emphasize nuclear readiness. This, in turn, led to a continual competitive development of nuclear systems, culminating in a state of Mutually Assured Destruction as outsized strategic arsenals of America and the Soviet Union faced each other. The collapse of the Soviet Union in 1989 also collapsed the basic rationale for NATO. But instead of looking for a military drawdown and despite earlier informal assurances, NATO integrated several East European nations into its system. Russia naturally took this as a military challenge—there was certainly no other focus for NATO forces—and objected strongly. Russia also strongly objected to American plans for a limited anti-missile system in Eastern Europe.

While this was going on, Vladimir Putin was turning Russia's nascent democracy into a shell. Economic difficulties dramatically reduced the size of the Russian armed forces and initially limited Russian foreign affairs. The Western failure to engage gave Putin a major boost, enabling him to blame the West for Russian economic problems, building on centuries-old trends of Europe-Russia confrontations and skillfully manipulating traditional Russian ambivalence. Stressing the need to counter NATO, he rejuvenated the army, a source of pride for the average Russian. Emphasizing Russia's rightful position as a world leader, his confrontational stance gained broad domestic support. In this context, Western denigration of Russia was normal, and Russia was simply defending its own culture. Military confrontation fit neatly into this narrative.

Global Disruption

Despite membership in such Western groups as the World Bank and participation in the G-8 economic summits, Putin became heavily involved with separatist movements at home and abroad. Domestically, the largest conflict was in Chechnya where the Russian military basically destroyed the capital city of Grozny and installed a strongly pro-Russian government under Ramzan Kadyrov. Regionally, Russia maintains a military base in Moldova's breakaway Transnistria province, which the Council of Europe recognizes as "a Moldovan territory occupied by Russia." Similarly, in 2008 Russia used actions by South Ossetian separatists as a pretext for a military invasion of Georgia. The Georgian government severed diplomatic relations with Russia which then recognized Abkhazia and South Ossetia as separate republics. Most recently, Ukrainian attacks on the Russian naval base at Sevastopol have led Russia to sign an agreement with Abkhazia to establish a new Russian naval base in the disputed territory. In Central Asia and Belarus, Russia has supported autocratic governments suppressing internal opposition.

Nowhere in the region was Russian support of separatists more significant than in Ukraine. Growing domestic discontent resulted in an Orange Revolution in 2004, protesting election rigging. More demonstrations in 2013/2014 led pro-Russian President Viktor Yanukovych to flee to Russia. Russia reacted violently, initiating military operations against Ukraine, using its navy to annex Crimea and then launching an open invasion of the Donbas in August 2014. This conflict settled into an uneasy frozen state until Russia launched an invasion of Ukraine in April 2022. Ukraine's strong response with significant help from the West limited Russia's gains to a small part of the country. But Western reluctance to directly confront Russia also led to a stalemate by early 2024 with ongoing military operations by both sides but minimal expectations of a resolution by military means.

In addition to its regional disruptions, Russia has also been broadly involved in the international sphere. In Syria, Russian support for the autocratic regime of Bashar al-Assad played a major role in ending democratic pressures from the Arab Spring in the Middle East. This has resulted in thousands of deaths and is a primary cause of refugee flows into Europe, but it protects Russia's Mediterranean naval base at Tartus. Similarly, Putin's strong support for Venezuelan President Nicolás Maduro has been critical for his survival, while support for dictatorial regimes in Cuba and Nicaragua has undermined efforts to promote democratic governments throughout Latin America. In Africa, Russia and China are working together to increase influence, with Russia actively involved in both the Central African Republic and in a recent coup in Niger. More broadly, the war in Ukraine has significantly worsened global starvation as Russia has blocked food shipments from Ukraine. The war has also pushed militarization globally, undermining resources for economic development while global political fragmentation greatly complicates efforts to address global warming and the increasing numbers of local disasters.

The West had initially hoped that it could develop positive relations with Putin's regime and its responses to Russian activities were restrained. But these hopes steadily faded as his autocracy intensified, systematically eliminating internal dissent. Even minor objections are promptly met with police responses and incarceration. Putin has broadly promoted a warped vision of Russian history, incorporating deep-seated aggressive forms of patriotism, Soviet nostalgia, and pride in the past. This vision of an imperial legacy stresses the need to confront a threat from the West and has drawn extensive public support, partly because of a widespread reluctance to be seen as opposing the regime on any level.

The invasion of Ukraine transformed what been a great power squabble into a fundamental attack on universal values. Not since Hitler has one man so thoroughly controlled a major country and set it on such a destructive path. The fundamental quest now is not for territory in Ukraine, but for global stability. Except for nuclear considerations, Russia does not pose a direct military threat to the United States, though it does pose a military threat to a number of NATO members. More importantly, it is systematically undermining the structure of international order that is critical to US development and to global peace. So long as Russia actively supports autocratic regimes globally and continues military operation in Ukraine, there can be no peace in Europe, indeed, no real peace globally.

Cyber Threat

The cyber threat is another matter. Russia has a long history of propaganda and disinformation. The rise of the internet and cyberspace has greatly expanded the playing field. Social media has further expanded this reach. Some discussions between America and Russia have occurred on setting standards for cyber engagement, but no agreements. There is general agreement that cyber attacks are equivalent to military attacks, but no agreement at all on what that means in practice. In recent decades, Russia has extensively exploited cyber potential in several ways:

- Intrusions into individual business and personal accounts. One 2014 intrusion, attributed to Russia, stole data on 500 million Yahoo accounts. In another instance, federal agents shut down two global cyberfraud operations, apparently operated out of Russia, that infected between 500,000 and a million computers and cost people more than $100 million in direct and indirect losses.

- Focused attacks on nations. In 2007, when Estonian authorities began removing a bronze statue of a World War II-era Soviet soldier from a park in Tallinn, they expected violent street protests by Estonians of Russian descent. Instead, they got a month-long cyber attack that came close to shutting down the country's digital infrastructure. The Estonians tied the attacks to a Russian official; the Russian government denied any involvement. Similar attacks were noted in Georgia during the 2008 war with Russia. In 2017, Ukraine became a scorched-earth testing ground for Russian cyberwar tactics. A worm introduced into Ukrainian government computers rapidly raced out to countless machines around the world, crippling several multinational companies, particularly Maersk. The result was more than $10 billion in total damages. American intelligence agencies confirmed that Russia's military was responsible; the Russian foreign ministry declined to comment. These incidents exemplify how Russia's current concept of hybrid warfare, often employing proxies, greatly complicates attribution.

- Infrastructure targeting. A Trump administration alert had accused Russia of a coordinated "multi-stage intrusion campaign" to hack into critical American infrastructure networks and conduct "network reconnaissance" on critical infrastructures: energy, nuclear, commercial facilities, water, aviation, and essential manufacturing. These efforts have been going on for years. The alert depicts an adversary probing for vulnerabilities and preparing to use them with advanced malware, if and when it deems it advantageous.

- Public propaganda. The most obvious case of Russian public propaganda is the widely discussed Russian meddling in the 2016 Presidential campaigns, starting with intrusion into the Democratic National Committee's servers, extracting 50,000 emails belonging to the Clinton campaign, and then astutely disseminating them to embarrass Hillary Clinton. This was part of an extensive three-year surreptitious campaign that reached well over 100 million Americans with false, misleading, and inflammatory postings on Facebook, messages on Twitter, and over 1,000 videos on YouTube. The intelligence community concluded that President Putin and other senior officials in Moscow also sought to influence the 2020 elections. In 2018, Microsoft thwarted hacking attacks against two conservative think tanks by a group with known ties to the Russian government.

- Internet intrusion. In October 2020, America unsealed criminal charges against six Russian intelligence officers in connection with some of the world's most damaging cyber attacks, including disruption of Ukraine's power grid and the release of a mock ransomware virus (NotPetya) that infected computers globally, causing billions of dollars in damage. Only a few months later, Russia was implicated in a wide-ranging intrusion that compromised major parts of the American government, demonstrating how cyber operations have become a key plank in Russia's confrontation with the West.

Russia, with its deep experience producing propaganda and extensive involvement in a wide variety of cyber efforts, clearly has a more advanced cyber capability than America. Almost certainly, it has identified significant American vulnerabilities. With its open society, America is intrinsically more vulnerable, as vividly demonstrated by the incoherent efforts to control even domestic content on Facebook and Twitter. Russia, on the other hand, has extensive internal controls on the internet, making cyber intrusions more difficult for the American government. Internally, Russian media mocking America resonates with the Russian public, while any American media mocking Russian activities has minimal traction in America.

Especially in the absence of any agreed standards, America cannot easily address the cyber challenge, particularly since it is so difficult to attribute cyber activities to specific sources or to demonstrate actual Russian government involvement. America can build some deterrence with cyber intrusions of its own. Indeed, it has recently acknowledged digital incursions into Russia's electric power grid. Limited efforts like this can even be counterproductive, allowing Putin to bolster his domestic standing by demonstrating that Russia is under attack. He has minimal concern that America would actually damage Russian systems since Russian retaliation could be severe. Because of this imbalance, a tit-for- tat situation is hardly attractive. It simply perpetuates a covert competition where America is at a real disadvantage.

For America, the best defense against cyber attack is a good working relationship with an adversary nation. That is what is needed with Russia. Right now it is unthinkable that former enemies Germany and Japan would support cyber confrontations with America. In the meantime, the best counter to Russian cyber activities is American broadcast activities, along with defensive measures and diplomatic pressures.

Public Opinion

The intrusion into the Democratic National Committee was apparently a Russian response to revelations in the so-called Panama Papers. In the spring of 2016, an international consortium of journalists began publishing revelations from a vast trove of documents belonging to a Panamanian law firm that specializes in helping wealthy foreign clients move money out of their home countries. These revelations included ties to money from several prominent Russians. Putin was apparently furious at this, attributed it to Western intelligence, and ordered retaliation. It seems that Western governments were not actually involved, but the claim allowed Putin to depict the information as simply Western propaganda. It also showed Kremlin sensitivity to light being shed on corruption.

In contrast to cyber, in the more public area of open broadcasting, America has a considerable advantage. In early 1953, the American government began broadcasting into the Soviet Union with Radio

Liberty, showcasing independent, contemporary voices, and providing critical discussion of current affairs while countering disinformation. By 1955, its broadcasts in 17 languages were a major challenge to the Soviet government, which spent more on jamming them than it did on its own broadcasts. However, once Mikhail Gorbachev became head of state in 1988, jamming the broadcasts stopped as part of the Soviet Union's new openness. By 1990, Radio Liberty had become the most listened-to Western radio station in the Soviet Union. During the 1991 coup attempt on Boris Yeltsin, it was instrumental in allowing him to stay in touch with the Russian people. In appreciation, he allowed [Radio Liberty](#) to open a permanent bureau in Moscow—Radio Svoboda.

In 2014, in conjunction with the Voice of America, Radio Liberty launched a new Russian-language TV news program, *Current Time*, to provide audiences worldwide with a balanced alternative to the disinformation produced by Russian media outlets. It had reported on such sensitive topics as Russian intervention in Syria, the poisoning of a Soviet refugee in London, and the revelations by the Panama Papers of Russian money being hidden abroad. Radio Svoboda has also expanded its coverage with video blogs, original documentaries, and new digital tools. In 2018, its website had over [90 million visits](#), its Facebook page had some 600,000 followers, and it was active on YouTube, Twitter, and other social networks. The Russian state TV had regularly portrayed Radio Liberty journalists as spies, while cyber efforts sought to discredit its reporting and attack its journalists online. In December 2017, the government officially labeled Radio Free Europe/Radio Liberty (RFE/RL) and Voice of America as [foreign agents](#). Clearly, open broadcasts have a significant potential to influence developments in Russia. By January 2021, the Russian administration was threatening multimillion-dollar fines and possible criminal charges against REF/RL employees based on [newly restrictive requirements](#) expanding the scope of "foreign agents." This effort essentially shut down any independent radio commentary.

It is understandable that the Russian populace wholeheartedly embraced a strong leader who, aided by spikes in energy prices, brought stability and pride back to Russia. By and large, the population was happy to trade economic improvements and international prestige for freedoms which they never really enjoyed anyhow. Nevertheless, democratic ideals do have resonance in Russia and Western economic sanctions, imposed after the invasion of Ukraine, are starting to have an impact. The more difficult everyday economic situations become, the more difficult it is for the government to suppress opposition. Putin declares that the "liberal idea has become obsolete" even as he is pushed to respond to unrest over low living standards. Independent candidates make electoral politics increasingly contested, and the government reacts with voter suppression. In July 2019, 1000 people protested in Moscow over barring opposition candidates from the city ballot. Open broadcasts have a significant potential to influence developments in Russia. A wave of arrests against journalists in 2019 vividly illustrated the Kremlin's concern about popular protests. In 2020, thousands marched to mark five years since the assassination of an opposition politician while the arrest of a regional governor brought widespread protests and a petition with more than 30,000 signatures in Khabarovsk in Russia's Far East. Two following events underlined Kremlin concerns on the opposition: the poisoning of opposition leader Aleksei Navalny and the self-immolation of independent journalist Irina Slavina in Nizhny Novgorod. After recuperating from the poisoning in Germany, Navalny has since returned to Russia where he has been held in maximum security prisons. More recently, opposition figures are working to get involved in upcoming elections.

Summary

Although Putin has worked hard to reassert Russia's position on the world stage, health and demographic issues undermine Russia's economic position, and a reliance on raw material sales downgrades the potential for longer term economic development. Cooperation with China in an effectively anti-democratic partnership also offers few benefits for Russia, which would inevitably be the junior member of any Sino-Russian partnership.

Russia poses only a minimal military threat to America or NATO, despite its strong nuclear capabilities. Its belligerent military development is fundamentally a show for the Russian people and does little to change Russia's position of military inferiority. Any NATO effort to focus on Russia as an enemy simply supports Putin's claim of a threat from the West.

Nonetheless, Russia is the major short-term challenge to global stability. Its invasion of Ukraine brought war to Europe for the first time in almost 80 years. On a broader scale, Russian support for autocracy undermines peaceful development in the region (Moldova, Georgia, Central Asia) as well as in Syria, Africa (Central African Republic, Niger) and Latin America (Venezuela, Cuba, Nicaragua) and bolsters Iran and North Korea. Support for China also buttresses Xi's dominance of China. More broadly Russian cyber actions undermine internet operations globally, while complicating efforts at promoting global economic development, restricting actions on global warming and promoting global military expansions. America has to respond to the current Russian military threats in Europe, but resolving the confrontation requires energizing the Industrialized World to commit to continuing pressures promoting the emergence of a more progressive Russian government.

THE ISLAMIC WORLD: CLASH OF CIVILIZATIONS

"Clash of Civilizations" is the title of a 1993 article by Samuel Huntington that drew attention to the growing frictions between the

Christian European and American cultures on the one hand and Islamic culture on the other. These frictions go back centuries. The Middle Ages were an Islamic Golden Age when science and economics flourished in much of the Islamic World on a par with Europe. By the 12th and 13th centuries there were already active military confrontations as the Crusades sought to recover the Holy Land from Islamic rule. In the centuries that followed, European Renaissance and the Holy Roman Empire led to a dramatic scientific and economic expansion and on to an Age of Discovery when European control expanded over much of the world. This was also the time of the rise of the Ottoman Empire, which in the 16th and 17th centuries twice laid siege to Vienna. By the 19th century, the Austro-Hungarian Empire dominated the continent, and the Industrial Revolution gave rise to radical economic, cultural, and social change in Europe. The fading Ottoman Empire was finally dismembered in the aftermath of World War I. With European control of the Middle East and north Africa, much of the Islamic World was relegated to a second-tier status both economically and politically.

Significant American involvement in the region only began during World War II when Iran became a major conduit of American aid to the Soviet Union. After the war, as oil became a strategic commodity in the evolving Cold War, America developed close ties with both Saudi Arabia and Iran, the two countries having the largest oil reserves. In 1951, Mohammad Mosaddegh was democratically elected as the Prime Minister of Iran and became enormously popular after he nationalized Iran's oil industry. America and Great Britain, considering him unreliable and fearing a Communist takeover, orchestrated a coup d'état in August 1953. This coup remains the underlying reason for deep US-Iranian enmity. It strengthened an increasingly repressive rule by the Shah, Mohammad Reza Pahlavi.

In February 1979, a year of strikes and demonstrations forced the Shah to flee to America; cleric Ruhollah Khomeini returned from exile and set up an Islamic Republic. The end of that year saw increasing turmoil in American relations with the Islamic World. In November, a group of Muslim students seized the American Embassy in Tehran and took 52 personnel hostage after America refused to extradite the Shah. A subsequent failed rescue attempt then helped force President Carter out of office. The hostages were released January 20, 1981, just minutes after American President Ronald Reagan was sworn into office. American relations with Iran remained strained.

Afghanistan

In the middle of this turmoil with Iran, the Soviet Union invaded Afghanistan in December 1979. America began an extended effort to support Afghan guerilla forces. The effort itself was largely carried out by Pakistan working with radical Islamic elements inside Afghanistan. With American approval, Saudi Arabia also supported this effort, even as it promoted its own radical Islamic Wahhabism globally. Then Saddam Hussein invaded Iran, hoping to take advantage of its post-revolutionary chaos, but instead initiating an Iran-Iraq War, which would last almost a decade. During that time, America actively provided intelligence and logistic support to Hussein.

The last decade of the century began with positive developments for American relations with the Islamic World. The final Soviet troops left Afghanistan in 1989 and Afghanistan descended into civil war. With the Soviets gone, American attention temporarily shifted elsewhere. In August 1990, Saddam Hussein invaded and annexed Kuwait. America formed an international coalition and initiated Operation Desert Storm, entering Kuwait in February 1991 and devastating Iraqi forces. The coalition declared a cease-fire after only 100 hours, but allowed Iraqi forces to take much of their military equipment back to Iraq and did not seek Saddam Hussein's removal. This was the period when Huntington was writing his article, when the Clash of Civilizations was becoming evident. At that point, America had complex relations with the Islamic World, having stood up in defense of Kuwait, being strongly at odds with Iran, and having close relationships with autocratic governments in Saudi Arabia and Egypt. Through this decade, the American relationship with Islam remained basically stable; cultural differences were not a driving factor.

But Afghanistan was looming in the background. It remained in a complicated civil war, as a radical Taliban group emerged and took control of most of the country with Pakistani backing. Other radical Islamic groups began to emerge, particularly al Qaeda. A transnational extremist Salafist organization founded in 1988 by Osama bin Laden. He used it to oppose the Soviet occupation and use Afghanistan as a springboard for radical Islamic promotion. Al Qaeda was implicated in 1998 bombings that killed more than 200 people at American embassies in Dar es Salaam in Tanzania and Nairobi in Kenya. American intelligence recognized al Qaeda as a threat but did not consider it a pressing one.

This changed dramatically in the new century when terrorists commandeering airplanes struck the World Trade Center and the Pentagon on September 11, 2001, killing almost 3,000 Americans. Al Qaeda specifically claimed credit for the strikes, calling them a response to global actions against Muslims. Other motives may include the "humiliation" resulting from the Islamic world falling behind the Western world, especially visible with ongoing globalization. President Bush promptly initiated a Global War on Terror, defined largely by military intervention and efforts to reshape the politics of the Middle East. The most immediate result was the American invasion of Afghanistan in October 2001 as the Taliban government declined to hand over Osama bin Laden, the mastermind behind the 9/11 attacks. This invasion has been a disaster. The opening moves set the events on a purely military course. President Bush had campaigned against nation building, though he apparently changed his mind as actions progressed. Nevertheless, economic assistance remained disjointed and disunified. This allowed the Taliban to regain control of the nation in 2021 amid a chaotic US withdrawal.

Operations in Afghanistan were the most extensive aspect of American involvement with the Islamic World. Recognizing that the effort could not rely on military might alone, America began a "civilian surge" to bring more nonmilitary expertise into the battle area, but this was too little, too late. A corrupt government, a resilient and determined insurgency, a flight of brains and capital from the country, a badly discouraged American public, and a declining international commitment badly undermined American control. Perhaps the most telling statistic is jobs: despite almost 20 years of effort and perhaps a $6 trillion cost of the Global War on Terror, there were over 2 million unemployed Afghans, half of them educated. Peace negotiations between America and the Taliban, without Afghan government inclusion, were difficult with no clear American objectives. Direct negotiations between the Taliban and the United States resulted in a Doha Agreement in February 2020, basically delegitimizing the Afghan government while seeking some kind of peaceful exit. President Biden's subsequent decision to withdraw US troops from Afghanistan directly led to Taliban overrunning the country in August 2021 as the government fled. Since then, the country has been in turmoil, its economy devastated while the United Nations and most of the international community refuse to recognize the government.

Afghanistan's other neighbors also impacted the American relationship with the Islamic World, particularly Pakistan. Although allied with America in the struggle against the Taliban, Pakistan's intelligence system, initially supported by America, was largely responsible for creating the Taliban in the first place. It had clearly maintained a range of surreptitious ties as a hedge against total American withdrawal. In fact, the Pakistani Army had every incentive to support selected radical

Islamic elements to maintain tensions with India and justify its own privileged (and highly profitable) position within Pakistan. Some of the problems with American-Pakistani relations have already been mentioned; there is certainly no other American ally relationship with a higher level of mutual distrust. This is particularly troubling because of Pakistan's nuclear capabilities. Security measures are not shared with America, and the unsettled political situation makes some kind of seizure by radical elements a possibility. Rising friction with India has raised the likelihood of military confrontation a number of times. Recent Pakistani efforts to force the return of over a million refugees to Afghanistan have further complicated the situation. Relations with the United States remain strained.

The Central Asia countries (Kazakhstan, Kyrgyzstan, Tajikistan, Turkmenistan, and Uzbekistan) also figure in both the Afghanistan operations and the Islamic World challenge. A major approach to stabilizing Afghanistan had been the promise of greatly expanded regional trade on the model of the traditional Silk Road, now incorporated into China's Belt and Road Initiative, an important element of its global efforts. NATO use of these routes from Central Asia into Afghanistan had been fraught with tensions, especially with Kyrgyzstan where an American air base became a point of controversy with Russia until it closed in 2014. By and large, Central Asian nations are more interested in shoring up their own autocratic governments than in promoting regional cooperation. However, Uzbekistan had been supporting commerce with Afghanistan, including rail connections, while distancing itself from Russia

Islam and Governance

The Iraq War, the terrorist threat of al Qaeda, the rise of a militant Iran, and increased levels of violence in Palestine and Lebanon all gave credence to a Clash of Civilizations. Radical Islamic forces insisted on a conservative Islamic view of the world, a theocratic Caliphate strictly applying Islamic Shariah law. Several aspects of this confrontation are particularly noteworthy:

- The major struggle is within Islam, where the overwhelming majority of Muslims reject such dogmatic, inflexible, and violent interpretations of their religion. But there is no central Muslim authority to denounce such extremism, so there is relatively little moderate Islamic opposition to the flood of virulent extremist propaganda promoted on the World Wide Web and in many individual mosques. The official state religion of Saudi Arabia is a strongly conservative version of Islam, Wahabism, which the Saudi government promotes worldwide with generous funding. Wahabism rejects Western values and supports a world-wide religious training that is in many ways supportive of radical Islamic views. Nevertheless, except for Iran, Muslim governments do not stress cultural conflict with the West and generally envision global economic cohesion.

- In the aftermath of the 9/11 attacks, the Islamic World generally was sympathetic to America and initially supportive of actions against the Taliban in Afghanistan. As the American response widened to include Iraq, Muslim opinion shifted, with a widespread belief that American actions were aimed at Islam in general. These misgivings were reinforced by the reports of American excesses in Abu Ghraib and Haditha.

Obviously, radical Islamists do their best to reinforce these views, complicating American appeals to the Islamic World.

- It is unclear to what extent the general economic backwardness of the Islamic World helps to fuel radicalism. Radical Islamists denounce Western exploitation, and this certainly resonates with many deprived and downtrodden individuals in the Islamic World. But this is seen mainly as an economic and not a cultural challenge.

- The Iranian theocracy, seeking to dominate the region, echoes many of the same charges against America, despite its considerable divergence with radical Islamists. The Iranian involvement exacerbates Sunni-Shiite frictions and promotes further destabilization in the entire Middle East. This is particularly worrisome in Iraq, where Iranian influence is significant. Iran's support for radical groups, particularly Hezbollah, throughout the Middle East is also concerning. Israel sees Iran as a fundamental threat, particularly due to its potential development of nuclear weapons.

President Obama began his term in office with a broad outreach to the Islamic World, but it was quickly overtaken by events. A widening conflict in Afghanistan meant a continuing confrontation between America and Islamic elements. Backlash from the vivid violations of Abu Ghraib and Haditha continued with a murderous rampage by a deranged sergeant, thoughtless burning of Korans, and ongoing civilian casualties. But the broader Islamic World became the focus of attention in December 2010 as the Arab Spring erupted—a series of anti-government protests, uprisings, and armed rebellions that spread across much of the Arab world. Starting with a self-immolation in Tunisia, it energized internal forces to overthrow governments in Tunisia and Egypt. In Libya, Muammar Gaddafi's overthrow was greatly assisted by NATO aerial and logistics support to rebels; the country remains fragmented into ethnic and tribal groups. Yemen also had a new leader, but bitter fighting among tribal and religious groups brought active American involvement with drone strikes against Islamic radicals. Then American logistic and diplomatic support of Saudi military strikes created a major humanitarian crisis. The Arab Spring also initiated a still ongoing Syrian Civil War that created millions of refugees, many flooding into Europe. Turmoil in Syria brought strong Russian military and diplomatic support of Bashar al-Assad's repressive government.

The Arab Spring faded by 2012, as many demonstrations were met with violent responses and the movement itself lacked any organized leadership. The region had barely begun to quiet down when another radical movement burst onto the scene. In early 2014, the Islamic State of Iraq and Syria (ISIS) suddenly declared a caliphate and seized part of eastern Syria and western Iraq, driving out Iraqi government forces whose military leadership had been largely replaced by political appointees. ISIS captured Mosul (Iraq's second largest city) and overran an area inhabited by a minority Yazidi community, killing hundreds of men and carrying women into slavery. This brought American forces back into Iraq, leading an international coalition that eventually eliminated all ISIS territorial gains, particularly thanks to Kurdish forces in northern Iraq and eastern Syria. Continuing frictions in Iraq, fomented by Hezbollah, led to an American assassination in January 2020 of Iranian Major General Qassem Soleimani who had been orchestrating Iranian-supported elements. One immediate result was the Iraqi parliament voting to expel the American troops in Iraq, resulting in heightened tension. In December 2021, The United States formally concluded its combat mission, leaving some 2,500 to serve as trainers and advisors. In January 2024, US support forces and an Iran-backed militia group traded missile strikes, leading the Iraqi Prime Minister to seek a quick and orderly exit of US forces, describing their presence as destabilising amid regional spillover from the Gaza war.

Syria remains in turmoil, riven with its own ethnic and religious divisions while the Assad regime does its best to bloodily repress a growing and fragmented insurgency. The few American forces that had been operating in north Syria in conjunction with Kurdish troops infamously withdrew, undermining the Kurdish efforts. Diplomatic efforts to calm the situation have been totally ineffective, partly because Russia provides much backing to the regime despite American objections.

Turkey has been particularly challenging. It is a NATO member and for years sought to join the European Union. Since President Recep Tayyip Erdogan became Prime Minister in 2003, he has focused on maintaining his leadership, moving the country away from the strongly secular framework set by Kemal Ataturk in the 1920s. He initially reached out to improve relations with the large Kurdish minority, but quickly saw this as a political liability and has since returned to the long-standing repression of the Kurds. After establishing control over the military and spurred on by the Arab Spring uprisings, Erdogan launched a new set of global and Middle Eastern initiatives in 2011. Aimed at reviving Turkey's Ottoman-era influence, this was a conscious reassertion of Turkey's place as a Muslim and Middle Eastern power. He purged opposition elements from the government and stressed an Islamist orientation, citing a coup attempt in 2016 by supporters of an opposition politician, Fethullah Gulen, exiled in America.

The Syrian civil war raised a whole new set of problems, with refugees streaming through Turkey to Europe. In 2016, after a spike in migration to Europe, the European Union pledged 6 billion euros for Turkey to hold refugees. Subsequent fighting in the border areas brought Turkey into direct conflict with forces supported by Russia. Nevertheless, Turkey has been collaborating with Russia in several areas, including purchases of S-400 air defense systems and becoming a major consumer of Russian petroleum products. To address the fighting in Syria, Erdogan hosted an April 2018 summit in Ankara with Russia, Turkey, and Iran, essentially sidelining Europe.

More recently Erdogan has challenged Greece over energy explorations in disputed areas near Cyprus in the eastern Mediterranean and has supported anti-government rebels in Libya. He has also supported Azerbaijan in its local war over the Nagorno-Karabakh region, an Armenian populated area within Muslim Azerbaijan. Russia was central in arranging a cease-fire in the region, but what will be the final outcome is still uncertain.

Erdogan's continuing Islamist orientation is illustrated by his recent claim that "thoughtless imitation of the West has caused Turkey the greatest damage" as well as his controversial reclassification of the historical Hagia Sophia as a mosque—built in the 500s, this had been a major Christian cathedral for a thousand years, then a mosque, and finally it was turned into a museum when Turkey was secularized in the 1930s. With enemies at home and abroad, the Turkish president is doing all he can to cultivate nationalism among the populace. He has been reluctant to join in sanctions against Russia, complicated Sweden's bid to join NATO, and maintained ties with Hamas despite its attack on Israel. But its economy is very stressed and the United States has an opportunity to demonstrate US support for the Turkish people and push for a more normal relationship with Turkey.

American relations with the broader Islamic World have been stable, though at times problematic. Initially, because of a need to protect oil sources, America established a strong relationship with the Saudi monarchy. Even though this need has largely disappeared, America still maintains its relationship with this repressive regime and continues to support its destructive campaign in Yemen. Similarly, America continues to support a repressive military regime in Egypt. On the other hand, it has provided minimal support to Tunisia, the only democratic government to emerge from the Arab Spring. Libya remains in turmoil, with Turkey and Russia supporting some warring factions, even as the European Union tries to negotiate agreements. Friendly and relatively progressive monarchies in Morocco and Jordan as well as a troubled democracy in Indonesia, have been able to largely maintain the allegiance of their populations despite internal challenges. But American support for them has also been minimal. America does provide some support to African governments struggling against radical Islamic groups, but confrontations with Islamic groups have not gone well. As in Afghanistan and Iraq, this support is heavily military. Overall, historical American support for autocrats dismays democratic forces and undermines American credibility, reinforcing radical Islamist charges that the American support of freedom is a sham.

The direct threat to America from the Islamic World is minimal and almost totally from radical elements rather than governments. A spectacularly successful terrorist attack, as on the World Trade Center, would certainly be disastrous at some specific location, but would hardly impact the nation as a whole. Such an event is also very unlikely now with heightened intelligence and surveillance operations. Nuclear challenges are more of a problem, particularly regarding Pakistan where radical elements could possibly seize control of some nuclear assets. A Pakistani nuclear war with India, which could have severe global impacts, is also possible but unlikely. Regional military confrontations with Iran could severely impact global oil trade, but the importance of oil is steadily declining. Overall, the main threat from the Islamic World is global disruption, including a threat to free movement and personal security for Americans worldwide.

There has been one recent major disruption in the Islamic World – a broad attack by Hamas on Israel on 7 October 2023 that killed 1,200 people and took some 240 hostages. A retaliatory assault by Israel on Gaza has killed over 25,000 Palestinians, most of them women and children, as it sought to destroy Hamas. Western governments have strongly supported Israel, with the United States opposing a UN resolution to end the Israel-Hamas war and President Biden specifically stressing that "We stand with Israel. And we will make sure Israel has what it needs to take care of its citizens, defend itself, and respond to this attack." But the Israeli response has been so grievous it has stirred widespread support for the Palestinians, including demonstrations in the United States denouncing the destruction in Gaza. The United States recognizes that Palestinian civilians are not to blame for Hamas's atrocities and that lasting peace and security for Israelis and Palestinians may require two states for two peoples. Hamas itself has done a poor job of representing the Palestinian people. Israel's occupation of large areas of Gaza has clearly shown how Hamas spent major resources building its own capabilities while doing little to promote Palestinian development. There will certainly not be any short-term resolution of the Israel-Palestinian confrontation. This is clearly a cultural clash but it is strongly focused on Israel and is not part of a broader clash of civilizations.

US relations with the Islamic World remain complex. Prospects for broader democracy are, to say the least, somewhere off in the future. But the worrying clash of civilizations is happening only at the level of fragmented terrorist threats. Overall relations with the Islamic World remain generally cordial, with only Iran actively challenging the West.

TERRORISM

The Federal Bureau of Investigation (FBI) is the primary government organization responsible for protecting America from terrorist threats: the unlawful use of violence and intimidation by individuals and/or groups to further ideological goals, such as those of a political, religious, social, racial, or environmental nature. Responses to Bush's Global War on Terrorism focused almost totally on Islamic radicals, but in recent years it has become clear that the terrorist threat is much broader. For starters, Islamic radical views have spread well beyond Islamic radical organizations, as evidenced by the American citizen killing 50 people in an attack on the Pulse nightclub in Orlando, Florida, in 2016. But terrorist threats were well established before the World Trade Center attack in 2001. The previous worst act of domestic terrorism was the Oklahoma City bombing in April 1995. A truckload of explosives was detonated in front of the Alfred P. Murrah Federal Building, killing 168 people in a violent attack on the US government. The nation now faces a kaleidoscope of threats ranging from white supremacists, neo-Nazis, and shadowy anarchist elements to a fringe of violent incels—politicized involuntary celibates fueled by a hatred of women. These are loosely networked movements with amorphous goals and no clear leadership structure, but they share a common objective of disrupting society.

Thankfully, recent terrorist attacks have been largely by lone actors and small groups of individuals and have not had national impacts. But these smaller operations happen all the time. In 2022 alone, the FBI listed 39 incidents, ranging from a mass killing of 10 to attempted kidnapping.

A couple major areas of potential terrorist activity are well documented and very troublesome.

Industrial and Terrorist Threats

It is difficult to separate these two categories, partly because the consequences can be similar and partly because a terrorist attack could result in a major industrial accident.

Industrial and transportation accidents would be local incidents and unlikely to rise to high levels of casualties. Toxic gas releases during a 1984 industrial accident in Bhopal, India, killed at least 10,000 people and severely affected another 100,000, but also resulted in major safety improvements worldwide. Industrial accidents in America have typically killed a handful of people, though occasionally they have resulted in evacuations of thousands who were at risk. However, an intentionally caused event, designed to produce maximum casualties, could potentially be on the same scale as Bhopal.

A skillfully executed terrorist use of chemicals could possibly kill thousands. Nevertheless, the experience of the Japanese Aum Shinrikyo doomsday cult shows that this is not an easy task. In 1995, at a cost of some $30 million and with a team of trained scientists, they succeeded in producing sarin nerve gas and releasing it in crowded subway cars. Total deaths were 12, certainly a cause for concern, but hardly a spectacular success. Though the cult had plans for much wider dispersion of purer batches of sarin, the attack disrupted the Tokyo transportation network only for a day or so. Within days the police initiated widespread raids on the group; key leaders were arrested and eventually executed.

Industrial plants that pose a significant accident hazard are required to have response plans. These plans are not available to the public, so they cannot easily provide a blueprint for terrorists or malcontents. However, they are often available to emergency response groups, creating a potential for leakage of information. In many plants, attractive targets (e.g., large gasoline storage tanks) are readily identifiable. It is hard for outsiders (including terrorists) to judge the proficiency of plant security and emergency response personnel, and this, of course, makes any attack planning relatively difficult. On the other hand, there are probably few industrial plants that could withstand a sudden attack by a heavily armed group. But mounting such an attack would require extensive preparation, which significantly raises the potential for discovery.

Transportation accidents are more troublesome, regularly occur, and could be intentional. A 2005 freight train derailment in South Carolina sent over 500 people to hospitals and killed eight from exposure to a single punctured chlorine tank car. According to one estimate, a single breached chlorine tank could lead to 17,500 deaths, 10,000 severe injuries, and 100,000 hospitalizations. Although there is a systematic effort to route hazardous cargo around major cities, this is not always practical. In one widely publicized instance, the Washington, DC, local government made a concerted effort to re-route hazardous cargoes from a rail line that runs within four blocks of the Capitol. This resulted in extended court battles and highlighted the risks. Oil and chlorine shipments remain a hazard.

Past intentional explosive incidents have killed hundreds—257 people in the 1988 embassy bombings in Nairobi and Dar es Salaam and almost 300 people in the 1999 apartment bombings in Moscow; all these bombings were attributed to radical Islamic elements. By comparison, the Oklahoma City bombing by local terrorists killed 168 people.

Car bombs and terrorist explosions are unlikely to kill more than a few hundred people. The four Islamist terrorists who hit the London subways on July 7, 2005, for example, killed a total of 52 commuters and injured over 700 people. The March 11, 2004, Islamist terrorist train bombings in Madrid were more successful, killing some 190 people and injuring almost 2,000. Nevertheless, the impact of such incidents is significant—again because there is a relatively high casualty toll in a single event. The

Madrid bombings were certainly a factor in Spain's unexpected decision to withdraw troops from Iraq.

Airplanes as weapons remain a possibility; the airplane strikes on the World Trade Center killed about 2,750 people. Despite greatly improved airport security since then, terrorists remain interested in this option. Twenty-four men arrested in England in August 2006, were planning to destroy planes with liquid explosives carried on board, prompting a flurry of new security measures. Even if they had been successful, the casualty toll would have been well under a thousand people.

To rise into the high thousands, a terrorist explosive strike would have to be spectacularly successful, but there are certainly potential scenarios, such as an explosive-laden plane (even a light plane or a larger drone) crashing into a major sports event. Dozens of other potential scenarios have been discussed in the media.

Likewise, the Environmental Protection Agency (EPA), as the lead federal agency, partners with the water supply sector to safeguard water supplies from terrorist acts. They have a clear awareness of the potential for hostile agents to contaminate a water supply system, as vividly demonstrated in February 2021 by a cyber intrusion into the control system of a Florida water supply plant. This is addressed in the National Infrastructure Protection Plan, which envisions an integrated approach to identify threats and reduce vulnerabilities. Critical infrastructure partners are expected to set multi-year priorities and review them annually. Unfortunately, the plan was issued back in 2013 and has not yet had a wide impact. EPA has been partnering with research organizations and member utilities to develop systems that could rapidly detect the presence of contaminants in drinking water.

Bio-Terrorism

All pandemic threats are natural threats. It seems unlikely that a terrorist group would be able to initiate a medical disaster of such magnitude, or even that it would want to, as it would inevitably affect their own preferred populations. Nevertheless, the widespread availability of sophisticated biogenetic equipment and the worldwide availability of many lethal viruses, including those originally collected for biowarfare purposes, mean that this is a possibility. Some extremist group or even some perverted scientist could produce an agent that turns out to be much more lethal or effective than anticipated. Project Bioshield, signed into law by President Bush on July 21, 2004, was specifically focused on terrorist actions, as is the policy behind it: Biodefense for the 21st Century. According to the Department of Health and Human Services, a lesson learned from the COVID-19 pandemic has driven emergency preparedness for existing viruses, such as pandemic influenza.

One geneticist recently startled the scientific world by creating the first live, fully artificial virus in the lab. It was a variation of the virus that causes polio, yet different from any virus known to nature. New techniques developed by other scientists could allow the creation of synthetic viruses in mere days, not weeks or months. Hardware unveiled in 2005 by a Harvard genetics professor can churn out synthetic genes by the thousands for a few pennies each. Along with synthetic biologists, a separate but equally ardent group is pursuing DNA shuffling, a kind of directed evolution that imbues microbes with new traits. Another group seeks novel ways to deliver chemicals and medicines, using ultra-fine aerosols that penetrate deeply into the lungs, or new forms of microencapsulated packaging that control how drugs are released in the body. Still another group is discovering ways to manipulate the essential biological circuitry of humans, using chemicals or engineered microbes to shut down defective genes or regulate the production of hormones controlling such functions as metabolism and mood.

An unclassified CIA study in 2003 titled "The Darker Bioweapons Future" warned of a potential for a "class of new, more virulent biological agents engineered to attack" specific targets. "The effects of some of these engineered biological agents could be worse than any disease known to man," the study said. One likely source could be a "lone wolf": a scientist or biological hacker working alone or in a small group, driven by ideology or perhaps personal demons. "All it would take for advanced bioweapons development," one specialist warned, "is one skilled scientist and modest equipment—an activity we are unlikely to detect in advance." More recently, research on the potential for bird flu to mutate into a much more deadly form was initially suppressed out of concern that it could aid bioterrorists. In the end, publication was considered more advantageous, but the controversy underlined once again the potential for good research to be put to bad ends.

So, the explosive development of biotechnology not only expands our ability to address emerging threats, but it also expands the potential for threats to emerge. It seems clear that in the years immediately ahead, a designed pathogen could threaten the lives of millions of Americans as well as many millions more globally.

Every year, an estimated 3,000 Americans die from food-based diseases; another 125,000 people are hospitalized. The Food & Drug Administration estimates that food-based sickness probably afflicts almost 50 million Americans annually. Tracking and preventing such incidents is a state responsibility, so programs vary widely. It is obviously possible for someone to purposely initiate such an outbreak and potentially cause hundreds or even thousands of deaths. In response, the Department of Agriculture has been a lead agency in developing a Strategic Partnership Program Agroterrorism (SPPA) Initiative to work closely with states and industry to secure the food supply. More recently, a Food Safety Modernization Act of 2011 has allowed for a more proactive national approach towards food safety.

Summary

The terrorist threat is something that has always been with us, the threat of violent individuals wreaking havoc. The modern situation has made it a major player thanks to several developments:

- The modern world has a wide range of integrated networks that are critical to social functioning but vulnerable to focused attacks that could kill thousands, even millions, in a single act;

- Weapons possibly available are not only modern military weapons but have expanded to include nuclear weapons and materials, as well as computer and cyber options;

- The global information and social networks allow isolated radical individuals to identify and contact with one another as well as reaching out to wide groups of potential collaborators.

The result is that terrorism is no longer an isolated phenomenon, threatening local destruction. It has evolved into an unpredicted and unexpected threat to global stability.

CHINA

China is the major strategic challenge for the twenty-first century. It is not only a growing challenge to American world leadership, but also a direct challenge to ideals of democracy. The most populous nation on earth, it is seeking recognition as a major power. It is now a country of contradictions. It has widespread affluence and dynamic cities; it also has widespread poverty and environmental degradation. Its economy is largely decentralized, but its political system remains strongly centralized. American policy towards China has undergone severe stresses with the COVID-19 pandemic originating there.

America must keep the focus on its core objective: integrating China into a peaceful and prosperous world order. In 2001, it seemed like this long-term objective might be within reach when President Clinton strongly supported China's entry into the World Trade Organization, with high optimism that "We have a far greater chance of having a positive influence on China's actions if we welcome China into the world community instead of shutting it out." Unfortunately, this optimism proved premature.

China's entry initiated a flood of inexpensive Chinese imports but also caused the loss of well over a million American jobs. At the time, China was moving in a liberalizing direction, opening their market and reducing their tariffs. The clear benefits to American consumers came at a cost to some producers, particularly in textiles and solar panels. In 2006, President Bush and Chinese President Hu Jintao launched a US-China Strategic Economic Dialogue (SED) to manage immediate tensions and to expand economic issues of interest to both countries. The economic recession of 2008 forced some re-assessments, particularly in regard to Chinese currency manipulation.

Economic Dominance

Beijing's Made in China 2025 initiative in 2015 signaled an effort to achieve manufacturing dominance by 2025. It envisioned modernizing ten key sectors, such as aerospace, automation, artificial intelligence, and quantum computing, through extensive government support. One aspect of this program was intellectual-property theft and the forced transfer of foreign technology as a condition of accessing China's market. An independent commission estimated costs to America as between $225 and $600 billion annually. The large trade deficit and associated losses of American jobs were primary drivers of President Trump's raising tariffs and initiating a trade war. This led to some $250 billion of American tariffs on Chinese imports and a subsequent increase of Chinese tariffs on imports from America.

An agreement in January 2020 eased the trade war, but the impact of COVID-19 vividly demonstrated an excessive dependence on China for a range of pharmaceuticals and supply chain elements, particularly for such critical technology materials as rare earth elements. This "phase one" trade deal sought a modest increase of farm and energy exports, but did not force China to alter its "state capitalist" economic model or even concede that it has a history of forcing American firms to hand over their technology.

In fact, technology theft remained a key issue as evidenced by the July 2020 closing of the Chinese consulate in Houston with American officials describing it as an espionage hub, and China promptly closing the American consulate in Chengdu in retaliation. The result was intensified confrontation as the COVID-19 pandemic made clear an excessive American dependence on Chinese supply lines for industrial components, technology materials, and critical medical supplies

The main Chinese threat that America now faces is a threat of economic and technical dominance. China is seeking to replace America as the dominant nation while it supports autocratic governments and undermines Western solidarity. It has asserted exclusive jurisdiction over nearly the entire South China Sea, claiming a spurious Nine-Dash Line as the outer limit of its sovereign territory, reflecting China's deeply felt 200 years of humiliation at the hands of Western powers. Its uncompromising assertions spurred the Philippines to bring suit under the terms of the UN Convention on the Law of the Seas (UNCLOS), a convention that the United States has never ratified. The Hague Tribunal Permanent Court of Arbitration completely rejected Beijing's assertion that the land formations and waters in the area have historically fallen exclusively under the control of the Chinese state. But China has brushed aside any objections and has been steadily building up its presence, expanding the land area of islands and reefs while supporting air and naval activities leading to some regional confrontations. Supported by its allies, America has countered these efforts by systematically conducting freedom of navigation operations. These naval patrols have raised the potential for US-China military clashes. China also regularly talks of the need to integrate Taiwan, raising another potential for military clashes with the United States over a clearly regional issue against the setting of ongoing global confrontation.

A major change in recent decades has been that the Chinese leadership has shifted its basis of legitimacy from ideology to economics. It has become the world's largest manufacturer and merchandise trader. This has made it the largest American trading partner—the biggest source of American imports and the third-largest export market. Economic development has supported a broad Chinese effort to bolster its international position. In April 1996, China led the formation of a "Shanghai Five" with a treaty signing in Shanghai by representatives of China, Russia, Kazakhstan, Kyrgyzstan and Tajikistan. This group eventually set up a formal Shanghai Cooperation Organisation and added Uzbekistan, looking to unify efforts on social and political issues. It served as a vehicle for China-Russia cooperation, though Russia blocked Chinese efforts to set up a development bank within the organization.

More recently, China set up an Asia Infrastructure Investment Bank and has expanded its outreach with a 2013 Belt and Road Initiative, promoting infrastructure not only on traditional Silk Road routes into Central Asia, but globally. Some 150 countries, many of them in Africa, have joined this initiative. Top Chinese officials have described it as a vast network of roads, rail lines, and maritime shipping routes radiating outward from China. It is projected to eventually include a railroad in Kenya; hydropower dams in Cameroon and Zambia; and dozens of other projects across Asia, Africa, and Europe. Pakistan has been a major partner in this effort, which could help spread Chinese investments into the control of Afghan mineral resources. A 10th anniversary forum in October 2023 included some 130 countries, highlighted it as China's Grand Strategy For A New World Order. But the reality is that more than $1 trillion loaned to over 100 countries have failed to earn the returns that China expected while burdening numerous countries with huge debt overhangs.

Chinese technology development has become the center of an economic confrontation. China values artificial intelligence as a critical force multiplier. It sought to gain parity with America by 2020, and wanted to establish China as the global leader by 2030. As part of this thrust, it expanded its development on space technology, as demonstrated by its December 2020 moon landing. Its efforts to establish technology dominance in the past were severely restricted by its dependence on foreign integrated circuits. This spurred an intensive expansion of its own chip production efforts as well as aggressive acquisitions and continuing theft of intellectual property. The Chinese economy is now facing multiple challenges and facing a period of slow growth.

A recent Digital Silk Road project included a significant expansion of investment as well as expansion of 5G internet networks. China, an early developer in this area, has set up much more extensive networks than any other country and is broadly promoting them on a global basis. Based on security concerns, America has set restrictions on China producing 5G network equipment using American technology or software and pushed American allies to support these efforts. It has also greatly restricted sales of advanced chips to Huawei, the main Chinese circuit manufacturer

Competition with America has also spread into social media areas, particularly when America placed restrictions on TikTok. This is basically a video-sharing platform but has a billion users worldwide and an ability to collect significant data on them. New restrictions on TikTok prohibit it on official devices while it engages in extensive discussions with the White House on how it will operate in the United States.

Technology is the long-term challenge. America still retains a clear advantage in artificial intelligence, but American restrictions have pushed China to invest heavily in development of its own technology. Homegrown Chinese innovation, not intellectual property theft, will become America's biggest tech worry. By one 2019 report, China was increasingly close to achieving technological parity. One result has been a significant increase in federal support for research and development. Building on the CHIPS and Science Act, The Biden administration's research priorities focus on prioritizing national technological competitiveness.

Regional Influence

The Belt and Road Initiative has also raised concerns about support for autocrats. At least 18 countries—including Zimbabwe, Uzbekistan, Pakistan, Kenya, the United Arab Emirates and even Germany—are using Chinese-made intelligent monitoring systems, and 36 countries have received training in topics like "public opinion guidance," which is typically a euphemism for censorship. Moreover, the project can become a debt trap for countries, especially as the COVID-19 crisis has undermined the ability of a number of nations to repay loans. In 2018, China used such a debt to force Sri Lanka to give China exclusive control of a new port city. America attempted to counter this Chinese program by setting up an International Development Finance Corporation to better align development and foreign policy goals. By 2023, this effort had $41 billion total portfolio exposure in 112 countries, but was still dwarfed by the $1 trillion Chinese effort.

The on-going trade disputes with America are legitimately based on intellectual property rights and Beijing's manipulation of its currency. But they have reached the point where they are simply tearing apart a deep economic relationship without anything to replace it. Concerns over a heavy dependence on Chinese components and pharmaceuticals decrease demand from the Industrialized World. Nevertheless, America has a stake in helping China build domestic prosperity. America has much to offer economically, particularly with environmental technologies and open markets. Promoting positive relations with China depends significantly on mutually beneficial economic relations.

China's military has initiated a [broad modernization program](), seeking to amass national power to achieve "the great rejuvenation of the Chinese nation" by 2049. It seeks to strengthen its nuclear deterrent and sees no limits in its partnership with Russia, discreetly providing material support to for its war against Ukraine. But China poses only a negligible direct military threat to America. It is threatening to some American allies, and gives China has a clear military advantage in that part of the world.

America has minimal interest in these territorial disputes, but it does have a strong interest in supporting friends and allies against Chinese belligerence and in promoting generally accepted international standards. A [military response]() is a [poor option](). It not only entails a needless risk of escalation, but it also allows China an opportunity to paint America as the cause of the problem and to stoke Chinese nationalism in an effort to justify military increases and buttress legitimacy. It also discourages regional countries by pushing them to take sides in a confrontation.

Japan, the Philippines, Vietnam, and Malaysia have all challenged China's domination. China is at a significant diplomatic disadvantage because the South China Sea has been used for millennia by all its bordering countries. China's military emphasis directly contradicts its claim to a "peaceful rise." In an area of limited global significance, every effort needs to be made to keep confrontation in economic and diplomatic channels. Military belligerence only facilitates China's efforts, domestically and internationally, to divert attention from its maritime claims. And the confrontation raises the possibility that actions could spring out of control, as vividly portrayed in 2034: A Novel of the Next World War. The allocation of rights within the South China Sea is properly an issue for negotiation among the coastal countries. International recognition of any Chinese sovereignty depends on negotiated agreements and recognition of international standards. A growing international backlash may push China to resume talks. The primary American interest should be international cooperation, supporting China's peaceful rise in the context of global economic development.

Domestic Control

Chinese leaders are working hard to maintain total control of the population, but success is far from assured. An ossified political regime is trying to control a dynamic and creative new generation. The critical year in this struggle was 1989 when protests spread to some 400 cities, and as many as a million protestors assembled in Tiananmen Square at the entrance to the Forbidden City, a place of high cultural significance, including the Mausoleum of Mao Zedong. Hopes for expansion of democracy were crushed by the fateful decision of primary leader Deng Xiaoping on June 4, 1989, when troops violently cleared the square; something like a thousand people were killed. Ever since, the leadership has tried to suppress all memory of the event, which epitomizes the central threat to the regime: popular uprising.

A crackdown on dissidence was the immediate result. This has steadily expanded to the point that today China is blanketed with a surveillance network that employs facial recognition technology to identify any individuals in public places. This is supplemented with required identification cards that contain extensive personal information, along with biometric data and a composite rating score assessing political reliability. Then Uighur riots in 2009 in Xinjiang and the Arab Spring in 2011 raised the specter of ethnic revolt and resulted in an intensified suppression of dissent and increased surveillance. The COVID-19 crisis provided the leadership an opportunity to greatly increase surveillance and control measures.

Domestically, Hong Kong has been one focal point of attention. Controlled by Great Britain for over a century, it was a vivid example of China's subordination to the West. The British lease on Hong Kong ran out in 1997; diplomatic negotiations with China resulted in a 1984 Sino-British Joint Declaration, in which the United Kingdom agreed to return Hong Kong to China. China guaranteed Hong Kong's political independence for 50 years but continually worked to reign in democratic efforts there. In September 2014, a new requirement for pre-screening of electoral candidates resulted in large street protests. China, of course, claimed that they had been instigated by the West and refused to give any political concessions. It also claimed that the Joint Declaration had become void; British objections had minimal impact. A new crisis erupted in July 2019 when the city council proposed broadening the scope of extradition from Hong Kong to China. After a week of major protests, the Hong Kong government withdrew the proposal, but did not remove it from consideration. Then in June 2020, the Chinese government imposed a sweeping national-security law that allowed mainland Chinese officials to conduct secret trials for charges of sedition and collusion with foreign powers. These could be applied even to petty, non-violent activities. China even issued arrest warrants for Chinese living abroad, including at least one American citizen living in Washington. America ended Hong Kong's special economic status and several bilateral agreements, including reciprocal tax exemptions. Hong Kong was essentially integrated into mainland China.

The other focal point of repression has been religious and ethnic minorities, particularly the Muslim Uighurs in Xinjiang, an isolated area above the Taklimakan Desert deep in Central Asia. Since 2016, the Chinese government has detained more than one million Uighurs in reeducation camps designed to strip them of their culture, language, and religion. Uighur women have been systematically sterilized, and some 8,500 mosques have been destroyed. Nevertheless, global objections to these genocidal measures have been very limited. America has imposed sanctions on officials responsible for carrying out the crackdown and placed some restrictions on imports. The European Union has been relatively quiet, though France has called for an international mission under UN supervision to travel to the Xinjiang region to evaluate the treatment of the Uighurs. The Islamic World has basically been silent, as well illustrated by Turkish President Recep Tayyip Erdogan who has welcomed big Chinese investments for his beleaguered economy. Although he stridently promotes Islamic values in Turkey, he has been largely silent on the treatment of Turkic Muslims in Xinjiang, an about-face from a decade ago when he said the Uighurs there suffered from "simply put, genocide" at the hands of the Chinese government.

Global Influence

On a global scale, this acceptance of Chinese repression has been very disturbing . In July 2019, America led 22 mostly Western ambassadors in a letter to the UN Human Rights Council expressing concern about China's mass detentions in Xinjiang. China responded by publicizing police repression of blacks in America and mistreatment of prisoners at the detention center at Guantanamo Bay. It delivered its own letter of response, signed by more than a dozen member countries of the Organisation of Islamic Cooperation (OIC), supporting China's policies in Xinjiang, stark testimony to Beijing's ability to leverage its growing economic clout. Similarly, when the Human Rights Council in Geneva was considering an inspection of Xinjiang by Michelle Bachelet, the UN human rights chief, China's presentation got positive reviews of its human rights record from more than 120 countries with fewer than three dozen expressing real concern. Michelle Bachelet made no trip. Shortly after, China, concerned that a UN Security Council meeting set to discuss human rights violations in Syria would veer into one on Xinjiang, pressured the Ivory Coast to block a necessary quorum.

However, action at the United Nations has continued. In October 2020, Germany presented a letter to the human rights committee signed by 39 countries, including America, objecting to the Chinese treatment of the Uighurs; some other countries declined to sign due to Chinese pressure. In 2022, fifty UN member states issued a joint statement condemning the Chinese government's oppression of Uyghurs and other Turkic peoples in East Turkistan. A UN review meeting in January 2024 saw Western countries chide Beijing for its treatment of Xinjiang Uighurs while many non-Western countries provided China varying degrees of support. The topic remains highly visible globally while China lobbies hard for international support.

When China curtailed political freedoms in Hong Kong in 2020, two rival declarations circulated at the United Nations Human Rights Council. One, drafted by Cuba and commending Beijing's move, won the backing of 53 nations. Another, issued by the United Kingdom and expressing concern, secured 27 supporters. At the end of the Cold War, the United Nations was expected to promote democracy and human rights. Instead, Beijing's clout helps China legitimize its claim to be a superior alternative to Western democracies. This is a stark demonstration of China's growing international influence. On these lines, the House Intelligence Committee warned that America is at risk of being unable to protect the nation's health and security and compete with Beijing on the world stage. This assessment comes amid a wider rebalancing of American national security priorities to contend with renewed competition with Russia and China as well as ongoing threats from rogue states, such as Iran and North Korea. The report also stressed the need for intelligence officials to become more adept at analyzing nonmilitary threats, such as health, the economy, and climate change.

For years there was an expectation that sooner or later, somehow or other, China would assert control over Taiwan. China proposed a "one country, two systems" style unification that Taiwan promptly rejected, partly no doubt because of China's obvious manipulation of Hong Kong's "one country, two systems" status. But the other direction for Chinese unification is also possible: The Taiwanese system would spread to the mainland, and the appeal of its democracy in conjunction with events in Hong Kong could force the Chinese leadership to be much more open. The Chinese constitution sets democratic centralism, power to the people, as the basic principle of government organization. Taiwan can offer China unification based on China's own declared democratic standards and provide Taiwan's own Statement of Democracy. Economic pressures have the most obvious potential to promote such a shift, especially if the Chinese leadership cannot easily point to an enemy to stir patriotic support. Clearly China holds a very hard line in regard to Taiwan, recently sending military aircraft into Taiwanese airspace when a senior American official visited to show America's continuing support. The unrest in Hong Kong and democratic efforts in Taiwan are not only reminders of China's historical failures, but they also represent an alternative way of life that poses the major threat to Chinese autocracy. Taiwan can set the example for China, specifically what the Chinese Communist leadership is afraid of.

Summary

With political legitimacy depending on economic development, the Chinese leadership has to promote popular enthusiasm or face a leadership crisis. America should do everything it can to avoid making confrontation a choice for the Chinese leadership. Against this background, American policy has been ambivalent. Major American corporations have provided critical support to Chinese economic development, even as the American government funded military programs to counter Chinese challenges. Overall, policy is reminiscent of containment, biding our time while internal evolution inevitably forces political modernization.

America has a major advantage in the effort to push China into a positive global role—the universal appeal of American ideals of democracy and equality. This is what led to the formation of a peaceful Europe after World War II, what provided hope and encouragement to Eastern Europe in the Cold War, and what helped drive the changes in the Soviet Union. Democratic forces are the single most important challenge to the Chinese leadership. Unrest in Hong Kong has highlighted both the appeal of democracy and the difficulty the Chinese leadership, still haunted by the specter of Tiananmen Square, has in dealing with it. The recent Chinese takeover of the Hong Kong government, stifling democratic protests, has all but eliminated its special status. America needs to promote democracy but cannot do this effectively until it can make a convincing display of its own democracy and domestic prosperity.

OTHER NATIONS

A short review cannot begin to provide an in-depth analysis of the full spectrum of international challenges to freedom and liberty, but some other major challenges need to be at least acknowledged:

- Africa, the continent with the youngest population, is hobbled by ineffective governments. Not a single vibrant democracy exists on the entire continent. It is a continent of great riches, but also great misery and great neglect. With its young population, it could be a dynamic region in the decades ahead. Or it can continue to be a land of misery and neglected opportunities, fueling instability and autocracy. Islamist violence; corruption; and struggling economies, hard-hit by insurgency and the COVID-19 pandemic, continue to undermine democracy in much of the continent. America has supported a wide variety of diplomatic and economic efforts in Africa; military aid also increased with low-profile efforts sensitive to African skepticism on American motives. America's Prosper Africa initiative works to unlock opportunities to do business in Africa while strengthening partnerships with democratic nations throughout the region.

- Immigration has become a global problem that cannot be solved within the Industrialized World. It is driven by a lopsided distribution of wealth within poorer countries, with potentates of various sorts skimming fortunes from their unfortunate subjects. Many refugees are fleeing crime ridden areas and violence where their lives are at stake. This global refugee flood, with its high percentage of unemployed men, is driving the current turmoil in the Middle East, complicated by the results of the Arab Spring and COVID-19. Refugees from Central America are a problem for the United States, but they pale in comparison with more than a million refugees flooding into a Europe which has just overhauled its immigration policies to make it easier to deport failed asylum seekers and to limit entry of migrants into the bloc. Human rights organizations have roundly criticized this agreement. Globally there are some 36 million refugees, while over 100 million people have been forced to flee their homes.

- Failed states flourish, driving their populations into poverty, while China and Russia enable repressive regimes to survive and destabilize wide aeras of the world. Failed States represent countries where the government does not have effective control of its territory and is not perceived as legitimate. Typically, such governments cannot provide domestic security or basic public services to its citizens, and they often experience widespread internal violence. Countries at the top of this list pose a direct challenge to international order, including Syria, Somalia, and Yemen.

India

India is the world's largest democracy. Like its rival, China, India is also a land of contradictions. Relations with America have been ambivalent for years, and Indian rivalry with Pakistan complicates the situation in Afghanistan. Internally, India has areas of high technology prosperity contrasted with widespread misery. It has become increasingly autocratic and repressive of its minorities. On January 22, 2024, Prime Minister Narendra Modi consecrated a giant new temple devoted to the Hindu deity Rama in Ayodhya, on the site of a Muslim mosque that had been destroyed by a Hindu mob in 1992. With upcoming elections, the government is strongly demonstrating support for its Hindu majority

The United States has a wide range of common interests with India and sees it as a major strategic partner, though there have been recent tensions over an assassination attempt on a Sikh separatist leader in New York. While India looks outward at a larger integration with the global economy, neighboring Pakistan looks inward and stagnates. The Pakistani Army supports elements of Islamic radicalism and trumpets an Indian threat to justify its own dominating position within the Pakistani economy.

Latin America

Latin American has been largely neglected for many years. During much of that period there was at least passive American support for a range of autocrats. The American economy was both admired and envied as Latin American economies failed to flourish, but many American actions also led to widespread resentment. Cuba represented the only direct challenge, and it was effectively quarantined. More recently, leaders in Venezuela, Bolivia, and Nicaragua have built on these resentments to mount their own challenges to internal democracy and external

American influence. Haiti poses another direct challenge, though of a quite different type. It was the focus of concerted American efforts to eliminate a repressive dictatorship, but this brought no real development. Even before a devastating earthquake in 2010, unemployment hovered at 70 percent and more than half of the people lived in extreme poverty. In 2021 the president was assassinated just as another earthquake struck. Since then, local criminal gangs have taken over parts of the country as it has descended into turmoil. With US support, the UN Security Council has authorized an armed intervention to be led by Kenya. At the moment, this is still pending. Overall, Latin America faces several major challenges:

- Drug use in America fuels drug production in Columbia, Central America, and Mexico. Grisly cartel wars in Mexico resulted in almost [35,000 murders](#) in 2019, largely driven by organized crime. Corruption by cartels reached into the [highest levels](#) of the Mexican government, including a former Secretary of Defense and the former head of Mexico's Federal Investigation Agency. Besides Mexico, drug impact is felt throughout Central America and Columbia and penetrates deeply into America itself.

- Wealth inequality throughout Latin America feeds [widespread poverty](#), which, in turn, significantly increases the attractiveness of the drug culture and fuels illegal immigration into America. For Latin America COVID-19 was a [double shock](#): a brutally painful tragedy in its own right and the definitive end of decades of poor economic growth, despite steady economic growth increases elsewhere on the globe.

- Central America poses a particular problem. As noted above, refugee floods have overwhelmed American border areas and are the center of major political controversies. The core problem goes back a hundred years when American businessmen basically took control of Central America and set up "banana republics" that strongly supported American commercial interests at the expense of the indigenous populations. Poor economic conditions, exacerbated by global warming and drug cartels, continue to push refugees north. In January 2021, several thousand Hondurans were attempting to reach America, but were confronted by Guatemalan and Mexican forces. The only solution lies in the countries of origin, providing economic support to help them stabilize so that their citizens do not become refugees.

In addition to the competitive situations outlined here, there is a potential for much more intense confrontations that could significantly impact our nation.

Nuclear Threats

The biggest hostile threat to American lives is nuclear. In some cases, nuclear actions could lead to catastrophic consequences and, therefore, require serious attention. A strong American nuclear posture helps deter nuclear challenges, but also highlights the importance of nuclear forces. Especially in an uncertain world, this could promote nuclear proliferation, intensifying the threat to America rather than decreasing it. New nuclear states would be less capable of providing in-depth protection and perhaps also be susceptible to control by radical elements, worsening the only significant nuclear threat America faces: terrorists.

Strategic Nuclear Exchange

For many years, America lived with the threat of a comprehensive nuclear strike from the Soviet Union. Continuing nuclear force expansions and warhead developments by both countries resulted in a posture of Mutually Assured Destruction: each side had tens of thousands of warheads aimed at the other. In a full scale nuclear exchange, one researcher estimated that 100-160 million American citizens would die in the first few days. Firestorms and ozone depletion would add to this destruction, and a resulting Nuclear Winter would approximate the effects of an asteroid strike, spreading the destruction globally.

The potential for such an exchange to occur was higher than almost anyone realized. Robert McNamara, the Secretary of Defense during the Cuban Missile Crisis, recently outlined how that crisis came close to initiating nuclear war. In another chilling episode, a Russian colonel described how a false alert resulted in launch instructions for 5,000 Soviet missiles, instructions that the colonel declined to carry out.

With the demise of the Soviet Union and improved US-Russian relations, the likelihood of this threat was significantly diminished. These improved relations led to the 2002 Moscow Treaty, in which each nation agreed to reduce strategic nuclear forces to about 2,000 deployed warheads. The subsequent New START Treaty signed in 2010 reduces the number of strategic nuclear missile launchers but does not limit the number of operationally inactive stockpiled nuclear warheads that remain in the high thousands in both the Russian and American inventories.

However, relations between the two countries have continued to deteriorate while no additional nuclear reduction steps have been taken in recent years. In the meantime, Russia has pushed ahead with its most massive intercontinental ballistic missile testing and upgrading program since the collapse of communism. America is moving ahead with its own plans, including a major upgrade for its nuclear missile forces. Although it had suspended its participation in the Intermediate-Range Nuclear Forces, by late 2020 America was promoting an extension of the New START treaty, due to expire in February 2021. In January 2021, following an American withdrawal, Russia also withdrew from the Open Skies Treaty. Despite a Putin announcement in February 2023 on START suspension, Russia is still adhering to the treaty but has restricted its participation.

Recently, Putin has boasted of powerful new weapons, including a Hypersonic Cruise Missile, that he says could make American defenses obsolete. Yet these and other new additions to the Kremlin arsenal do not change the big picture. Russia is militarily much weaker than America and its allies. In any real confrontation, it loses. The actual significance of the new weapons is domestic: they exist to support Putin's posture and demonstrate to Russians that their country is standing up to a NATO threat, thus justifying the tax rubles pouring into his military-industrial complex. Russia is simply not capable of occupying any significant NATO territory, and any such incursion would have major economic impacts on Russia. Russia could potentially seize some individual areas, such as Russian-settled areas of the Baltics, where an earlier Soviet influx of Russians diluted the native populations. For NATO to rely on significant military forces is a poor way of addressing this threat; putting resources into making these countries, including their Russian minorities, prosper would make much more sense.

Russia has also developed a new 9M729 ground-launched cruise missile system. America, backed by its allies, has complained that this breaches the 1987 Intermediate-Range Nuclear Forces Treaty, which prohibited the development of missiles with ranges between 500 and 5,500 kilometers (roughly 300 to 3,000 miles). For several years, American officials complained of Russian violations of the terms of this pact and formally withdrew in August 2019. Russia insists it complies with the treaty. Regardless of its treaty status, the new missile does give Russia more potential for a limited incursion into NATO territory. But any nuclear use would bring immediate and major international condemnation, both diplomatic and economic, and would only exacerbate a bad situation. This capability certainly bolsters Putin's claim to be responding to NATO threats, but hardly makes a Russian incursion any more attractive.

The threat of a nuclear exchange with the Russians remains and once again grows; even a limited exchange could spin out of control. It is practically impossible to put any quantitative probability on this threat, though it would certainly seem to be higher than the probability of an asteroid strike or a supervolcano eruption, probably even larger than the proverbial "one-in-a-million" chance. Yet even with a minimal American deterrent force, it is hard to imagine what could bring the Russian leadership to take such a clearly self-destructive step. Maintaining a minimal deterrent is clearly a responsible action but increasing current nuclear capabilities or upgrading existing systems would offer little benefit.

Currently, no other nations pose a threat of a comprehensive nuclear exchange, and only China would seem to have any potential to pose such a threat in the future. At present, China has perhaps [300 nuclear weapons](#) and has been upgrading its capabilities, but it is not really in a nuclear race with America. This is consistent with China's historical inclination not to compete against opponent's strengths, but rather to focus on their weaknesses. A relatively small number of strategic nuclear weapons gives China essentially a countervalue capability against America. A significant increase in numbers would provide China little additional capability and would require a major refocusing of assets away from economic development, which is clearly occupying the current leadership. Overall, the probability of a Chinese comprehensive nuclear strike in the years immediately ahead is significantly lower than for a Russian strike.

Local Nuclear War

Both India and Pakistan have considerable stocks of nuclear weapons that do not directly threaten America, but they do threaten each other. India blamed a bloody November 2008 terrorist attack in Mumbai on Pakistan, where an unstable political situation certainly poses the possibility of some situation getting out of control and a nuclear war ensuing. A February 2019 suicide bombing in Kashmir provoked an Indian air attack on a training camp inside Pakistan; an Indian fighter jet was shot down and a pilot captured. In the days following, thanks to strong international pressure, a [more conciliatory exchange](#) resulted in the return of the captured pilot and a lowering of military alerts. This incident starkly demonstrated the potential for some individual confrontation to rapidly escalate. Relations between the two countries remain strained.

Aside from the immediate catastrophe a nuclear engagement would pose for the two countries, it also raises the possibility of a [global Nuclear Winter](#), which could ultimately result in the deaths of tens of millions of Americans, or more. This potential underlines the importance of stabilizing the political situation in South Asia.

The only other real potential for local nuclear war is in Korea, where North Korea has been systematically improving its nuclear capabilities. In December 2023, it [tested a long-range Intercontinental Ballistic Missile](#) (ICBM) that could carry a small nuclear warhead the nation claims to have. It also claims to have a submarine with nuclear missile capabilities.

Individual Weapon Detonations

While a comprehensive nuclear strike could destroy America, a single weapon detonation could probably destroy a major city. This could kill a million or more people and make a huge mess, but it would basically leave the country intact. Such a strike could come from several sources, including an intentional strike by a major power, a strike (perhaps covert) by a minor nuclear power, or an unauthorized strike launched by a rogue commander.

- The only major powers now capable of launching an intentional strike would be Russia or China. Russia, with its reliable, high-yield thermonuclear weapons, is a particular concern. Retaliation would surely follow, so such a strike would almost certainly be in some extreme situation. It might be theoretically possible for China to launch such a strike and then tell America that it is prepared to destroy America while absorbing whatever retaliation America could muster. But China is in no position now to even suggest such a risky gambit, for it has only a minimal nuclear force. With Russia, we are still in a position of Mutually Assured Destruction, so it would make little sense for Russia to commit national suicide by mounting a nuclear attack against America. Such scenarios lack even minimal rationality. Considering that actors are not always rational, the scope of forces in place, and the potential for very basic misunderstandings, such an exchange remains possible.

- Only a few minor nuclear powers could launch a strike against America with relatively low yield weapons. Iran, starting around 1999, conducted a coherent, systematic program to develop nuclear weapons with the approval of its senior leadership. This program was suspended in 2003 as Iran opened negotiations with Great Britain, Germany, and France. However, extensive uranium enrichment programs continued, much to the distress of America and the international community. This was intensified in September 2009 by the disclosure of a secret enrichment facility in the vicinity of Qom. The Obama administration engaged in formal negotiations in November 2013 between Iran and the five permanent members of the United Nations Security Council plus Germany. In July 2015, an agreement on a Joint Comprehensive Plan of Action (JCPOA) was reached and formally endorsed by both the UN Security Council and the European Union. It limited Iran's enrichment efforts and gave the International Atomic Energy Agency regular access to all Iranian nuclear facilities. Four days later, Iran's Supreme Leader Ayatollah Khamenei asserted that the agreement was not even necessary since Iran already had a fatwa (religious ruling) declaring nuclear weapons to be religiously forbidden under Islamic law. In Washington, an Iran Nuclear Agreement Review Act had given Congress 60 days to approve, disapprove, or do nothing. After intense public and Congressional debate, Congress failed to pass any resolutions and the agreement went into effect. In January 2016, after the International Atomic Energy Agency (IAEA) confirmed that Iran met the relevant requirements, all nuclear sanctions were lifted by the UN, the European Union, and America. American President Trump certified Iranian compliance in April 2017 and reluctantly in July, but in October 2017, he declined further certification, accusing Iran of violating the "spirit" of the deal and citing a need to "address…many serious flaws." The IAEA continued to assess that Iran was in compliance with JCPOA, and the other parties have worked to preserve it. Nevertheless, America officially announced in May 2018 that it withdrew from the treaty. In October 2020, the Trump administration imposed sanctions in defiance of European humanitarian objections. Shortly after, the UN Security Council terminated sanctions against Iran with American allies abstaining on the vote. Then a November 2020 assassination of Iran's top nuclear scientist was followed by a law directing enrichment to resume if sanctions were not lifted. Iran clearly has a capability to produce nuclear weapons, but has not mastered all of the necessary technologies. It has been heavily involved in the current turmoil in the Middle East, including support for Houthi attacks in the Red Sea, but has been careful to avoid any direct confrontation with America. Nevertheless, it is possible that the conflict will broaden into a regional war.

- North Korea does have nuclear weapons. It has conducted five weapon tests along with continuing missile development, including a 2017 test of an intercontinental missile capable of reaching anywhere in America and an October 2020 display of an even newer missile along with claims to claims to have submarine nuclear missile capabilities. As noted above, in December 2023, it tested an Intercontinental Ballistic Missile (ICBM) and claimed a submarine missile capability. Only days later, North Korean leader Kim Jong Un called for bolstered war readiness to repel what he said were unprecedented United States-led confrontational moves. Of course, North Korea knows well that any missile strike on America would result in swift retaliation and certainly lead to the fall of the regime. Nevertheless, if the regime felt it were failing anyhow, it could turn to some kind of final thrust against a long-term enemy. For America, this is the most worrisome challenge if war erupts on the Korean peninsula.

- Pakistan, is an ally at present, but an unstable one. A takeover of all or part of the country by extremist elements remains possible. Suicidal elements could launch a strike on American assets regardless of consequences. Pakistan lacks a missile capable of reaching America, but it could certainly turn to alternative delivery means.

- In the longer run, America could face a much wider range of nuclear armed nations. North Korea's nuclear tests and Iranian nuclear efforts have spurred a new interest in nuclear weapons. Sovereign nations have an inherent right, recognized in the Nuclear Non-Proliferation Treaty, to develop nuclear weapons for their own defense. As many as 40 more countries have the technical skill, and in some cases the required material, to build a bomb—Taiwan, Brazil, Egypt, Saudi Arabia, South Korea, and Japan are among those countries that could potentially develop nuclear weapons. Strengthening the Nuclear Non-Proliferation Treaty would seem to be an important objective, but recent actions have gone in the opposite direction, including American support for increased Indian nuclear programs and similar Chinese support for Pakistani programs.

- An unauthorized launch could potentially be carried out by some rogue commander in the Russian or Chinese forces as well as within our own forces or those of our French or British allies. *The Hunt for Red October* film dramatized such a scenario. In our own forces, we have worked hard to put extensive safeguards in place to negate such a possibility, and we have doubtless shared some of this technology with our allies and probably also with Russia. Nevertheless, no system is foolproof. The larger the size of existing forces, the larger the potential for some unauthorized actions. Many of these protection systems are computer based; hackers have certainly demonstrated that such systems often have unexpected vulnerabilities.

Support for nuclear nonproliferation is languishing. The failure of America and Russia to continue reductions in their nuclear arsenals is not only in direct violation of Article VI of the Treaty on the Non-Proliferation of Nuclear Weapons, but also means that Russia maintains a troubling strike capability. In addition, it sets a tone of disregard for the treaty itself. American nuclear support for India, although it does improve relations with this important nation, also undermines support for the treaty, as does the continuing reluctance of America to ratify the Comprehensive Test Ban Treaty. One result is an increased likelihood that additional nations will seek nuclear weapons.

Nonmilitary actions to address threats of nuclear strikes have been mainly diplomatic efforts focused on the Iranian and North Korean programs. These are complex negotiations involving a number of countries with varying interests. They are also complicated by the facts that Iran insists that its intentions only involve peaceful use of nuclear energy, while North Korea has already detonated test devices and has as many as 30 weapons. North Korea did agree, at least in principle, to eliminate its program. President Trump met twice with the North Korean leader Kim Jong-un, but the effort seems to have gone nowhere, despite President Trump's praise of Kim. By 2020, it appeared that Kim's entire negotiating team had been banished, and prospects for successful negotiations had all but disappeared. By January 2021, Kim Jong-un was pledging to advance the country's weaponry. Results with Iran are still far from certain. Efforts by the Trump administration to structure sanctions and international pressure were met with considerable skepticism. The Biden administration has not promoted any significant nonproliferation initiatives.

Protective military actions fall into two basic groups: potential American strikes against Iranian or North Korean nuclear targets and active programs of anti-missile defense to blunt not only these threats but also threats of individual missile launches from other quarters. Military strikes are highly problematic, not only because of their uncertain effectiveness, but also because of their potential to initiate broader military confrontations as well as impact negatively on international relations. Both nations have gone to considerable effort to conceal program elements by placing them in protected locations, particularly underground, so it is unclear what air or missile strikes could even accomplish.

American anti-missile programs have been ongoing for a number of years. They are specifically intended not to be comprehensive protective systems, but rather systems capable of thwarting strikes by one or a few ballistic missiles. Unfortunately, the systems have not performed well in tests. Shorter-range anti-missile weapons have performed very poorly in combat; the systems are vulnerable to a range of [countermeasures](); and they offer no protection against shorter-range, sea-launched missiles or smuggled weapons. Although the system capabilities remain problematic, the costs have been substantial; current missile defense budgets are a bit over $10 billion a year. The Trump administration initiated a 2017 [Ballistic Missile Defense Review]() to address hypersonic and cruise missiles as well as ballistic ones. Additionally, future developments are tied with space weapons as [Russia develops]() both hypersonic cruise missiles and hypersonic glide vehicles (maneuverable warheads that can be launched into space and navigate autonomously).

Overall, despite some $400 billion spent on various missile defense programs, it is questionable if the system [could even address]() the continually expanding range of opposing systems and it would be totally incapable of addressing a major missile attack.

Radiation Dispersal Incidents

A significant reactor accident occurred in 1979 at Three Mile Island in Pennsylvania. In this instance, the main feedwater pumps stopped running, caused by either a mechanical or electrical failure that prevented the steam generators from removing heat. Then a pressure-relief valve failed, unknown to the operators, and eventually caused a loss-of-coolant accident resulting in the meltdown of the reactor core. But there was no breach of the containment walls, no significant release of radiation, and no fatalities.

In 1986, Chernobyl provided another illustration of how no system is foolproof. The reactor crew took advantage of a shutdown for routine maintenance to perform some emergency reaction tests. Violating a number of safety procedures, they pushed the reactor into a very unstable situation. Then a sudden temperature surge led to a catastrophic steam explosion resulting in a fire, a series of additional explosions, and a nuclear meltdown. Large areas of Ukraine, Belarus, and Russia were badly contaminated, resulting in the evacuation and resettlement of over 300,000 people. There were 56 direct deaths from the accident and estimates that as many as 9,000 others might eventually die from some form of cancer induced by the accident, though actual deaths appear to have been less than anticipated.

The most recent reactor accident in 2011 was at Fukushima, Japan, in the wake of a tsunami. Automatic systems immediately shut the reactors down, but the failure of all external electricity sources and the flooding of some critical equipment areas meant that the reactor cores could not be cooled. This triggered a chain of events leading to fuel melting; three of the units were heavily damaged and a large quantity of radiation escaped into the environment. International best practices were not followed before the accident, and the threat was underestimated.

The experience with these three accidents indicates that reactor accidents and radioactive dispersal incidents are unlikely to rise to high levels of immediate deaths. While economic consequences may be significant, including a need for widespread and semi-permanent evacuations, the overall impact on the nation would be modest. Yet, over one-third of the American population lives or works close to of one of the [54 nuclear power sites](), and risks from earthquakes or coastal flooding at some locations are a concern.

[Terrorist groups]() have considered causing a radiation dispersal incident, including crashing an airplane into a reactor or employing a Radioactive Dispersal Device ("dirty bomb"). The [Nuclear Regulatory Commission]() has assessed that existing preparedness training regarding safety issues also cover potential terrorism challenges. The potential for disruption from a Radioactive Dispersal Device is modest, particularly because terrorist organizations would be unlikely to have access to significant amounts of highly radioactive substances. One specific concern would be with [cesium-137](), which is used in a wide variety of devices, including radiation therapy devices for treating cancer and industrial gauges that measure the flow of liquid through pipes.

Overall, it seems very unlikely that the results of a reactor incident (either accidental or intentional) or a Radioactive Dispersal Device would rise to a level of extreme damage, certainly not in terms of direct fatalities. On the other hand, we can hardly ensure that terrorists will be unable to get possession of a significant amount of highly radioactive material. Dispersing such material in a major downtown area could clearly have a severe economic impact and eventually significant deaths from radiation poisoning. Extensive intelligence networks that can identify and thwart potential smuggling attempts are now the major protection.

Improvised Nuclear Devices

Constructing nuclear weapons remains a very sophisticated process and will probably stay well beyond the capabilities of any subnational group. Nuclear weapons need to be in a relatively small, self-contained, and deliverable package. They need to make efficient use of nuclear materials and be robust enough to sit in an arsenal for a number of years. They must above all be reliable, exploding with their expected yield when a detonation signal reaches the warhead. On the other hand, improvised nuclear devices do not have to meet any of these requirements. One could potentially be bought by terrorists, or it could be built from the components of a stolen weapon or from scratch using nuclear material (plutonium, uranium, or highly enriched uranium). They could be large and unwieldy, perhaps built inside a 40-foot shipping container or a large truck or assembled in the basement of a commercial building or warehouse.

Even a relatively small explosion of 10 kilotons in a major city could kill several hundred thousand people, destroying everything within a half-mile radius and causing severe damage for miles beyond. In the end, years of cleanup of 3,000 to 5,000 square miles could be needed and some areas would probably have to be permanently closed.

Terrorist groups have been actively seeking nuclear capabilities though they face many hurdles. Because of known ties between al Qaeda and a black-market nuclear network run by Pakistanis, it can be assumed that terrorists have the know-how to construct a crude improvised nuclear device. The biggest challenge they face is obtaining key nuclear materials: highly enriched uranium (HEU) or plutonium.

Russia poses the largest concern because of the size and dispersion of its nuclear weapons complex. Security is often inadequate; at the same time, the rise of criminal organizations and the relative poverty of many workers in the nuclear complex make for a worrisome combination. Recognizing the dangers of loosely controlled nuclear materials, America initiated the Nunn-Lugar Cooperative Threat Reduction Program in 1991—a systematic effort to improve physical security and material accountability at scattered Russian nuclear facilities. This initiative resulted in a wide range of cooperative programs between America and the nuclear successor states of the Soviet Union. But Russia's suspension of participation in START discussions has undermined the global nonproliferation efforts.

Multilateral programs have had a wide impact. First, the G8 launched a Global Partnership against the Spread of Weapons and Materials of Mass Destruction in 2002, a $20 billion program with four primary goals: increasing security of nuclear and radiological materials, securing alternative employment for former weapons scientists, disposing of chemical weapons, and dismantling nuclear- powered submarines. By 2022, 177 nations had ratified the Comprehensive Test Ban Treaty and were voluntarily taking part in sharing intelligence on nuclear terrorist threats as well as pledging to work toward better security practices over nuclear and other radioactive materials. America has signed, but not ratified, and the treaty is not yet in force.

These initiatives resulted in a substantial increase in efforts to improve the security of nuclear materials. International efforts to prevent nuclear terrorism have entered a new era of uncertainty. Terrorist threats are evolving, and it is increasingly unclear if nuclear security protections against them will keep pace. If improvements to nuclear security do not adapt to these threats, the risk of nuclear terrorism will grow.

Pakistan poses an entirely different set of problems. It possesses nuclear weapons and has an unstable government. Prime Minister Imran Khan was elected in 2017, but then forced from office, arrested, and sentenced to prison as he challenged the military establishment. Within the country, wide sympathy for Muslim extremists raises the potential for insider cooperation with a terrorist organization as well as the potential for cooperation of individual nuclear technicians or scientists. Although the Pakistani nuclear complex is much smaller than the Russian one, there is no international program to help ensure security of materials and weapons, nor is much known about the actual security measures in place. The prior extensive nuclear black market conducted by Pakistan's senior nuclear scientist, A.Q.Khan, also calls into question the degree of government control over the complex.

The United States has had complicated relations with Pakistan for years, imposing sanctions after nuclear weapons tests in 1998 and then welcoming it as a partner after the 9/11 attacks. The relationship was tense with concerns that Pakistani elements were aiding the Taliban in Afghanistan. The 2011 killing by a US strike force of Osama bin Laden in a compound in northern Pakistan reinforced these misgivings. In 2018, President Trump refused further aid, denouncing Pakistan's lies and deceits as it gave safe haven to Afghan terrorists. The Taliban takeover of Afghanistan further worsened US relations with Pakistan. Nevertheless, recognizing broad overlapping interests, there have been recent efforts to revitalize relations with Pakistan through innovative diplomacy. The Biden administration was interested in re-defining the relationship and there have been a series of commercial meetings. These efforts have not been helped by Pakistan's recent actions forcing the return of perhaps a million Afghan refugees back out of Pakistan, at the same time denouncing the Taliban regime in Afghanistan for supporting an anti-Pakistan insurgency. The situation remains unsteady.

Although Russia and Pakistan pose the most urgent concerns, dozens of countries (including North Korea and Iran) pose some potential for leakage of highly enriched uranium or plutonium. Thankfully, production of either of these materials requires substantial industrial capability, something that terrorist groups would be unlikely to acquire or operate surreptitiously.

Having HEU would greatly simplify the task for terrorists as it can relatively easily be fashioned into an improvised nuclear device. Because of the higher radiation flux from plutonium (especially from reactor grade plutonium), its use in weapons requires a high degree of sophistication. It would also be difficult to construct an improvised nuclear device with plutonium. Such a device would be much more likely to produce a fizzle of a result, something that would be a gross failure for a weaponeer. But for a terrorist, even an explosion equivalent to only several tons of TNT would be a great success. An explosion of this magnitude is still large by conventional standards. It would not destroy a city, but it would certainly destroy a number of buildings. It would vaporize essentially all of the plutonium and would create a huge contamination problem in an urban area, not to mention potential fires. And the very fact that terrorists had actually caused a nuclear explosion would spread panic at the scene and would greatly heighten security concerns ever after. It would also be a major public relations *coup d'etat* for the terrorists, heightening the enthusiasm of their supporters, demonstrating the vulnerability of America, and raising the bar for the severity of the next attack.

We have to assume that terrorists have sufficient knowledge to build some improvised nuclear device. And it is likely that they could get the cooperation if not the dedicated support of knowledgeable nuclear technicians and maybe even weapon scientists. Knowledge is not the barrier, rather getting sufficient HEU or plutonium is the barrier. Preventing this has been the focus of efforts to thwart terrorist nuclear capabilities.

Preventing delivery of an improvised nuclear device would be much more difficult. Both uranium and plutonium emit alpha radiation, which can be effectively shielded even by a sheet of paper. However, some of the radiation decay products do emit more penetrating radiation, so shielding these materials from radiation detectors is more difficult. Nevertheless, a detector would have to be extremely sensitive to detect a smuggled device or smuggled materials for use in a locally constructed device.

Overall, the potential for terrorist use of an improvised nuclear device remains significant.

Electro-Magnetic Pulse (EMP)

Sudden surges of electromagnetic energy can cause corresponding power surges within complex electronics, destroying the chips that are at the heart of all our computerized devices as well as melting copper windings in the high voltage transformers that interconnect the entire American power grid infrastructure. Such transformers weigh over 100 tons apiece, usually cannot be repaired in the field, and because of their size, cannot be flown in from overseas factories, where there is already a several year backlog of orders. By destroying consumer electronics along with the distribution transformers, EMP could turn off all of our lights, refrigerators, water-pumping stations, TVs, and radios, leaving the nation with little ability to provide food and water. In worst case scenarios, millions of Americans could eventually starve to death. There are two major possibilities that could result in such catastrophic effects: solar storms and high-altitude nuclear explosions.

The most energetic solar storm ever recorded occurred when the world was only on the threshold of our electronic economy. On September 1, 1859, Richard Carrington, a foremost English astronomer, observed two bright beads of white light form over an enormous group of sunspots. The next day, stunning auroras were seen as far south as the Caribbean, while telegraph systems worldwide went haywire. Even when telegraphers disconnected the batteries powering the lines, aurora-induced electric currents in the wires still allowed messages to be transmitted. Such an event today could cause catastrophic damage. This Carrington Event is unique in its magnitude, so we cannot know whether the next similar solar storm will be in 100 years or 100,000 years.

But smaller solar storms have regularly caused significant problems. On March 13, 1989, for example, two solar blasts knocked out the Hydro-Quebec electrical utility, causing it to go from fully operational to complete shutdown in 92 seconds; millions of customers lost power, but this was largely restored within nine hours. Other major solar storms will certainly occur. A continuing series of lesser events indicates that this will not, like an asteroid strike, probably be off in a far distant future. Any catastrophe caused by a major solar storm would be global, so America could not expect any assistance from other nations. Government leaders are well aware of this potential. A 2014 Congressional hearing on Electromagnetic Pulse (Emp): Threat To Critical Infrastructure addressed the issue, and it is included in the 2017 Critical Infrastructure Protection Act.

A nuclear version of a solar storm first occurred on July 9, 1962. A high-altitude nuclear test near Johnston Island blew out street lamps, television sets, and telephone communications in Hawaii nearly 1,000 miles away, unexpectedly demonstrating the potential of EMP disruption. Since then, the threat of an EMP attack has been extensively analyzed. It is clear that the damage from even a single nuclear burst that did not directly kill even a single person could still be catastrophic. While Russia or China could certainly mount such an attack, this could also impact their own systems and obviously invite retaliation. More disturbingly, unstable countries such as North Korea, Iran, or Pakistan might also be capable.

Attribution and even retaliation might be difficult. In one scenario, a short-range ballistic missile such as the venerable Scud could be mated with a crude warhead and launched from a ship off the American coast. Non-nuclear scenarios are also possible, with specially designed weapons configured to produce strong EMP pulses. The technology base that may be applied to the design of electromagnetic bombs is both diverse, and in many areas, quite mature. Key technologies include explosively pumped Flux Compression Generators (FCG) and explosive or propellant-driven Magneto-Hydrodynamic (MHD) generators.

Overall, American infrastructure remains broadly vulnerable to EMP, as detailed in a 2008 Congressional report. The most likely instigation would be some kind of hostile activity. But the sun remains a direct concern, particularly because some scientists assessed the 2020 sunspot cycle as one of the strongest on record.

Shielding is the major method of protecting against EMP, along with devices to automatically disconnect equipment in the event of a sudden power surge, but such actions are not cheap. By one estimate, replacing major power transformers could cost $10 million each. For some pieces of critical equipment (like satellites), shielding is impractical. For millions of smaller devices, shielding might add only a couple percent to the cost, but the cumulative costs are high, and consumer product competition makes this unlikely without a much broader public awareness. The problem is complicated by the fact that investment in the grid itself has been sorely underfunded. The military includes some measure of protection in equipment specifications, but public information on this is very limited. The Navy, for example, has been applying EMP protection to some systems, but specifics are hard to come by. A major EMP event could cost $2 trillion during the first year in America alone with a recovery period of 4 to 10 years. One obvious protective step would be planning and preparations to disconnect power stations from a damaged grid so they could supply power to local users, the system in place before the broad national grid was even constructed. Overall, there needs to be much more attention placed on developing and applying cost-effective methods of protection.

Nuclear Overview

Campaigning in 2005, President Bush characterized the use of Weapons of Mass Destruction by radicals as the gravest danger the nation faces. The Trump administration also saw this as a grave threat and issued a comprehensive strategy for countering nuclear terrorism with three core elements: global efforts to close off terrorists' access, consistent pressure against terrorist groups by targeting their nuclear specialists and facilitators, and strengthening defenses at home and abroad. President Biden updated this strategy, stressing the need to involve the broadest range of partners. Improvised nuclear devices are the central concern. They could inflict extreme casualties as well as cause a major economic impact. Because of their low radiation signature, it is difficult to block the smuggling of required nuclear materials into the country. The use of radiation detection devices, although reassuring, is essentially useless against this challenge. So, efforts to enhance the security and control of such materials remains the most important means of countering this threat. Second to this, are intelligence efforts to identify radical elements and monitor their activities.

The main impact of a radiation dispersal accident would be economic and would be contained fairly rapidly, as was the case with Chernobyl and Fukushima. An intentional radiation dispersal incident within a major city could be much more damaging but would require a quantity of radioactive material that radical groups would have difficulty obtaining. The high levels of radiation emitted by such materials would also complicate an effort to smuggle it into the country.

Because of the high-yield weapons available, a Russian or Chinese nuclear threat poses a threat of larger magnitude, though of much lower probability. Little has been done in recent years to address the challenge of the needlessly large nuclear arsenals held by both Russia and America. Other nuclear powers, including North Korea and potentially Iran, pose threats of lesser magnitude. These nations lack a reliable means of delivery against targets in America, though North Korea seems to be approaching this capability.

Efforts to address these threats have fallen into several general categories:

- Diplomatic efforts have had uncertain results and have mostly ignored the threat of an unstable, nuclear-armed Pakistan. These efforts also face a basic nonproliferation dilemma: sovereign states inherently have as much right to develop nuclear weapons as America has. The Nuclear Nonproliferation Treaty also gives signatories an absolute right to withdraw from its obligations (as North Korea has done). So international efforts to restrain a spread of nuclear weapons must stress incentives and sanctions, both of which can require considerable time to implement and have an uncertain effect.

- Export controls on materials and equipment necessary for a weapons program have made it quite difficult for non-nuclear states to maintain an active weapons program. In Iraq's case, a combination of controls and sanctions effectively forced Saddam Hussein to eliminate his program; they also led Libya to do the same. But North Korea clearly shows that the controls cannot stop a determined state.

- Military strikes by Israel were effective against Iraq's program, destroying an unfinished nuclear reactor. Military options are less attractive against North Korea and Iran for a variety of reasons. Military defensive measures, particularly anti-missile systems, only address one aspect of the nuclear threat. This option could be attractive if it provided a reliably effective system at a moderate cost. Unfortunately, present systems provide neither. Cost is also substantially uneven—if a confrontational country has one missile, America must have hundreds of anti-missiles to try to protect against it.

- Intelligence efforts to identify weapon activities and locations in potentially hostile states are critical. These systems functioned poorly during the crisis leading up to the Iraqi War and seem to be only marginally effective in the Iranian and North Korean cases.

A strategic nuclear exchange with the Russians poses a threat very different from an asteroid or a pandemic. If a pandemic kills 100 million Americans, once the dead have been memorialized, the country will still have its cities and towns, its ports and power plants, its homes and office buildings, its infrastructure and farmland. The survivors can pick themselves up, dust themselves off, and move forward to revive the nation. But if a strategic nuclear exchange kills 100 million Americans, once the dead are memorialized, the nation will be left with radioactive rubble, radioactivity that will kill many of the initial survivors. And all survivors will face the uncertain effects of Nuclear Winter, which would only be intensified by any American retaliatory strikes. There will be no way to simply dust off and move forward. Because of this, the nuclear threat is much more alarming than a pandemic.

Arms reduction efforts are clearly an attractive alternative. In fact, decreasing weapon requirements and deployments would provide significant cost savings. Such efforts could also visibly improve American-Russian relations and support cooperative efforts, including efforts to secure nuclear and other materials from terrorists and radicals. Simply reducing the size of the nuclear complexes on both sides would also reduce the potential for leakage to terrorists or unauthorized actions by some deranged individual within the complex.

Mutual arms reductions would also support nuclear nonproliferation. This is under stress from Iranian and North Korean programs, which have made numerous other nations consider their own nuclear options. Invigorated American-Russian nuclear cooperation could do much to blunt this threat. On the other hand, current American efforts to improve nuclear capabilities to face a relatively low-level Russian threat can easily provoke Russian escalation. Such stepwise actions on both sides only make the threat worse.

Non-Nuclear Threats

Non-nuclear threats can seem large in the public view, but they have only a minimal potential to cause major damage to America.

Conventional War

For centuries major powers sought to overrun and occupy rivals. The two World Wars alone resulted in close to 100 million deaths. Now none of the major powers faces any significant threat of invasion and occupation. During the Cold War, NATO nations, indeed, faced a threat of being overrun by Soviet forces. But Russia is currently totally incapable of mounting such an extensive effort against West Europe. But its more restricted military actions, including the 2022 invasion of Ukraine, have raised the possibility of involvement of NATO troops in Europe. Efforts to end the fighting in Ukraine are important, but this has to be done with strong diplomatic and economic efforts promoting the emergence of a more progressive government in Russia to minimize any prospect of continuing war within Europe.

China could certainly become involved in regional military operations, but major involvement of American ground forces is unlikely. The one exception is Korea, where renewed Chinese support for North Korea could somehow get out of hand. Even then, the very idea of transporting significant additional American ground forces to Korea in the face of Chinese opposition would be daunting.

No major involvement of American ground forces has been initiated since the 2003 invasion of Iraq. Subsequent operations in Iraq and Syria were by relatively small contingents, including a [2019 concerted effort](#) to eliminate any territorial control by the Islamic State. Operations in Afghanistan had involved over 100,000 American troops, but mainly as anti-guerilla forces rather than standard military. The total US withdrawal from Afghanistan in August 2021 left the region in turmoil, but ended the only major US military operation.

Overall, America faces no prospect of invasion and minimal prospect of major casualties from ground force operations overseas. A confrontation with Iran is possible, but major involvement of American ground forces is unlikely. In any scenario, casualties, even in the thousands, are unlikely.

Electronic Disorder

The twenty-first century has added a whole new dimension to national threats: electronic threats. This has developed gradually over the last several decades as the country has become more and more computerized, telecommunications have become increasingly dependent on satellites, the national power grid has become the primary supplier of electricity to almost all users, and electronic devices have penetrated every corner of our lives. As our modern life has become strongly dependent on electronics, we have also become deeply vulnerable to their disruption.

When the internet was originally developed, not much thought was given to potential malicious use, so no effort was made to build in protections. Since then, as internet usage has mushroomed, so have malicious actions. Typically, for nefarious reasons some unknown party electronically probes for an unprotected point of entry into a system. Electronic viruses were an early challenge, often causing damage simply for the sake of causing damage, some kind of warped demonstration of superior computer skills. Viruses would be inserted, would sit dormant for some period of time, and then erupt in spectacular damage to the system. Such initial malevolent actions have evolved into a wide range of concerns, including a number that have national-level implications. More recently, artificial intelligence has created a whole new range of electronic possibilities that could substantially reduce the work force while facilitating the spread of artificially generated false information.

Military espionage is one major concern. The Department of Defense acknowledges several intrusions into highly classified systems. Some have apparently been traced to computers in China, though the Chinese government denies any role. As the American military has become more and more reliant on computer systems, there is a high concern that an intruder is doing more than collecting protected information but is working to identify ways to bring systems down, ways to impede or even prevent military operations.

The civilian equivalent is industrial espionage: stealing trade secrets, production know-how, or process details. Again, intrusions are often traced to computers in China as well as Russia. Some of them have been focused on military industries, others seem to be purely economic espionage. When a company does discover some computer intrusion, it can be reluctant to notify authorities, concerned that knowledge of an intrusion would affect the willingness of other companies to deal with it or damage its public reputation. There is also a broad concern that intrusions could be used for systematic damage.

This is not just a theoretical problem, as well illustrated by Stuxnet—a virus introduced into Iranian industrial nuclear control systems that caused widespread damage. Subsequent information tied this effort and a parallel Flame virus to Israeli and American intelligence agencies; they naturally declined comment. At any rate, the effort not only demonstrated that such intrusions could cause serious damage but also set a precedent for one country damaging another's industrial systems. Tying such an intrusion to America is of major concern because there have been continuous probes into various American infrastructure systems as well, including the electric grid. It is difficult for America to object to such intrusions if it has been doing them itself. The more systems use computers to make their operation more efficient, the more vulnerable they become to disruption.

Early on, crime was a prime motivator behind malicious use of the internet. Widespread intrusion into personal and business computers spread a variety of viruses. Many sat quietly on computers, unknown to the owners, until some remote operator directed them to carry out some activity, such as joining in an overwhelming burst of queries into some targeted system. Other intrusions simply gather information such as usernames, passwords, and credit card data as well as email lists to further spread malicious code. Recent intrusions into financial, commercial, and governmental institutions have resulted in the loss of financial information on thousands of individuals, raising serious apprehensions about identity theft.

It is difficult to identify the origin of any cyber attacks, probes, or intrusions. Stuxnet has been attributed to the Israeli and American governments. Numerous intrusions into American systems apparently originated in Russia or China. Yet proving the location of the perpetrator is usually impossible, much less initiating any official control, support, or direction. Other governments may have a direct interest in industrial espionage, but so do individual industries worldwide. There have even been reports that electronics imported into America come with built-in malware. Organization insiders can facilitate intrusions for whatever personal motivations they may have. Extremist organizations involved in cyber efforts have a wide range of motivations. Wikileaks made public massive amounts of restricted official documents, claiming it was operating in the best interest of an open society. Anonymous, a loose collective of more anarchic associates, has targeted a variety of organizations, including the Church of Scientology and research firm Stratfor. Radical and terrorist groups are certainly examining the potential to use computer attacks to undermine opponents and to extort ransoms. American intelligence warns of an increasingly dangerous cyber "Cold War."

Overall:

- US computer systems are subjected to a continuous stream of sophisticated probes and attacks. While identification of the perpetrators can be important, most important is what they are trying to do and how they are trying to do it. Adversarial countries and intelligence services are surely involved in some of these activities, although specific attribution is usually impossible. A major effort is clearly made by criminal organizations intent on collecting financial and industrial data. One recent report tells of information on 43,000 hacked servers for sale on the dark web.

- A clear threat to military and diplomatic systems is apparent, as well as precedents for such activities. When Estonia got into a dispute with Russia in 2007, government sites were overwhelmed with a massive "denial of service" attack that blocked computer availability across the nation. Subsequently, when Russian forces were invading Georgia, the Georgian government experienced a wide range of computer attacks that severely degraded its operations. Russia was the obvious suspect in both cases, but, of course, denied any government involvement.

- Probes into American infrastructure systems are particularly troubling because they could indicate a sophisticated operation aimed at crippling one or more systems, including planting malicious code that could be activated at some later date. If done by an adversarial government, such probes would probably be intended to develop a sophisticated understanding of control operations, to identify major vulnerabilities, or to design a devastating attack. Obviously, such an operation would have to contend with constantly evolving systems, and so require a continuous monitoring of the target. Nevertheless, a parallel operation by some radical or terrorist group might not be interested in preparing for some potential future activity, but intent on causing as much damage as quickly as possible.

As with EMP, a central protection is shielding, in this case not physical but electronic. Any protective efforts face a continuously evolving threat. The basic challenge is a multi-dimensional electronic version of spy versus spy with each actor continuously working to protect its own activities while probing for weaknesses in the other's activities. A successful protection at one minute can suddenly become useless. No one ever knows for sure what is safe and what is not. At a national level, the Department of Defense is directly addressing the challenge with its newly established Cyber Command while intelligence agencies, particularly including the National Security Agency, are heavily involved. Cybersecurity overlaps with cyber surveillance and the resulting systems have had a direct impact on individual privacy.

On the civilian side, it is much more difficult as each organization takes whatever steps it individually decides are appropriate for its situation. Many are simply oblivious to the threats they face. For the nation this is a particular challenge for infrastructure, which is almost totally in private hands. Although attacks on infrastructure could have a catastrophic impact, it is difficult for the government to require protective measures. So, for example, one 2012 effort in Congress to set security standards for industry was strongly opposed by the American Chamber of Commerce on the grounds that it would be a significant financial burden for companies, and the effort died in the Senate.

For key questions of exactly who is intruding, what are their motivations and capabilities, and what would be the actual result of some malicious action, there are no definitive answers. It is easy to construct a catastrophic scenario, but practical analysis shows that such dramatic scenarios are unlikely.

As almost every aspect of American life has become dependent on electronic systems, a whole new set of vulnerabilities has emerged. To date, their actual impact has been modest so it is difficult to raise public awareness of the challenges, much less willingness to spend significant resources protecting against threats that can seem vague and theoretical. As one assessment concluded, the current strategic environment is fundamentally unstable. This instability is highly dangerous for America; achieving stability primarily requires increasing resilience in our systems, and that requires substantial expenses.

MILITARY-INDUSTRIAL COMPLEX

> Every gun that is made, every warship launched, every rocket fired signifies in the final sense, a theft from those who hunger and are not fed, those who are cold and are not clothed. This world in arms is not spending money alone. It is spending the sweat of its laborers, the genius of its scientists, the hopes of its children.
>
> — Dwight D. Eisenhower

The quote above is obviously not from some starry-eyed pacifist but from a five-star general and former American President. He directly addressed the question of military budgets. These budgets are supposed to be supported for national security but in actuality are often supported for money.

Sitting at the intersection of wealth inequality and foreign policy, the Military-Industrial Complex continues to drain resources from critical programs. A main reason that this can happen is dysfunction at the top levels of government.

Avoiding a global meltdown is the core challenge of the twenty-first century. There is no military path. In fact, Eisenhower's warning about "a theft from those who hunger" becomes more pressing as hunger and poverty become more likely sources of global conflict. But Eisenhower also recognized that the military establishment is a vital element in keeping the peace; significant military reductions are only reasonable in a context of mutual agreements with potential adversaries. Absent this, it is almost certain that the world in general and America in particular will be unable to adequately address the underlying economic, social and environmental challenges to life, liberty and the pursuit of happiness. But continued major military expenditures worldwide simply drain away the needed resources.

National Security

National security is always presented as the underlying reason for continually large military budgets, stressing the need to protect the American people and the homeland from hostile nations and violent subnational groups. This is hugely exaggerated. Like a ventriloquist holding up his dummy and entertaining an audience with something obviously false, the Military Industrial Complex holds up its own version of an imminent threat that simply is not there. The world is in an unprecedented strategic situation. No major power threatens another with invasion or occupation. America simply faces no significant military threat.

The strategic challenges of the twentieth century were military and America met them directly. By the end of the century, neither a battered Russia nor a China only beginning to emerge was a significant rival. When Iraq invaded Kuwait in 1991, America was able to rapidly lead a broad coalition in a short, intense, and overwhelmingly successful Desert Storm. Entering the new millennium, America stood at the pinnacle of power, dominating the globe in a way few nations ever have.

It is true that Russian nuclear weapons could devastate the nation. China has a much smaller nuclear arsenal useful only for deterrence. But a Russian total strike, even if not answered, would result in a Nuclear Winter that would also devastate Russia (and everyone else). Such a strike would simply make no sense, ultimately devastating Russia as well as everyone else. A smaller strike would invite, really demand, an American retaliatory strike and could easily escalate into full-scale strikes and Nuclear Winter. The threat of a Russian nuclear strike is simply hollow, only useful for inciting fear. Additionally, there is almost nothing militarily that America can do to prevent it.

Overall, faced with growing global instabilities and uncertain conditions, there is a strong American tendency to strengthen its military capabilities to be better prepared to meet any kind of threat or challenge. Therein lies the problem—the major threats and challenges of the twenty-first century are not susceptible to military solutions, even for security challenges. Iraq and Afghanistan show the limitations of military solutions. Turmoil in the Middle East, radicalism and instability in Pakistan, intransigence by Iran and North Korea, and attacks by Somali pirates all pose challenges that military force cannot adequately address. The biggest problem is that the changing global situation poses new crises for which military force is irrelevant. Globalization with a newly networked world means that America can no longer dominate the global economy and enjoy a grossly disproportionate share of global resources.

It is easy to project a world of discord in the decades ahead. Both China and Russia have numerous internal problems, and their leaders are working hard to suppress any dissent. They are both becoming increasingly authoritarian and justifying this internally by the need to have a strong government in the face of external challenges, particularly from America. China is putting significant resources into military expansion and seems to be developing a strong capability to challenge American naval presence in the South China Sea. As internal problems worsen, both Russia and China maintain legitimacy by using denunciations of America to stoke patriotism, stressing contention rather than cooperation.

Opposing Russia and China with military developments only reinforces nationalist support for their autocratic leaders. The military threats they pose to American allies and friends are better addressed with diplomatic and economic actions. America supports international standards of conduct on the high seas. As mentioned earlier, any such standards need to have strong international backing. America has no primary responsibility for enforcing them, and the changing global situation requires working with allies to promote collaborative efforts. In 2007, the Chairman of the Joint Chiefs of Staff, Admiral Mullen, proposed creating a thousand-ship navy by collaborating with partner nations to support international standards, but nothing came of this.

Military forces have been used against smaller countries. Vietnam is the classic example, with almost 60,000 American deaths and a cost of $1 trillion in today's dollars. This debacle was then repeated in Afghanistan. Despite another $1 trillion and more than 2,000 American deaths over a period of almost 20 years, America was unable to demonstrate how democracy and development could lead to peace and prosperity. The problem goes back to the very beginning of the Afghan effort in 2001 when President George W. Bush announced, "we don't do nation building," and then shifted his focus to Iraq. Within a year, the Afghan countryside was no longer peaceful as the Taliban returned. America never veered from a military focus. In 2011, the top American commander in Afghanistan, Major General John Campbell, commented that "we can't kill our way out of this thing," but we kept trying.

The challenge of military confrontation was dramatically thrust back into the center of foreign policy by Russia's 2022 invasion of Ukraine. Suddenly there was once again war in Europe. The United States and NATO responded with major supplies of military equipment to Ukraine and a parallel major increase in their own defense expenditures. Globally military efforts were suddenly reemphasized, including the potential for China to invade Taiwan. Then the Hamas attack on Israel and its responding war in Gaza brought the global military focus to its highest level since World War II. Ukraine's reluctance to consider a cease fire and Russia's insistence on continuing military operations until it wins greatly complicate the situation. The United States is back where it was 50 years ago with the Soviet Union, confronting a Russia that seeks broad global control. The short-term military response is clearly appropriate. But the United States needs to do everything it can to shift from a military confrontation to a diplomatic and economic one, advocating a cease fire in Ukraine.

Militarization is not just a domestic problem as it reduces resources needed at home, but it is a global problem, now worsened by economic globalization. Working to build a stable world is a core challenge, and arms spending everywhere undermines it. This is particularly pertinent for America for two reasons. The first is that America helps to set the tone for global discourse. When America has high levels of military spending and supports major trades in arms, then of course other nations, both competitive and friendly, will do the same. And when America puts a large portion of its strategic resources into military assets, then there is less to put into development and other stabilization efforts. By being strong militarily, America increases its need to be strong because it promotes competitors to increase their military forces. This can easily become a vicious circle that undermines everyone's efforts to build better lives.

The central issue of globalization is that a prosperous America can only exist in a prosperous world. It is no longer external force that threatens to devastate America, but economic deterioration. For the first time in history, military forces are not central to addressing the major challenges facing the nation. Assets dedicated to nonproductive military use should be limited to directly addressing substantial current risks, allowing the maximum application of other assets to development and stabilization. As Afghanistan vividly illustrated, failure to promote development in a stable situation can rapidly lead to much larger military requirements. By shifting assets to developmental uses, America can set a global example for reducing the extensive diversion of assets into nonproductive military uses. Indeed, such a shift in focus is essential if the world is to avoid a global meltdown in the coming decades. Military missions need to be rigorously assessed in terms of overall national security requirements, which now broadly transcend military requirements. Overall, the new millennium presents an entirely new challenge: shrinking national assets as America increasingly faces nonmilitary security threats that are amorphous and harder to even define, much less address—global warming is a good example. So, it is too easy to keep focusing on the kinds of threats we are more familiar with—military challenges—even if this means that larger issues go unaddressed. The result is a growing mismatch between American strategic assets and the new range of challenges facing the nation.

President Eisenhower came back to this theme in his [Farewell Address](#) to the nation. He warned that "we annually spend on military security more than the net income of all United States' corporations. This conjunction of an immense military establishment and a large arms industry is new in the American experience. . . We recognize the imperative need for this development. Yet we. . . must guard against the acquisition of unwarranted influence, whether sought or unsought, by the military-industrial complex . . . each proposal must be weighed in the light of a broader consideration: the need to maintain balance in and among national programs—balance between the private and the public economy—balance between cost and hoped for advantage—balance between the clearly necessary and the comfortably desirable—balance between our essential requirements as a nation and the duties imposed by the nation upon the individual—balance between action of the moment and the national welfare of the future. Good judgment seeks balance and progress; lack of it eventually finds imbalance and frustration."

Indeed, the key word is "balance." When the survival of the nation was at stake, military priorities were naturally high. Now, with minimal direct threat to survival and a wide range of other threats and challenges for which military prowess is irrelevant, the situation is much more complicated. The central factor in deciding balance is risk. In contrast to asteroid strikes, usually neither the consequences nor the probabilities associated with specific threats or challenges can be quantified; in many cases they are even hard to describe. Yet these risks all need to be balanced. At the national level, it is the federal budget that reflects this balance, how the resources of the nation are allocated. In trying to balance dozens of often vague items, there will naturally be wide ranges of honest evaluation; therefore, the military budget can be particularly contentious.

Money

Money is the real driving force behind the military-industrial complex which, of course, has a vested interest in maintaining its position. Owners and executives of military support companies typically draw outsized compensation. Their dedicated work force also strongly supports the façade of critical protection for the nation and is also well paid. But these are [hollow jobs](#) that turn valuable resources into nonproductive, dead assets, and undermine the nation's ability to address the core challenges of promoting global stability and revitalizing America.

It is easy to tie almost any military expenditure to a supposed need to protect the American status in the world or to defend against some dire threat. The threats that the military could face can be vividly portrayed in contrast to vague challenges of cyber warfare, climate change, or potential epidemics, not to mention education shortfalls, infrastructure degradation or health care. So, it is relatively easy to build a compelling narrative in support of some specific military expenditure.

Money also drives America's role in the global arms trade where an emphasis on military expenses undermines economic development. America is the [leading nation in this trade](#), which supports American companies but shifts billions of dollars into non-productive and even counter-productive uses in countries that can ill afford it.

The military is not a jobs program, and military expenditures should be justified by how important they are in the overall context of national objectives. However, in practice, jobs are indeed critical. That is why Congress had to set up an independent [Defense Base Closure and Realignment Commission](#) to produce a list of bases for closing as the process was too divisive within Congress itself. When bases are being considered for closing, there is typically a strong outcry about why they are needed. If they survive a given round, only rarely does their community set up any kind of a planning committee to consider how best to address an eventual closing, something that would inevitably mark them as a prime candidate for a next round of closings. Instead, local communities and governments make every effort to reinforce their perceived importance. Similarly, there is strong Congressional pressure to support an [F-35 development](#) program even though it has been bedeviled with cost overruns and its military utility in twenty-first-century warfare is questionable. When significant cuts to defense industry were assessed in 2014, there were concerns about a half a trillion dollars in cuts to the defense budget over the next decade. But there was less concern about why these jobs were critical for the nation. An analysis by [Brookings Institution](#) showed how such cuts would be far less critical than presented by industrial supporters.

Military support jobs play a critical role in national elections. People employed in the military-industrial complex have strong incentives to support candidates who support military budgets. Moving significant resources out of non-productive military uses can be a plus for the nation. Such moves do not happen overnight and can be politically difficult. For example, if it makes military sense to reduce submarine manufacturing, it is real workers who make the submarines. Theoretically they and the resources they take can be put to more productive use, but that certainly requires planning, financial expenses, and time. Highly paid military design specialists have no comparable civilian jobs to move into. Of course, no workers with solid employment want to face having to find a new job. So it turns out that defense jobs are important for votes in at least four states (Arizona, Florida, Pennsylvania, Wisconsin), all critical in Presidential elections. This provides a strong incentive for thousands of workers to vote for pro-military candidates, generally Republicans and can be a critical factor in Presidential elections. Every major component of the military-industrial complex should be planning for eventual reductions, and the government needs to support this planning, but it is not happening. This is another major challenge in the years ahead that no one wants to address.

SUMMARY

From time immemorial, the central security challenge for cohesive groups has been physical protection against attack by enemies. America achieved its independence by military means and soon thereafter fought foreign invaders in the War of 1812. After that, thanks to protection by two oceans, direct physical challenge was minimal, but challenges to allied nations were severe. This drew America into two world wars and then conflict in Korea. The subsequent Soviet challenge, including direct nuclear threats, gave impetus to a strong military posture. Though the demise of the Soviet Union in 1991 greatly reduced the direct threat to America, the new millennium has not been kind to American primacy. Even in its first decade, there was a host of challenges to America, including:

- A newly assertive Russia, initially fueled by high energy prices, has a strong-willed, autocratically inclined leader, skillfully using Russian nationalism to support his determination to re-assert Russia's role as a global power;
- A rising China, buoyed by a surging economy and encouraged by American difficulties, is also stoking national pride, directly challenging American ascendancy, developing regional

dominance, and becoming a vague though very bothersome threat to American space assets;

- Radical Islamic groups, particularly al Qaeda, have stirred strong anti-American sentiments, especially in Pakistan but generally throughout the Islamic World, which is now in the throes of its own upheavals with largely unpredictable outcomes;

- Iran continues to frustrate efforts to restrain its nuclear program while actively supporting radical groups and Shiite minorities regionally, and is now reaching into the Western Hemisphere, notably building ties with an increasingly autocratic and anti-American Venezuela.

- The Global South has become a collective phrase for the world's developing and least developed countries, particularly in Africa. For 500 years, they were simply there, exploited by colonial powers and then the Industrialized World, with little opportunity to express any contrary opinions. But the impact of globalization and then the war in Ukraine has created a new situation, where realism leads these nations to challenge Western dominance in a multipolar world.

Nuclear threats are the most worrisome category of confrontational threats. Although the probabilities are low, results could be catastrophic. More efforts at broad arms control actions and improved relationships with major adversaries are certainly called for. Military measures have a minimal impact but maintaining a basic deterrence posture is important. Anti-missile capabilities are of limited use.

Nuclear activities are also the most important terrorist threat. This requires more international intelligence cooperation and better controls on key nuclear materials, particularly cesium-137. Biological threats are also significant; addressing them requires good intelligence including a specific focus on emerging biological research. Most other terrorist threats are relatively small in terms of potential impact on the nation as a whole. Protection against conventional attacks requires not only good intelligence but also local police and security measures at vulnerable locations. This is now much improved since 9/11, but attacks are still possible.

Against this background, the electronic environment faces both environmental and intended disruptions. Electro-magnetic pulse seems like a science fiction problem, but it is both real and potentially catastrophic. Cyber challenges have less potential to devastate the nation. Both challenges require extensive protective measures as well as the ability to rapidly disconnect or quarantine specific system elements.

In fact, America faces only a minimal direct physical threat. Russia's remaining nuclear arsenal could undoubtedly decimate America, but it is hard to construct any scenario where that would happen, particularly when faced with an American response, even a minimal one. China's arsenal is much less capable of delivering a devastating blow to America. China has a long history of playing to opponent's weaknesses and at any rate seems determined to be a regional rather than a global power. Iran and North Korea pose marginal direct threats to America. Terrorists do present a direct threat as illustrated by the 9/11 attacks. The American public is conscious of this threat, but the only strategic dimension of terrorism is with biological or nuclear attacks. In this regard, the stability of Pakistan is particularly troublesome as there is some potential for radical Islamic elements to take control of this nuclear-armed state.

The basic American response has been to address these challenges militarily. This has proven to be both very costly and of questionable effectiveness. In Iraq, a trillion dollars, hundreds of American lives, and tens of thousands of Iraqi lives have produced a fragile state that seems to be more subject to Iranian influence than American. A parallel effort in Afghanistan ended up with the Taliban government returning to power.

Overall, military actions address almost none of the major threats to life. Non-military threats put thousands of lives at risk and deserve a higher priority, but there are two major problems:

- Lives lost are specific people with names and addresses but lives saved are vague and uncertain. So, for example, you can count the number of people killed in traffic accidents, but you cannot count the number of people who are not killed because of increased vigilance or new laws, such as use of seat belts. No one knows who the people saved are. These saved lives contribute to a longer average life span and to overall economic improvements. However, this all seems theoretical. Roughly 120,000 people a year die from infectious diseases. In the last 15 years, the rate of infection has fallen by 45 percent. That means many thousands of lives have been saved—if we had not had this decrease, then 100,000 additional people would have died each year. But this is not countable. The average citizen has little appreciation of this significant reduction in deaths.

- People make unrealistic risk assessments, largely based on fear and emotional responses. Preference for car travel rather than air travel is one standard example. When a single event produces a large death toll, it has much higher psychological impact, so 100 people killed in a relatively rare plane crash make a much larger impression than the 100 people killed routinely every day in car crashes. Events that people have actually experienced or have been very forcefully made aware of, such as the World Trade Center attacks or the destruction of Hurricane Katrina, seem much more real than potential events, such as a major epidemic or an asteroid impact. In the months immediately following the World Trade Center attack, many people avoided air travel, and traffic deaths were a 1,000 above average—equal to more than a third of the people killed in the World Trade Center. Almost no one noticed.

Since few of the risk assessments can be addressed mathematically, they are answered subjectively with a natural bias towards personal history and potential personal impacts. Consequences are never clear. Will an asteroid be large or small, will a hurricane be Category 2 or Category 5, will a terrorist nuclear incident kill 50 people or five million? Likewise, probabilities are rarely clear. Are the Russians trustworthy, do scientists exaggerate threats, are radicalized Islamists 1 percent or 51 percent of the Muslim population? Such individual attitudes heavily influence individual assessments. The problem is obviously worsened when politicians focus on some specific threat or when they minimize potential consequences.

As a result, the nation does an erratic job of assessing risks and balancing one against another. So, the nation spends perhaps $5 million a year addressing the asteroid threat, some tens of millions addressing the pandemic threat, and hundreds of billions addressing the nuclear threat.

The resources available to address threats are limited. Insurance companies allocate larger amounts of resources to larger risks. The nation must do the same. This is the responsibility of our elected leadership. Although individuals understandably react emotionally based on psychological perceptions, the leadership has a responsibility to act more soberly, to make a more rational assessment of what is most important, and to explain such decisions to the electorate. The electorate also has a responsibility to step back from immediate emotional responses and critically examine the rationale for actions posed by the leadership. Unfortunately, such decisions are rarely taken so rationally.

4

NATIONAL STRATEGY

BACKGROUND

It seems that America has never had a real National Strategy—a statement of what is important for our nation, what we want to achieve, and how to do it. Such a National Strategy is an overall plan of how to best use resources to meet the challenges facing the nation. In addition to tax revenue and other monetary means, these resources include the time and effort put forth by federal officials and employees, as well as support from the states, non-governmental groups, local governments, and individuals.

The tangible embodiment of federal resources is the federal budget. Government expenditures in 2023 are estimated at $6.3 trillion. Of this, almost $3 trillion goes to mandatory programs (mainly Social Security and Health Insurance) and another $663 billion to interest on debt. Discretionary spending includes over $800 billion for defense, leaving less than $2 trillion for other discretionary programs, including retiree benefits, economic security programs and scientific research.

A National Strategy seeks to obtain the maximum benefits from the limited resources available by specifying what the nation wants to do, what competing objectives need to be balanced, and what approach to setting priorities will be used. The critical first step is to assess the threats and challenges facing the nation, and then develop an overall concept of how to address them in terms of national values and objectives.

Facing a threat of total destruction during the Cold War with the Soviet Union, an overarching concept of containment provided direction—limiting the reach of the Soviet Union and the spread of communism. Since then, there has been no concept to replace containment. A National Strategic Narrative developed in 2011 in the office of the Chairman of the Joint Chiefs of Staff stressed the need for global engagement and a focus on building prosperity, but it was never formalized.

The unfortunate situation is that our national strategic efforts are fixated on short-term military actions and simplistic solutions. As the larger strategic challenges of economic globalization, radical Islamic ideologies, economic inequalities, global warming, and real democratization come into closer view, our nation continues to allocate a large portion of available resources into programs that fail to address underlying problems or looming challenges. The Project on National Security Reform (PNSR) brought together a broad group of experienced statesmen and analysts. In 2008, PNSR's *Forging A New Shield* report directly addressed the need for linking resources and goals to produce a comprehensive National Strategy, but it had minimal impact on national policy and the organization ceased operating in 2012.

Since then, there has been no broad effort for producing a comprehensive National Strategy. The current National Security Strategy, focused on defense and threats of violence, only addresses military requirements. While it acknowledges the need for integrated federal responses, it fails to recognize socio-economic and environmental challenges as security issues, even though these are precisely the issues which have the potential to destroy the nation. One result is that a very large percentage of government discretionary funds is spent on a relatively narrow range of short-term military threats. This is because there is no system for looking at a broader picture, addressing the most critical threats and challenges facing the nation.

The major challenges we face are ambiguous and amorphous, and they call for national leadership inspired by a vision of a more distant future and with the foresight to lead the nation in a fundamental reorientation of organizations and policies. For many challenges, there will never be solutions. The best that can be done is to develop positive approaches, continually adjusted to manage the problem. Congress and the Executive Branch must oversee the effort, and government agencies involved have to assess how specific programs can fit into an overall strategy.

This chapter outlines the kinds of programs the nation can use to form an integrated strategy.

The first part, Fix America First, addresses actions the nation can take to be in the best position to move forward and achieve the nation's overall objectives.

The second part, Realign Foreign Policy, assesses actions the nation can take to meet external challenges from the global environment that are critical to American prosperity.

FIX AMERICA FIRST

The American government has to protect the rights and freedoms guaranteed by its fundamental documents and provide for the needs of even the least of its citizens. For years, America's [Beacon of Freedom](#) inspired people everywhere. America was the [indispensable](#) nation, uniquely founded on fundamental human principles of life, liberty, and the pursuit of happiness as expressed in its Declaration of Independence. Its postwar efforts embodied the American Dream: work hard and prosper. America used its fundamental principles to create an international framework of peace and stability, while its dynamic economy spread wealth and control widely.

But since the Reagan administration in the 1980's, the American Dream has faded due to a steady shift of wealth and control to the upper levels of society. Especially in rural areas, the middle-class economy worsened, promoting a natural tendency for people to cluster with their own socio-economic groups and blame others for the problems. Not only did technology help create this problem, but the internet publicized it. The American Beacon of Freedom dimmed drastically with America's visibly increasing domestic shortcomings and its support for autocratic regimes. The American failure to demonstrate that democracy leads to peace and prosperity is a fundamental cause of global turmoil.

Before America can even think of reasserting global leadership it has to address this shortcoming, making its Beacon of Freedom once again shine brightly. To once again be an example of the inalienable rights of democracy—life, liberty, and the pursuit of happiness—we need to Fix America First. Recent decades have clearly failed to show a positive economic situation, and COVID-19 only made it worse.

American Dream

As the American Dream has badly faded, America's reputation as a Beacon of Freedom also faded. The very first requirement for the nation is to rekindle the American Dream and its shining light of democracy and prosperity. As [Richard Haass](), President of the Council on Foreign Relations, argues, American national security depends on addressing its crumbling infrastructure, second-class schools, outdated immigration system, and burgeoning debt. Most recently, police violence and the nationwide protests that followed have vividly demonstrated the [hypocrisy of American democracy](), the pervasive racism that still continues to infect American society.

President Trump promoted an America First effort, but this mainly resulted in disengaging from global politics, disdaining allies, and befriending autocratic leaders. It did nothing to promote the domestic changes the nation so desperately needs to demonstrate how an effective democracy can provide for the needs of even the least of its citizens. President Biden has since stressed the need to grow the economy from the bottom up through public investments, empowering workers, and promoting competition. Public investment from the CHIPS and Science Act has attracted significant private investment. Nevertheless, despite strong economic performance, the public remains skeptical of current programs. Democracy has to be connected with bread-and-butter issues like health care and the economy.

America cannot promote global democracy if it cannot demonstrate it domestically. The first foreign policy requirement is socio-political change—at home. America needs leadership that works to unite the nation and vividly demonstrate that, indeed, all people are created equal and democracy can lead to broad prosperity.

Resilience

Resilience protects the life of the country and its citizens. It is the ability to handle negative events, to take them in stride, and move on. This requires monitoring for potential upcoming events, taking steps to minimize their impact, and being prepared to react to negative consequences. This requires significant expenditures up front. Many negative events have the potential of causing thousands and even millions of deaths, yet they remain vague and uncertain, often far in the future. This makes it difficult to fund necessary steps.

- Asteroid Strikes. The potential for damage from earthbound threats is fairly well understood, but the potential for asteroid impact is still uncertain. Because of the possibility of catastrophic damage, current monitoring programs are important but it is critical that we work harder to develop a real capability to deflect threatening asteroids.

- Pandemics. This is another area where assessment and monitoring have been inadequate. The White House pandemic office needs to be reactivated with more funding for pandemic preparations at both national and state levels. More collaboration across the globe is critical, particularly strong interaction with the World Health Organization. Another virulent pandemic is the most likely catastrophic threat the nation faces.

- Volcanoes and Earthquake Faults. These need to be continuously monitored with plans for response capabilities. Building code improvements are also important for reducing earthquake and tornado vulnerabilities. Insurance rate structures can also encourage stronger design and construction efforts.

- Global Warming. This needs to be addressed on a global basis. Administration efforts to reduce carbon emissions and build resilience with infrastructure improvements and response preparedness underline the need for continuing significant investments. On a global scale, a recent UN Climate Summit approved a global pact to transition from fossil fuels and promotion of clean energy alternatives. Implementation will require sustained pressures by America and the international community.

- Floods. Flood control efforts need to be improved, including a broad reassessment of levees and other protective construction. Coastal flood control is more difficult facing sea level rise which severely threatens hundreds of thousands of homes in the coming decades, while increasing storms threaten millions of others internally. Sea walls are at best an expensive and temporary approach; much broader assessments of managed retreat are needed at state level as thousands of threatened homes are in formerly reasonable locations. Insurance review is also important. Rates need to be set on risks and make insurance increasingly impractical in many areas. Building codes should not allow construction, especially re-building, in areas at high risk for floods and storms. In all areas, there needs to be more comprehensive assessments of how to best build resiliency with building codes reinforcing the need for stronger construction.

- Forest and Range Fires. Broadly forested areas need to have systematic programs to reduce the potential for extreme fire events. Wildland firefighters need to be part of an expert workforce put to work in calm months on prescribed burns and fire prevention projects. Insurance reassessments are also important, and costs need to depend on how well a property is protected. In addition, small towns in fire-prone areas need to develop detailed protection and response plans. The broad scope of wildfire destruction in recent years has driven home the need not just for prior preparation, to re-examine basic approaches to risk assessment and management.

- Water Management. Century-old frameworks for water management have proved totally inadequate for contemporary conditions. Water from a shrinking Colorado River, for example, supports drinking water, agriculture and electricity generation in seven states. Pushed by Federal oversight, the states are reluctantly agreeing to major realignments in water use that will force significant agricultural realignments. Similarly, in the mid-West and California ground water pumping has greatly increased flood risks even while major farm owners defy efforts to limit pumping. Nationwide, historic water allocations urgently need revision, often requiring agriculture to promote more efficient use of water and shift crop selections.

- Coordination Center. In order to address a broad spectrum of emergencies, the Federal Emergency Management Agency has to be able to rapidly establish a command center to integrate efforts of responding federal, state, local and tribal organizations. This requires extensive prior collaboration to ensure compatible systems and agreed responsibilities at all operational levels.

The basic requirements are that governments need to have dedicated organizations to monitor situations and minimize potential impacts, as well as facilities, equipment, and personnel capable of responding. It is clear that governments at all levels need more funding to address the range of challenges they are facing; early preparations are critical. A complex nation cannot be adequately managed by a small government that responds more to major organizations than to everyday people.

Equality

America was founded on the fundamental principle that all men are created equal. Nevertheless, there has been a long history of discrimination against Native Americans, Blacks, early Spanish settlers and later immigrants. The original white male elite did a great job of protecting their own position. More recently, monied elites have manipulated the economic system to their own benefit, so now economic inequality reinforces much of the earlier social inequality. People have become desperate and angry. Many have even come to question the basic democratic structure of the nation. The wealthy strongly protect their own financial and tax benefits, while millions of economically stressed citizens naturally insist on keeping taxes as low as possible. As a result, governments at all levels are hard pressed to pay for even immediate needs, much less meet any vague or future requirements.

The accumulation of wealth at the top of society is the underlying cause of society's worst problems. The system needs to institute pay systems that ensure that all Americans have an opportunity for jobs that offer a living wage and a sense of personal worth from contributions to society. The American Dream must be reinvigorated.

- Racism. This remains a central challenge for America; it has deep roots in most aspects of our society and is interconnected in so many ways. Society needs to modify or eliminate elements that disproportionately impact minorities. Equal treatment is central, starting with education systems that give everyone an opportunity for economic advancement and continuing on to employment opportunities based strictly on capabilities. A critical element for equal education is that education funding in the public school system be spread equally across entire states. All Americans will need to accept and embrace the fact that a fundamental part of American identity is multicultural consciousness.

- Tax System. The tax system has to limit excessive wealth accumulation. High tax rates on top income brackets should make such accumulation difficult. Special treatment of capital gains, dividends, large deductions for mortgage interest, and minimized inheritance taxes need to be reduced or eliminated. Specialized tax provisions that favor large corporations and the rich need to be transparent to the public and carefully monitored to insure they provide social benefits.

- Corporate Responsibilities. Corporations are the main economic engine of society and need to work for the benefit of society as a whole. The capitalistic emphasis on profit needs to be widened to ensure that the wealth they create is distributed fairly among all stakeholders: society, customers, and employees as well as shareholders. Worker input is particularly important in addressing minimum wages, benefits, and working conditions. When the American Dream was at its high point, unions were an important element in promoting broad stakeholder gains; this needs to be renewed. Social programs working to spread society's wealth much more broadly are neither capitalist nor socialist, they are simply humanist, and necessary.

- Financial System. The financial system supports the economy by providing loans and capital for businesses. Stock market profits also provide important income to many retirees. But the system should not support complex financial instruments and ultrafast transactions which mainly function to extract wealth from society at large and were a major cause of the 2008 recession. Regulations need to ensure it is a support system that works for everyone and not simply a system of extracting wealth for the benefit of those who already have it. An active press is probably the most essential actor in building public awareness of efforts to manipulate the system.

- Poverty. America continues to have a much higher level of poverty than other advanced countries. Significant improvements during COVID due to government support programs disappeared when the programs dried up. Improvements in the Supplemental Nutrition assistance Program (SNAP), child tax credits, better unemployment insurance and broader rental assistance programs are badly needed. Most important is that all Americans should be able to earn a living wage.

- Homelessness. Homelessness is a national problem addressed at the local government level. Governments at these levels should use construction permits and zoning to promote affordable housing and provide safe shelter for all and support for building sustainable lives. Restrictions on drug use and possession need to be relaxed, but homelessness cannot be solved until the underlying problem of wealth distribution is addressed.

- Tolerance. Acceptance of differences should be a highly regarded social value. Employers as well as government and social leaders need to be role models in treating others with respect and dignity. Workplace guidance should set the bar for respectful and inclusive treatment of coworkers, clients, and customers by establishing or reinforcing norms against hate, exclusion, or violence based on religion, race, gender, age, disability, or sexual orientation. Simplistic solutions to a number of major social challenges (conception creates a person; sexual intimacy is only for a married man and woman; gender is strictly binary) are often backed by religion and get broad support. It is certainly acceptable that each person can believe what of this they want, but it is not acceptable that they should force their belief on others. Members of a multicultural society have to be open to other people's views. How to structure social media so that it promotes discussion but not misinformation and hatred is a major challenge.

Economic inequality undermines basic values of American society. There is a fundamental need to broaden wealth distribution. Tax reform and unions promoting broader corporate support for society are two major requirements.

Economy

Providing every American with a meaningful job is a major economic challenge as both technology and globalization have significantly reduced the need for workers in major parts of the economy. Overall, the nation needs a whole new concept of a national work force.

- Growth. Economic success is no longer able to basically depend on growth, but on a dynamic, steady-state economy that is continuously improving, but not necessarily expanding. Thanks to modern production, the total needs of the population can actually be satisfied by a relatively modest percent of the population. Growth has been important element in increasing company profits, but is less critical for overall economic needs.

- Demographics. With a significant rise in the elderly population, there is a clear requirement for more medical and support workers. These have traditionally been poorly paid jobs; improved wages and benefits are necessary to make these jobs a vibrant part of the changing economy. Likewise, there can no longer be a gulf between a real economy with good jobs and a suppressed economy dependent on exploited foreign workers and immigrants. All jobs have to be good jobs. The other side of demographic changes is that workers will be a smaller share of the population. The economy has to be structured so that all people interested in jobs can work. Broader childcare programs can increase job opportunities, as well as shorter work weeks and less overtime with mandatory vacation and leave programs. Stiglitz raised the possibility of a universal basic income or some kind of guaranteed employment. He commented that hopefully the market will provide full employment, but if it does not, the government has to.

- Service Sector. The service sector has traditionally depended on income from the productive sector. With a much smaller productive sector, service sector jobs will have to be significantly increased and will depend more on money flows within the service sector rather than just from the productive sector.

- Higher Minimum Wages. Higher wages are certainly a challenge for many business operations. Nevertheless, the economy has to ensure that everyone is doing well so that larger customer bases for service operations mean those companies can pay higher wages. This is certainly a challenge for agriculture and service organizations where workers have been traditionally low paid. Better pay for everyone will obviously mean higher produce and restaurant prices, another indicator that earnings must be higher across the board so that everyone can benefit from a dynamic economy.

- Medical Care. Government oversight and legislation must limit profit-seeking by pharmaceutical, medical supply and hospital organizations. The Inflation Reduction Act addressed drug costs with much-needed reforms at different points, cost-sharing caps on insulin and allowing the federal government to negotiate prices for the most expensive and commonly used drugs. Further attention is needed on reforming patent protections as well as promoting fair price negotiation and inflation-based rebates. In addition, affordable medical insurance should be widely available; worker benefits should include reasonable medical insurance. Mental health facilities must be given the necessary support to meet the needs of their communities. Transparency at all levels is critical so that the public is aware of real costs involved and how they are distributed

- Agriculture. This needs to be fundamentally reorganized to support smaller farms, improve direct connections with consumers and businesses that use fresh produce, and adapt crops to changing climate zones. Less emphasis on meat consumption would be helpful. Large companies that consolidate operations, such as meat processing, in major facilities with poor work conditions and minimal wages should be broken up. New approaches, such as community gardens and vertical hydroponic farms in cities, need to be developed.

- Domestic Production. Tax and regulation systems as well as international trade agreements need to reduce the attractiveness of the shift of production jobs overseas. A reinvigoration of Buy American programs could slow the decline of production jobs but complicate international trade agreements. America needs to be part of a dynamic global economy but that cannot override a fundamental requirement that the economy provide for its own basic needs.

- Energy Transition. The economy must support a transition to more modern energy sources to reduce both dangerous jobs and the negative impact on global warming. Laws and regulations need to control fossil fuel operations more proactively, while governments can mandate broad use of more efficient lights, vehicles, and heating systems. The biggest challenge is how to transition the workforce. Companies and local governments must help workers acquire the skills needed in developing energy sectors.

- Military-Industrial Complex. This can no longer be a jobs program. Military forces need to be downsized; expenditures must have a credible rationale. Workforce transition is also a major challenge here as many military jobs do not have direct civilian equivalents. The government and major companies need to work together to transition large numbers of skilled and highly paid workers into new jobs.

Change is difficult. Two major sectors of the American economy need to be significantly downsized. Fossil fuel companies are slowly coming to recognize their need to reorient operations. Still, the Military-Industrial Complex remains oblivious to its deleterious impact on the American economy. The government needs to see that the economy works for the nation as a whole. Whatever is done has to be a much more fundamental shift than simply expanding the economy, and this poses another major challenge for the nation.

Government

Congress at the national level and legislatures at state and local level set the budgets and laws facilitating individual programs. Citizens need to vote for representatives that will work for the good of the nation and need to engage in and support legislative discussions. Government activities are also a significant source of service jobs. These jobs are created to serve the people, not to produce profit, thus allowing government workers to focus on the job they are doing, not its profitability. A key requirement of government managers is to set work force levels appropriate to work requirements.

- Transparency. Legislatures and government offices at all levels need to be as open and transparent as possible. Public input should be continuously solicited on legislative issues, and the impact of money on politics needs to be minimized. Campaign financing and lobbying should be strictly limited and transparent. A dynamic press is a central element in public oversight.

- Religion. Separation of church and state remains a fundamental requirement. Government money should not be used to fund religious functions, including education. A multicultural society simply cannot function smoothly without broad respect for other views.

- Education. Support of education is a major government responsibility. At grammar and high school levels, public education needs to provide all children a solid basis for full development according to their abilities. Scientific and technical topics should be integrated at lower grades. New methods of electronic instruction can supplement traditional methods to provide the broad subject range that the new economy requires.

State colleges and vocational-technical schools should be at minimum cost for residents, and they need to ensure that curricula meet modern educational needs. Higher education has to be broadly available and flexible to provide that wide range of skills needed in a modern economy. Governments at all levels need to provide education programs the resources they need to function smoothly. Requirements for required work authorizations – certifications, licenses, qualifications – need to be continuously reviewed to insure they are both pertinent and address contemporary needs.

- Prisons. America should be first in this and not last, to set an example for the world. This means starting at the beginning, reducing the number of people going into prison by reforming bail procedures and decriminalizing lesser offenses, as well as offering a range of alternatives to prison and providing judges more latitude in sentencing. Prisons also need to have active education and development programs. At the far end, as people are being released, there needs to be active programs reintegrating prisoners as productive members of society, providing assistance in meeting employment and housing needs. Use of for-profit prisons should be minimized. The starting point is an economy that works for all so that economically disadvantaged people do not see crime as an attractive alternative.

- Guns. The widespread ownership of guns increases the risks for everyone. The most important action is universal background checks for purchasing guns and ammunition. Background checks keep guns and ammunition away from those who should not have them, reducing both homicides and suicides. There also need to be restrictions on particularly dangerous weapons, especially assault rifles.

-

- Infrastructure development. This is a core responsibility and often postponed, but it is critical to a well-functioning economy. Development needs to be matched with continuing upkeep and maintenance efforts. At the national level, projects can be modelled after the Civilian Conservation Corps of the 1930's, but on a continuing basis and not just a one-time effort.

- Basic research. Federal research must be expanded to meet the technological challenge from China and to provide for continuing innovation. Current programs to support microchip development are an important element of this effort. Technology development has to involve close collaboration with universities and ensure that results are as widely available as possible. When government research leads to private development, transfer agreements should support the public interest and cap profits.

- Voting. Managing voting is a critical government responsibility. Procedures have to be open and transparent with election observers welcomed. Efforts to encourage broad participation are fundamental and have to include easy registration and voting procedures. Some helpful adjustments could be made easily, including a requirement for paid time-off for employees to vote, introducing automatic voter registration, and simplifying eligibility requirements. If specific requirements are introduced (e.g., photo identification cards), then there needs to be parallel efforts to facilitate compliance (e.g., expanded identification card issuance). Routine redistricting efforts need to be conducted by neutral and transparent commissions minimizing gerrymandering and there needs to be tighter controls on campaign financing.

- Public Parks and Lands. Offices managing parks and public lands need to be fully staffed and provide for routine maintenance as well as operations. Public input on activities and operations should be continually solicited, and operations need to be as transparent as possible.

- Police. Realignment of police forces is important. They need to be supplemented with mental health professionals and trained to be more sensitive to individual issues in confrontational situations; weapon use should be a last resort. Police need to be active members of their communities, hire personnel to identify and deal directly with racial profiling, and minimize the use of force. Programs that build relationships between communities and their police forces are critical. Courts and police departments must be more sensitive to unequal treatment and racial profiling.

- Regulations. Government action is necessary to protect broad public interests, especially in environmental and park areas, food preparation, and worker and product safety. Resulting regulations need to be continuously re-assessed so that they are not overly restrictive but focus on essential public interests.

- Immigration. The American economy can no longer support large numbers of immigrants, but has a moral obligation to help them, particularly since it has a major responsibility for the repressive governments driving immigration in the first place. Short-term efforts to accommodate current immigrants are essential along with enforcement of laws prohibiting hiring of illegal immigrants. But the immigration solution lies not at home but abroad. Working for better governance in countries of origin can also facilitate efforts to repatriate refugees.

A complex society requires a complex government to function efficiently. Ronald Reagan's emphasis on limited government was instrumental in reducing support of government at all levels, heightening a natural aversion to taxes. Broad prosperity is a fundamental requirement for an economy to support tax levels needed for effective government.

Government leaders at all levels need to look beyond short-term requirements and narrow constituencies to support longer-term efforts that are important for the nation as a whole. Wherever possible, government activities should be carried out by government employees and not shifted to other organizations where secondary considerations including profit and influence can take precedence over mission requirements.

REALIGN FOREIGN POLICY

As noted before, the optimism seen in the End of History proved premature as America failed to demonstrate the benefits of democracy. Now the threats and challenges facing the nation are often vague and hard to define.

During the Cold War, there was a narrow focus on anti-Soviet efforts, almost irrespective of the costs. This anti-Soviet focus also led to close ties with various repressive regimes as well as the undermining of popular movements in the Congo, Chile, and Iran. America's failure to promote democracy when the Soviet Union collapsed brought the Russians to see American values as simply ploys to facilitate domination. When the Arab Spring erupted in 2010, it was based on core American values of freedom and equality, but its leaders totally avoided any references to America, vividly demonstrating a sweeping skepticism of America's commitment to its own values. By the time Black Lives Matter protests and then a storming of the American capitol building became visible globally, American democracy was widely discredited. This provided autocrats everywhere a rationale for suppressing democratic activities. China particularly gets a major boost for its efforts to promote autocratic controls as a superior form of government. The American failure to demonstrate that democracy leads to peace and prosperity is a fundamental driver of the global turmoil challenging the nation.

American foreign policy needs to start with a vision of what kind of world we want to promote. Although premature, the End of History did provide such a vision, a global adoption of liberal democracy, based on the universality of the basic human values of the worth of the individual and the importance of freedom. Democracy is critical, but democracies without traditions of compromise and cooperation easily become dysfunctional or even repressive. Competent government is most important. Promoting global good governance requires real leadership, building consensus rather than taking unilateral or coercive actions.

American leadership postwar was critical for establishing a democratic system in Europe. Countries that fought against each other for centuries are now united in an economic union in which war is unthinkable. Now establishing democracy needs to be done on a global basis, not in a narrow effort to copy America's systems, but a broader effort to promote responsive governments incorporating their own positive cultural traditions. This is not simply an altruistic effort. America cannot prosper in a world of turmoil as vividly demonstrated by some 35 million refugees worldwide. These distressed individuals cannot fit into the Industrialized World, highlighting the need to promote development in their countries of origin. The world can no longer be compartmentalized; all nations need to work together.

America is indeed the indispensable nation. It remains the only nation in a position to provide the necessary leadership to bring nations together working for a common goal: global prosperity. This effort is complicated by global economic inequality that is central to autocratic regimes worldwide. Democracy suppression is particularly important to Russia and China, both of which support and promote autocracy globally. This is the fundamental challenge of the twenty-first century. Can we end up with a world of liberal democracy, or will autocracy prevail and global dysfunction simply continue?

Prominence Not Dominance

With dynamic globalization interconnecting so many nations and active regional organizations (such as the African Union), there is simply no real potential for any nation to achieve global dominance. What nations should aspire to is prominence—broad international recognition of their contributions to global peace and prosperity. So rather than competing, often militarily, for dominance, any number of nations can share prominence and enjoy the high regard of the global community.

This would require a world where basic American values are shown to be universal values of humankind. This cannot be democracies narrowly defined, forced into some sort of standard framework. It cannot be superficial democracies, demonstrating trappings of elections and courts which are manipulated for the benefit of those at the top. The most important attribute of democracy must be good governance, supporting broad prosperity and human rights for all its people. The exact political system is less important but must be compatible with local culture.

Promoting such a global network should be the ultimate objective of American foreign policy; creating a world where the major powers collaborate to make dramatic contributions to global peace and prosperity, where prominence, not dominance, is the ultimate objective. America cannot impose this framework. A world without a dominant nation [makes grand strategy difficult](). So foreign policy needs coordinated decision-making networks. America's long-standing alliances are critical, but they must be consultative and not simply extensions of American decision making. American leadership must stress fundamental human principles and work in collaboration with partner nations, alliance leaders, special envoys, and subject-matter experts.

Democracy Promotion

Democracy promotion is the central objective for American foreign policy with the aim of creating democracies that demonstrate the universality of human values. America has talked for years of democracy promotion, but the last time that it actually helped another nation to implement a democratic system and build a prosperous economy was South Korea in the 1960s and 1970s. I personally saw this dramatic change during two Army tours there. When I left in 1965, the main road in the country, Seoul to Pusan, was a two-lane dirt road. When I returned in 1977, it was a four-lane superhighway! The whole country had transformed; businesses were flourishing. The work America did with South Korea in those years is just what needs to be done with other nations now.

The support provided to South Korea was part of America's Cold War anti-Soviet focus. Since then, our foreign aid in developing countries has been a miserable failure. Trillions of dollars have been spent and thousands of lives lost with minimal results. Another South Korean success is nowhere to be seen.

Democracy promotion was originally an American effort, but there was a major increase in democracy assistance after the 1980's mainly by European countries. But these efforts typically promoted Western models without sensitivity to local context, oblivious to the fundamental requirement that democracy must proceed from the bottom up. European efforts were dramatically impacted by the war in Ukraine which was framed as a fight for global democracy. There were strong rhetorical commitments to defending democracy, but the war pushed the EU's immediate policy priorities away from democracy issues and toward more directly security-related concerns. The Global South was reluctant to join in Western support of Ukraine, seeing it as just one more instance where the major powers neglect the broader world. Prosperity, democracy, and freedom can no longer be compartmentalized.

Just as we cannot fix America without fixing conditions for those at the bottom, we cannot promote democracy abroad without ensuring that local citizens see benefits for themselves and a potential for their impact on policies. Democracy promotion efforts must nurture domestic drivers of change, promote citizen involvement, and support a free and active local press. Representative government cannot be just managed elections supporting a protected elite. The elements of good governance discussed above in the section on Fix American First are just as applicable in foreign democracies as in America's. American support for democracy has to be global.

Global leadership supporting democratic development and opposing autocracy is fundamental. America must support broad programs like the Millennium Challenge Corporation and the National Democratic Institute, ensuring not only adequate financial support but wide publicity of the positive impact of programs they promote.

Addressing this challenge requires a fundamental realignment of American national security efforts from protecting against enemies to building up friends, steadily reducing the need for military efforts both at home and abroad. The focus of American foreign policy must be on people, not their governments but the status of individuals. American foreign policy has to pressure governments to be responsive to their citizens, respect human rights and the rule of democratic law. America can only promote change with socio-economic development. It must provide support to positive programs, not only government programs, but programs by international organizations, local economic and cultural groups, and non-governmental organizations. Afghanistan vividly illustrates how failure to promote development in a stable situation can rapidly lead to turmoil. Admiral Michael Mullen, then Chairman of the Joint Chiefs of Staff, saw some progress in a "whole-of-government" approach, but concluded that a "whole-of-nation" approach was essential. That never happened. Resources for global development are scarce enough but we continue to drain off significant amounts for military expenditures, preoccupying national leaders with confrontational efforts rather than cooperative ones.

Any comprehensive appraisal of the governance in a country must address dozens of variables, such as corruption, media freedom, internal freedom, open voting, medical support, education, wealth inequality, equal opportunity, political freedom, ethnic and gender discrimination, treatment of minorities, neonatal survival rates, and life expectancy. Using evaluations by outside, independent organizations, such as Freedom House and Transparency International, can give more weight to such indicators.

Faced with this changing situation, how can America best promote global democracy? Where can we best focus our resources?

Latin America

There is no better place to emphasize democratic development than in our own neighborhood. Effective democracy promotion would directly benefit the United States by reducing flows of desperate refugees. It would also set an example for the rest of the Industrialized World on promoting economic development in former colonial areas. Strong economic, social, and political links make the United States well positioned to work with the region so all its nations can prosper. This should start with strong attention to Central America where the United States legacy of supporting repressive regimes has helped create the current governments, which are unable to provide their citizens anything close to peace, prosperity, and safety. The most important challenge is improving citizen security.

The basic approach has to promote broad regional prosperity and focus on the grass roots level. Agriculture and light industry must necessarily be at the center of any such program, but it must also include infrastructure, health, and education, as well as tourist services. Close monitoring to avoid misuse of funds is essential: tying development to governance improvements, applying anti-corruption measures, and reducing violence with rule-of-law. Programs must be transparent and subject to scrutiny by an active local press. Former Assistant Secretary of State Rick Barton has made several concrete recommendations starting with encouraging governments to broker peace deals between rival gangs while addressing underlying causes.

The current situation has record numbers of refugees fleeing to the United States, requiring urgent actions. El Salvador has stemmed its widespread gang violence. The new regime is highly regarded, but its gang suppression programs have raised concerns by human rights organizations. Supporting economic development here could be a good starting point and facilitate return of refugees for the United States. In Costa Rica, long a bright spot in the area, drug trade has brought rise in violent crime amid a backdrop of growing inequality, high unemployment and an erosion of investment in education. This is another country where immediate efforts to promote broad development could have a dramatic impact, focusing on specific industries and setting up Enterprise Zones insulated from broad political dysfunction. Cooperative outreach to all the regional governments is necessary for economic expansion. In the end, these populations all have to see a potential for real prosperity.

The obvious starting point is with those countries most open to cooperation. At the moment, that is clearly Guatemala where an anti-corruption candidate recently won the presidency. He certainly needs strong international support. Support has to include financial support; America could start some sort of mini-Marshall Plan. The original Marshall Plan in Europe was in countries with educated populations where there was a strong American political presence, even with Germany where America was an occupying power. Any Central American Marshall Plan must be tailored to the area, including a Regional Development Council to promote collaboration at the governmental level. Former Secretary of State George Shultz has recommended working with the Inter-American Development Bank which is already active in Central America. China has also pledged $150 million in support of development in El Salvador, and the World Bank has long been promoting jobs in the region.

Russia

Russia should be a primary focus of American foreign policy in the years immediately ahead for two reasons. First, with its war in Ukraine, Russia transformed what been a great power squabble into a fundamental attack on universal values, undermining the structure of international order that is critical to US development and to global peace. So long as Russia actively supports autocratic regimes globally and continues military operation in Ukraine, there can be no peace in Europe, indeed, no real peace globally. Second, there is a potential for Russia to abruptly shift toward democracy. A cooperative relationship between a new progressive Russia and the Industrialized World would dramatically transform the international situation. It could be a highly visible example of democratic development, strongly undercutting Chinese promotion of autocracy and minimizing cyber intrusions. It would also significantly reduce requirements for military forces globally, including the possibility of major reductions in nuclear weapons. Diplomatically, collaboration with Russia could help resolve confrontations in Afghanistan, Venezuela, Belarus, Ukraine, and Syria.

Putin's central objective is simply to stay in power, and his basic method is confrontation with the West. His central fear is not some Western intrusion, but internal transformation. NATO, now focusing on Russia as an enemy, only supports Putin's imperial narrative, while some misstep could actually result in armed conflict. Russian protestors want democracy but have few concrete options. The West needs to give them something—a strong statement focusing on what relations with a post-sanctions Russia could look like. The central task is doing what we should have done 30 years ago: integrate Russia into the Industrialized World, focusing on collaborative political, social, and economic actions, actively encouraging Russians to join in development efforts. The West needs to actively work with the Russian opposition elements to widely distribute this statement to the Russian people. Ideally, it would be part of a broader New Russia Vision by the Russian opposition to counter Putin's medieval version of imperial dominance.

Prior to the Ukraine invasion, the Brookings Institution had proposed a new security architecture, consolidating the neutral countries of eastern Europe and working with Russia to guarantee their sovereignty and security. NATO's own independent group report emphasized a need for transatlantic consultation. NATO could outline a potential shift of resources from military to developmental use. Instead of using 2 percent of Gross Domestic Product for military expenditures, NATO could envision shifting a small portion, say, initially 0.25 percent, to a new Russian Partnership Fund. The fund could work with Russian representatives to identify projects that might have maximum impact at minimal cost in a post-sanctions situation, such as:

- Cooperative Efforts. Expansion of currently successful efforts, including the long-standing and impressive joint operations on space exploration and reinvigoration of broad economic relationships.

- Arms Control. There has been long-standing cooperation on securing nuclear materials and knowledge. Significant nuclear weapon reductions would benefit both countries.

- Health Support. COVID-19 made medical shortcomings increasingly visible and still poses a worrisome threat. Broader medical collaboration including on vaccine development would certainly be welcome.

- Economic Development. NATO has a major opportunity to support economic development projects. Russia, for example, has a totally inadequate highway system, while Eisenhower's Interstate Highway System gave America broad experience in designing and constructing a national road network. Russia needs to broaden its economy from an oil and gas focus to creative uses of its wide mineral and resources, including helium.

- Technical Exchanges. There is a broad opportunity for scientific, economic, and educational exchanges with NATO nations. All organizations that had been involved need to be encouraged to begin discussions on possible re-starts.

The core principle needs to be an active outreach to the Russian people, stressing the total fiction of a Western threat while making Russian corruption and repression as transparent as possible. Creating a new approach to helping Russia become a true global partner with other countries is key. Programs that promote real economic advancement and provide Russia its own position on the world stage would have a strong resonance with the Russian people.

Rather than promote a new Cold War, now is the time to definitively end the last one.

China

China is not only a growing challenge to American world leadership but also a direct challenge to ideals of democracy. The American policy towards China has recently undergone severe stresses. As the COVID-19 impact wears down, America needs to re-assess this policy in the larger context of global challenges and accept that competition with China will be a permanent international reality.

American strategy must focus on its core objective: integrating China into a prosperous and peaceful world. China poses only a minimal direct military threat to America. Military confrontation only reinforces the Chinese communist leadership in its effort to use Chinese patriotism to distract attention from internal autocracy. Every dollar America spends on military confrontations with China is a gift to General Secretary Xi. He has worked hard to distract popular attention from the provision in China's own constitution that "the Party shall develop a broader, fuller, and more robust people's democracy." The Communist Party has loudly denounced democracy as a Western construct. It suppressed democratic efforts in Hong Kong, denigrated minorities as anti-Chinese, and pictured democratic Taiwan as a rogue province. All the while, Xi has sought broad international support for Chinese autocracy, relying heavily on his Belt and Road Initiative.

Regional issues, including the allocation of rights within the South China Sea, are properly an issue for negotiation among the regional countries. UNCLOS should be the basis for resolving these issues, but China disputes its applicability. It makes no sense for America to promote military confrontation defending an international convention that America itself has not ratified. America should minimize its military presence and issue a strong declaration that, as recently reaffirmed by the UN Permanent Court of Arbitration, it is inappropriate for any one nation to claim exclusive rights to these regional assets.

The international community has a legitimate interest in pressuring all stakeholders to respect one another, to negotiate within international norms, and to honor the free access rights of all nations. As discussed above, America needs to pursue not dominance, but prominence. Both China and America can enjoy prominence as America promotes Chinese integration into a cooperative world environment that works for everyone. Outreach is a much better option than containment. With the Soviet Union, confrontation led to arms races, global bipolar competition, and the eventual stalemate of Mutually Assured Destruction. China has much more economic clout than the Soviet Union ever had, and much more potential to play a leading role in a prosperous global economy. It is the only nation with any significant influence on the North Korean regime which regularly threatens conflict with South Korea; extended hostilities could not take place without Chinese support.

America needs to significantly expand its outreach to the Chinese people, promoting political evolution while stressing clearly and continually the importance of democracy and human rights. America has a major advantage in such an effort—the universal appeal of American ideals of democracy and equality. Democratic forces are the single most important challenge to the Chinese leadership. Unrest in Hong Kong highlighted both the appeal of democracy and the difficulty the Chinese leadership has in dealing with it as they are still haunted by the specter of [Tiananmen Square](). Taiwan is also of high concern to the Chinese leadership because it represents the alternative way of life that poses a [major threat]() to Chinese autocracy. China talks of overwhelming Taiwan, but in the end it could be Taiwan's democratic system that overwhelms China. Russia's strong support of autocracy also helps to support Xi's own autocratic programs; emergence of a new, more progressive Russian government could also support democratic efforts in China.

During the Cold War, no one expected the Soviet system would suddenly be swept away by democratic forces, so no one worked to help make that happen. But such a shift is exactly what is needed today with China, and America can help make that happen. America has much to offer economically, particularly with environmental technologies and open markets. With its allies, it can pressure China to live up to international standards on human rights as well as its own standard of a "peaceful rise." It should also invite China to join in setting agreed-upon international norms, including on sea control and rights of access. America can also promote broader cooperative efforts, cultural exchanges, arms control agreements, and environmental collaboration. Because of the centralization of power under Xi Jinping, Communist party rule has become far more brittle, bolstering the case for an American strategy of sustained pressure to induce political change.

America needs to issue strong statements that include the following:

- America supports basic human ideals of equality and freedom and works hard to demonstrate how they lead to a peaceful and prosperous society;
- America supports Chinese prominence on the world stage, demonstrating China's economic and technical development.

Encouraging these actions, American priorities should be—

- Minimize any military confrontation with China;

- Ratify the United Nations Convention for the Law of the Sea and work with China and the United Nations on drawing up broadly agreed-upon international norms;

- Put maximum diplomatic pressure on Chinese elements of repression and human right violations, while supporting minority rights within China;

- Engage in an active trade relationship with China, recognizing the need to avoid excessive dependence on supply chains and to protect key technologies or share them with transparent agreements;

- Expand people-to-people contacts, including tourist programs, educational exchanges, and collaborative regional projects;

- Support China's integration into the global economy and encourage maximum technical and educational exchanges;

- Energize Trans-Atlantic collaboration on a cohesive set of policies and actions toward China, including interaction with the Belt and Road Initiative.

Muslim World

It is clear that relations with the Islamic World are problematic. Prospects for broader democracy are, to say the least, somewhere off in the future. But the worrying clash of civilizations is happening only at the level of fragmented terrorist threats. Overall relations with the Islamic World remain generally cordial, with only Iran actively challenging the West. The most important steps would be to promote economic development within the Islamic World.

Regional stability was dramatically disrupted when Hamas initiated a broad attack from Gaza on Isarel, killing a thousand Israelis and taking several hundred hostages with a wide scope of war crimes. Although antisemitism clearly played a role, the central motivation was not that Israelis are Jews, but that they were oppressors. Israel naturally responded with intense military actions in Gaza. This counterattack quickly turned into its own series of war excesses, killing nearly 30,000 Palestinians and carrying out widespread destruction in the first month of response. The West in general with strong United States involvement supported the Israel counteractions, even as the [Israeli Defense Minister](#) described Palestinians as "human animals" and decreed that no fuel, electricity, water or internet access would be allowed into Gaza. As the scale of destruction became rapidly apparent, the West called for restraint on actions affecting civilians but has been reluctant to label the Israeli excesses as criminal. There have been [widespread pro-Palestinian demonstrations](#) across America. Although occasionally denounced as antisemitic, supporting organizations include pro-peace Jewish groups. The protestors clearly denounce Israel not for being Jewish, but for the extensive killing and destruction in Gaza. On these same lines, [South Africa directly charged Israel](#) with violating the 1948 Genocide Convention, established in the wake of the Holocaust. It asked the International Court of Justice to order an immediate end to military activities in Gaza. Although it might be several years before the case is decided, the court did issue ["emergency measures"](#) instructing Israel to avoid acts which might be considered genocidal and to enable humanitarian assistance to the people of Gaza. The White House dismissed the case as meritless and counterproductive, continuing its reluctance to label any Israeli actions as criminal. But it is working hard with other regional countries to push for a cessation of hostilities and eventually a separate Palestinian state, a position directly at odds with the current Israeli objectives.

America has to support the Jewish people who were historically devastated by Nazi genocide, but obviously should not support the extensive killing and destruction Israel is currently conducting against the Palestinians. The United States and Western governments need to separate their support for the international Jewish community from automatic support for the Israeli regime, while pressing for a democratic and prosperous Palestine.

Elsewhere in the Islamic Word, there remains a wide range of confrontations. The fighting in Gaza threatens to involve Israel in a wider war with Lebanon, while the Houthi group controlling much of Yemen has used attacks on Red Sea shipping to underline its support for the Palestinians, leading to NATO attacks on military targets in Yemen and straining American efforts to stop the war from spreading. As with Ukraine, a shift from military efforts is badly needed. None of this can be resolved militarily; broad economic development and democratic expansion are what is required.

Other Countries

The Committee to Destroy the World (the tongue-in-cheek title awarded by *Foreign Policy* magazine to the collective of heads of failed nations) flourishes, driving their populations into poverty while building their own personal fortunes. A main reason that repressive nations can continue operating is the support they get from China and Russia. China resolutely refuses to judge the actions of other sovereign rulers. Partly this allows China to lock in favorable long-term resource contracts with countries that most industrial nations avoid. More importantly, it allows China to reject efforts by other nations to critique Chinese internal practices, including suppression of minorities and human rights violations. Russia's approach is similar, though its acceptance of the Partnership and Cooperation Agreement with the European Union included vague commitments to democracy and human rights. Overall, the support by China and Russia to repressive regimes enables these regimes to survive and destabilize the parts of the world where they are located. Reducing Chinese and Russian support for autocratic regimes is an essential step toward global development.

African countries face a particular challenge in the years ahead as demographic projections envision population increases that will only make good governance all the more difficult. Democracy promotion globally has to depend on supporting economic and social development with transparent programs that contrast markedly with Russian and Chinese programs that bolster autocracy.

Minorities are a challenge globally. America works hard to integrate its own minorities and sets an example, but the task remains demanding. Almost everywhere else minorities are a constant challenge; a few examples include the Roma in Europe; Muslims in India, France, and Russia; Hungarians in Romania; tribal groups in Africa, including the Tigray in Ethiopia; indigenous groups throughout Latin America; Kurds in Turkey, Iran, and Iraq; the Rohingya in Burma, and of course the Uighurs and Tibetans in China. Nations everywhere need to do a better job of helping their minorities flourish. Broader democratic governance is critical.

Global Warming

America needs to take two key steps to address global warming:

- Reduce Carbon Emissions. America needs to set the example on this. A critical element is a shift away from fossil fuels. It is important not only to make renewables cheaper, but to integrate them into the power grid, finding ways to store surplus electricity on a much larger scale and reassessing the potential for nuclear energy. Transitioning the work force is a particular challenge. Setting up local Environmental Councils that include executives from regional companies as well as representatives from federal agencies, unions, educational institutions, and social organizations could be very helpful. Such inclusive groups could actively expand comprehensive development plans with strong local support. Each location would have to set up its own response plans for potential emergencies and decide what preventative measures would be appropriate.

- Rejoin the Kyoto Protocol. Congress should ratify America's participation, an action long overdue. America should devise a climate-centered foreign policy that uses the country's political capital and economic resources to drive the decarbonization of the global economy. Such a policy could put America at the forefront of a clean energy future, enhancing the competitiveness of American firms and allowing all Americans to benefit directly from emission reductions.

The Executive Branch needs modernization, which should include the creation of a National Climate Council. The consumption of fossil fuels lies at the root of global inequality. Developing countries are bearing the brunt of global change impacts including drought, basically caused by carbon emissions from the developed world. Wealthy countries need to put significant investment in developing countries to shift investment from fossil fuel industries to sustainable alternatives.

STRATEGY DEVELOPMENT

Our nation definitely needs a comprehensive National Strategy to identify all our main nonmilitary and military objectives and assess how to best attain them.

As the review of threats and challenges above makes clear, there are two fundamental national goals:

- Demonstrate that democracy can indeed lead to a peaceful and prosperous nation while developing the resilience necessary to ensure national survival.

- Provide the necessary leadership to create a democratic world that addresses global warming.

The broad range of actions and programs necessary to Fix America First requires several basic efforts. The central challenge is to address inequality, both racial and economic, based on the excessive accumulation of wealth. This cannot happen without deep changes in the attitudes of many Americans, changes centered on a better balance between individual rights and responsibilities to society and with a renewed commitment to tolerance, providing respect and dignity to all people. Domestically, the government must ensure that the economy functions for the benefit of society as a whole, allowing everyone to live the American Dream.

On a global scale, the Beacon of Freedom has to light the way forward. America cannot impose democracy, but spreading it is the basic challenge. America can no longer seek military dominance. Instead, it must promote prominence, reinvigorating the State Department and emphasizing soft power to lead the world into a new era of prosperity. Promoting collaboration with Russia can lead to broader collaboration with China in a new world where prominence and collaboration are central values. In the longer run, many resources need to shift from military to developmental uses. It is not only military nuclear forces that need to be considered unnecessary and eliminated, but conventional forces need to be minimized as well.

The West has to build a vision of a democratic world with a New Europe that includes a dynamic Russia cooperating on development and democracy. America has an opportunity to lead the world into a new era of prosperity. COVID-19 and then the war in Ukraine forced everyone to see many of the inadequacies of current systems and focus on new approaches to the threats and challenges facing the nation and the world. This needs American leadership. Despite all its problems, the United States remains the indispensable nation, the only nation capable of pulling the West together and leading in a positive direction. It has to reinvigorate its post-war leadership, working to bring nations together but not dictating what international policies should be. As Max Bergmann has outlined in detail, the West needs to focus on achieving a democratic and prosperous world. The route to that is promoting the emergence of a new and democratic Russia actively working with the Industrialized World, as should have happened 30 years ago.

The United States has to move away from its fixation on military solutions. America has to show that democracy works, shifting money from the top and invigorating actions at the grass roots level. Secretary of State Antony Blinken recently spoke of revitalizing a free, open, secure, and prosperous world, emphasizing the need to build new coalitions and strengthen international institutions, reinvigorating support for real economic and democratic development. Central America can certainly be a good starting point, but development efforts elsewhere in Latin America, in Africa, and in the Middle East need support. Secretary Blinken recognizes the need to work cooperatively with all governments, but the United States needs to keep attention on everyday people and pressure governments to recognize international norms. Reinvigorated US leadership is the key to global stability and prosperity.

A National Strategy has to prioritize critical projects discussed earlier in this chapter to best allocate necessary resources. The National Security Council has the broad membership necessary for this task and has to broaden its scope beyond its traditional military focus. Government leaders at all levels need to look beyond short-term requirements and narrow constituencies to support longer-term efforts that are important for the nation as a whole.

WORKS CITED

(This is a partial list. For full documentation, including hyperlinks, see the online version.)

"China's Claims to the South China Sea Are Unlawful. Now What?". (July 27, 2020) *New York Times.* www.nytimes.com.

"The Darker Bioweapons Future". (November 3, 2003). Freedom of Information Act. The Electronic Reading Room. https://www.cia.gov/readingroom/document/0001298811

Denning, Steve. "The Origin of the World's Dumbest Idea: Milton Friedman". (June 26, 2013) https://www.forbes.com/sites/stevedenning/2013/06/26/the-origin-of-the-worlds-dumbest-idea-milton-friedman/?sh=1070907a870e

"Erdogan Says 'Thoughtless' Imitation of West Caused Largest Damage to Turkey." Globalsecurity.org from Sputnik News. (October 19, 2020) https://www.globalsecurity.org/wmd/library/news/turkey/2020/turkey-201019-sputnik01.htm?m=3n%2e002a%2e2903%2etz0ao0emf5962e2lix

Fukuyama, Francis. "The End of History."www.wesjones.com/eoh.htm. taken from The National Interest, Summer 1989.

"Full Text of Clinton's Speech on China Trade Bill". (March 9, 2000) *New York Times Archive* https://www.iatp.org/sites/default/files/Full_Text_of_Clintons_Speech_on_China_Trade_Bi.htm

"General: We Can't Kill Our Way Out Of Afghanistan". (Interview by Rachel Martin, May 28, 2011). *All Things Considered.* www.npr.org.

"Governor Polis Signs Executive Order Directing Action on Equity, Diversity, and Inclusion". (August 27, 2020) https://www.colorado.gov/governor/news/2851-governor-polis-signs-executive-order-directing-action-on-equity-diversity-and-inclusion

Huntington, Samuel P. (Summer, 1993). "The Clash of Civilizations?" https//www.foreignaffairs.com/articles/united-states/1993-06-01/clash-civilizations

Karma, Roger. (April 15, 2020). "'Deaths of despair': The deadly epidemic that predated coronavirus." www.vox.com.

Kimmelman. Michael. "Lessons from Hurricane Harvey: Houston's Struggle is America's Tale". *New York Times*. November 11, 2017.

Krystek, Lee. (2011). "Is the Super Volcano Beneath Yellowstone Ready to Blow?" www.unmuseum.org/supervol.htm.

National Security Strategy (October 2022). https://www.whitehouse.gov/wp-content/uploads/2022/10/Biden-Harris-Administrations-National-Security-Strategy-10.2022.pdf

Preble, Christopher. "A Credible Grand Strategy" (January 2024). https://www.stimson.org/wp-content/uploads/2024/01/Grand-Strategy-Report-WEB.pdf.

Polyakova, Alina et al, "A New Vision for the Transatlantic Alliance" (November 30, 2023), https://cepa.org/comprehensive-reports/a-new-vision-for-the-transatlantic-alliance-the-future-of-european-security-the-united-states-and-the-world-order-after-russias-war-in-ukraine/

"Reimagining European Security," 2023, https://us.boell.org/en/re-imagining-european-security

"Russia Can Repel Asteroids to Save Earth" (October 24, 2006) Space Daily.com, https://www.spacedaily.com/reports/Russia_Can_Repel_Asteroids_To_Save_Earth_999.

Shabecoff, Phillip. "Global Warming Has Begun, Expert Tells Senate". *New York Times.* June 24, 1988.

Soldatov, Andrei, and Irina Borogan. "In From the Cold: The Struggle for Russia's Exiles" (December 12, 2023). https://cepa.org/comprehensive-reports/in-from-the-cold-the-struggle-for-russias-exiles/

"Transcript of President Dwight D. Eisenhower's Farewell Address". (1961). www.ourdocuments.gov.

Woodruff, Sasa and David Brancaccio. "Why economist, Joseph Stiglitz is advocating for "progressive capitalism". (May 30, 2019). https://www.marketplace.org/2019/05/30/economist-joseph-stiglitz-progressive-capitalism-people-power-profits

www.ingramcontent.com/pod-product-compliance
Lightning Source LLC
Chambersburg PA
CBHW020456030426
42337CB00011B/127